The Modern Nations in
Historical Perspective

ROBIN W. WINKS, *General Editor*

The volumes in this series deal with individual nations or groups of closely related nations throughout the world, summarizing the chief historical trends and influences that have contributed to each nation's present-day character, problems, and behavior. Recent data are incorporated with established historical background to achieve a fresh synthesis and original interpretation.

ERNEST K. BRAMSTED, *author of this book, was born in southern Germany. He holds doctorates in history and sociology from the Universities of Berlin and London and is a Fellow of the Royal Historical Society, London. After working with the British Broadcasting Corporation during World War II, he taught modern history for many years at the University of Sydney, Australia. Among the books written by Professor Bramsted are two of the standard works on German history:* Aristocracy and the Middle Classes in Germany: Social Types in German Literature, 1830–1900 *and* Goebbels and National Socialist Propaganda, 1925–1945.

ALSO IN THE EUROPEAN SUBSERIES

The Balkans *by Charles and Barbara Jelavich*
France *by John C. Cairnes*
Ireland *by Oliver MacDonagh*
Italy *by Massimo Salvadori*
Poland and Czechoslovakia *by Frederick G. Heymann*
Russia *by Robert V. Daniels*
Scandinavia *by John H. Wuorinen*
Spain *by Richard Herr*

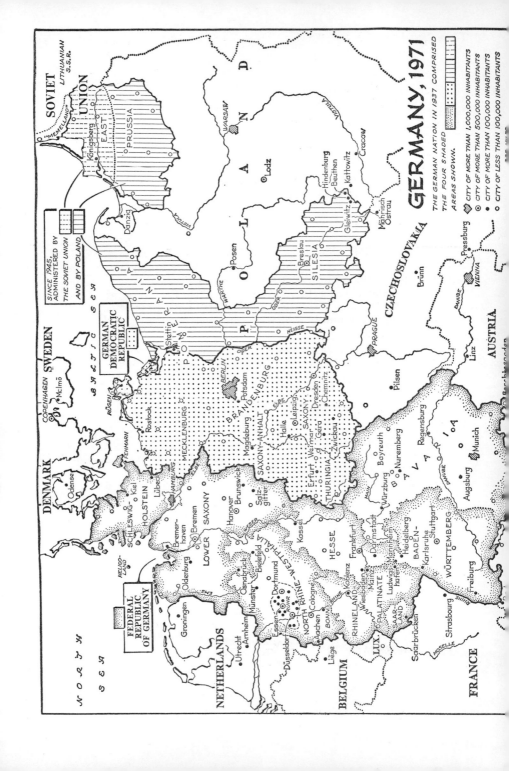

GERMANY, 1971

THE GERMAN NATION IN 1937 COMPRISED
THE FOUR SHADED AREAS SHOWN.

● CITY OF MORE THAN 1,000,000 INHABITANTS
◎ CITY OF MORE THAN 500,000 INHABITANTS
● CITY OF MORE THAN 100,000 INHABITANTS
○ CITY OF LESS THAN 100,000 INHABITANTS

SINCE 1945, ADMINISTERED BY THE SOVIET UNION AND BY POLAND

GERMAN DEMOCRATIC REPUBLIC

FEDERAL REPUBLIC OF GERMANY

NORTH SEA

SOVIET UNION

LITHUANIAN S.S.R.

"MEMELLAND"

EAST PRUSSIA

Königsberg

Danzig

P O L A N D

WARSAW

Lodz

Posen

Breslau

SILESIA

Hindenburg
Beuthen
Gleiwitz
Kattowitz

Cracow

Mährisch Ostrau

Pressburg

VIENNA

CZECHOSLOVAKIA

Brünn

PRAGUE

Pilsen

AUSTRIA

Linz

Berchtesgaden

Munich

Augsburg

BAVARIA

Regensburg

Nuremberg

Bayreuth

Würzburg

SWEDEN

COPENHAGEN
Malmö

DENMARK

Odense

BALTIC SEA

RÜGEN

FEHMARN

HELIGOLAND

Kiel

SCHLESWIG-HOLSTEIN

Lübeck

Rostock

MECKLENBURG

HAMBURG

Bremer-haven
Bremen

LOWER SAXONY

Oldenburg

Hanover

Brunswick

Salz-gitter

MAGDEBURG

SAXONY-ANHALT

BRANDENBURG

Potsdam

BERLIN

Stettin

ODER

NEISSE

WARTHE

VISTULA

ELBE

Leipzig

Halle

SAXONY

Dresden

Chemnitz

Zwickau

Gera

THURINGIA

Erfurt
Weimar

Kassel

HESSE

Frankfurt

Darmstadt

Mainz

Wiesbaden

Koblenz

RHINELAND

Bonn

RHINE

Cologne

Aachen

Dortmund

RUHR

Essen

Düsseldorf

NORTH RHINE-WESTPHALIA

Münster

Osnabrück

Bielefeld

Groningen

Arnheim

Utrecht

NETHERLANDS

BELGIUM

Liège

LUX.

SAAR-LAND

Saarbrücken

RHINELAND-PALATINATE

Ludwigs-hafen
Mannheim

Heidelberg

Karlsruhe

BADEN-

Stuttgart

WÜRTTEMBERG

Freiburg

Strasbourg

RHINE

MOSELLE

DANUBE

FRANCE

The Modern Nations in Historical Perspective

GERMANY

Ernest K. Bramsted

PRENTICE-HALL, INC.   *Englewood Cliffs, New Jersey*

A SPECTRUM BOOK

Map credits: "Germany and Austria in 1945" (p. 5)—from DTV Atlas zur Weltgeschichte, by H. Kinder and W. Hilgemann; trans. Ernest A. Menze; may drawn by Harald and Ruth Bukor. Copyright © 1966 by Deutscher Taschenbuch Verlag GmbH & Co. KG. and by Penguin Books Ltd. Reproduced by permission of Doubleday and Company, Inc., and Penguin Books Ltd.
"The Growth of the German Empire, 1864–1871" (p. 140) —from A History of Europe from the Beginning of the Eighteenth Century to 1937, by H. L. A. Fisher (London: Eyre & Spottiswoode Ltd., 1952). Reprinted by permission of Eyre & Spottiswoode Ltd.

For Eleanor

10 9 8 7 6 5 4 3 2 1

PRENTICE-HALL INTERNATIONAL, INC. (*London*)
PRENTICE-HALL OF AUSTRALIA, PTY. LTD. (*Sydney*)
PRENTICE-HALL OF CANADA, LTD. (*Toronto*)
PRENTICE-HALL OF INDIA PRIVATE LIMITED (*New Delhi*)
PRENTICE-HALL OF JAPAN, INC. (*Tokyo*)

Contents

Preface

While working on this volume the author has sometimes remembered a comment by the English historian J. M. Thompson: "There never was and there never can be such a person as everybody's Napoleon." This insight might be adapted to a nation. Indeed there cannot be such a concept as everybody's Germany when one considers her long and varied past and her complex and divided present. As with other nations, historians have disagreed little in their acknowledgment of the major facts of the evolution of Germany, but the situation is quite different when it comes to the emphasis on facts and factors and on their interpretation. The background of the writer, his own political preferences, the generation to which he belongs, and whether he sees the history of the nation from within or without—all these circumstances are bound to make their impact. With the changes in the political and social structure of a country the image of its history changes, too.

The German liberals of the last century looked at Germany's past differently in 1848–49, when they hoped for unification through a national assembly, and after 1871, when Bismarck's authoritarian empire had been established. Again, German socialists interpreted it in terms different from those of Prussian conservatives or South German Catholics, not to mention the historical ideologies of the various types of nationalist and racialist from Heinrich von Treitschke in the Bismarckian empire to Alfred Rosenberg in Hitler's Third Reich. Today the competitive coexistence of the two German republics, with their contrasting political systems and international affiliations, has led to versions of German history that sometimes have little more in common than chronology.

Perhaps in most countries nowadays historians are more aware than were their predecessors of the role of traditional patterns in the history of a society on the one hand and of the significance of social and political change on the other. The history of both—human beings and social institutions—crystallizes from time to time in a variety of specific attitudes. A number of them can be discerned in the development of Germany since 1500. To mention only a few: the deference of the subjects to the multitude of rulers and their courts; the rivalry of Christian creeds and of their followers from Luther's Reformation to Bismarck's *Kulturkampf*; the militaristic and bureaucratic behavior of the establishment in Prussia; the high premium on *Kultur* in the classicist society of Weimar around 1800; the long-lasting political insignificance of the middle classes, so different from the situation in France and England; the juxtaposition between industrial expansion and *Realpolitik* in the age of Bismarck and Alfred Krupp; the political isolation and even "ghetto" attitude of the German Social Democrats until 1914; and, finally, the specific shape of German nationalism, with its roots in the romantic school of the early nineteenth century and its various later branches of imperialism and racialism—an ideology and behavior pattern that after 1933 reached its perverted climax in the concentration camps of Dachau, Belsen, Auschwitz, and Treblinka.

A short history of a country's past and present has also to consider its new starting points, the fresh beginnings, the crises of reform or revolution. Germany has had many reformers but few revolutionaries. There is no parallel in German history to either the French or the Bolshevik Revolution. A great German revolutionary like Karl Marx lived most of his life outside the country of his birth. There were outstanding reformers like Luther in the sixteenth and Baron vom Stein in the early nineteenth centuries; there were the two—in the last analysis abortive—revolutions of 1848–49 and of 1918–19, which were efforts to establish democracy; there was Bismarck's unification of the nation from above in 1870–71. Present-day Germany, however, has perhaps been most affected by the breakthrough of Hitler's totalitarianism in 1933–34 and by the collapse of his Third

Reich in 1945, after it had challenged the world. Its result was the Four-Power occupation of the country by the victors, and with it the gradual emergence of the present two German states, one oriented towards the West, the other towards the Soviet Union.

Within the limitations of a short volume relating the present to the past and vice versa, one has to strike a reasonable balance between significant events and patterns of attitudes, a balance, too, between political, socioeconomic, and cultural history. As this is not a handbook but a survey of essential strands, the aspects of cultural history has had to be confined to the significance of some major literary figures and movements. To consider Goethe and his concept of world literature, the romantics, Heinrich Heine, and later Thomas Mann and Bertolt Brecht can help us to a better understanding of the society and politics of their time.

Germany's position in the center of Europe has been a source of both weakness and strength from the Middle Ages to the present day. It was the cause of much mental claustrophobia and insecurity, of a marked inferiority feeling of many Germans before 1870, and of an aggressive self-assertiveness afterwards. One has to realize that from the sixteenth to the nineteenth centuries Germany served and suffered frequently as a battleground for foreign armies, as a target of invasion and exploitation by others. During the days of William II and, later, of the National Socialists, the boot was on the other foot. In a bid for world power the trained German armies twice between 1914 and 1941 marched into Western Europe and Russia, to be beaten only after prolonged and grim struggles, with dire costs for both sides.

Today it seems that the age of nationalism has by and large ended in Europe and an era of regional integration and supranational interdependence has arrived. The issue of confrontation or coexistence of the two German states affects many other people. It forms an important factor on the chessboard of international power politics. Against such background, both the Western orientation of Dr. Adenauer's foreign policy and the new *Ostpolitik* of Willy Brandt have to be seen.

On a personal note, perhaps it should be added that the writer spent the first part of his life in Germany and the second in the Anglo-Saxon world. This, he believes, has enabled him to look at the theme both from the inside and from the outside, involved and yet detached.

The author wishes to express his thanks to the Australian Research Grant Committee and to the University of Sydney for grants
that have assisted in the preparation of this book. He is also grateful
to The Wiener Library, London, and to *Inter Nationes*, Bonn–Bad
Godesberg, for the material put at his disposal. The author alone is
responsible for the opinions and comments expressed in this book.

Weybridge, Surrey   E. K. B.

1

A Divided Country

INTRODUCTION

The basic fact about Germany today is her division. There are two German republics, each with its own government, which for twenty years have not recognized each other: the Federal Republic of Germany in Bonn and the German Democratic Republic in East Berlin. West Germany has a population of about 60 million people; East Germany about 18 million. Both are highly industrialized states, but organized on different economic and political lines. West Germany is a partner with France, Italy, and the three Benelux countries in the European Economic Community (E.E.C.), or the European Common Market; East Germany is a member of the E.E.C.'s counterpart among the East European Communist states, COMECON, the Council for Mutual Economic Aid. The Federal Republic belongs to NATO, the North Atlantic Treaty Organization; the Democratic Republic to its opposite number, the organization under the Warsaw Pact that combines the military forces of the Soviet Union with those of the East European Communist states. The 828 miles of strictly guarded border that separates the two Germanies also divides Europe to some extent.

There are other divided nation-states on the map today, like the two Koreas and the two Vietnams. However, in Europe no other nation-state has lost its national identity and unity since 1945. Seen in historical perspective, the paradox of Germany is that her division is both old and new. In its present form it is entirely new—the outcome of the Four-Power disunity after the collapse of the united Germany that was founded by Bismarck in 1871; it was transformed from a monarchy into a republic in 1918, and changed to the National Socialist totalitarian state in 1933. This *Reich* was of relatively short duration, as history goes—it lasted for seventy-four years. Before 1870 there had been no one Germany, only separate Germanies—three dozen of them in fact between 1815 and 1870, and more than three hundred under the moribund and shadowy First Empire, which had long ceased to be of any significance before it officially expired in 1806.

It is an important aspect of Germany's history that she became a unified nation-state much later than either England or France. Unification came about only under the pressure of modern industrialization and technology—in the age of railways and new military techniques. The period before unification was dominated by the rivalry and competition between two major German states, Prussia and Austria. Conflict between them began during the three wars provoked by Frederick the Great in the middle of the eighteenth century, and ended with the loss of Silesia by Austria. Later, during the Napoleonic Wars and in the era of the Austrian chancellor Metternich, the two states cooperated as conservative powers against the new ideas of liberalism and constitutionalism. But in the 1860s Bismarck and Moltke in Prussia engineered a decisive conflict that terminated with the defeat of the Austrian army at Königgrätz in the summer of 1866. The Prussian victory meant the implementation of the second of two blueprints for a united empire which had been discussed for thirty years by liberals and conservatives: a Greater Germany with Austria included, or a Lesser Germany under Prussian leadership without Austria. Lesser Germany was headed by Bismarck and the Hapsburg monarchy now had no say in its affairs of Germany. At the same time the dream of many German liberals of a liberalized and democratic empire was not fulfilled. The alternative between individual freedom or national unity ended with the greater emphasis on the latter in Bismarck's Second Empire.

Industrialization and national unity based on decisions by arms came late and their impact was all the more intense. There was a change in attitude and in the prevailing human type. The largely introverted nation composed of burghers and accustomed to order and obedience heeded the warning from the police president of Berlin after Prussia's defeats by the Napoleonic armies in 1806: "To keep quiet was the first duty of the citizen." The lack of rebels and re-formers during the two centuries from 1648 to 1848 was perhaps compensated for by the remarkable sequence of great philosophers, musicians, and poets at the beginning of the nineteenth century. But after 1870 a new type appeared on the enlarged German scene—the successful German who put efficiency, drive, and if necessary, ruth-lessness above everything. There was little left of the sleepy, order-loving, obedient, and honest "German Michel" of earlier days who was portrayed with his peaked cap both at home and abroad. The tough, new, successful personality had its exemplars in men like Bismarck, Krupp, or Carl Peters, the colonial pioneer.[1]

Along with these different images of the German personality a variety of traditions, difficult to pin down, has also influenced the German mentality. There is the voice of self-cultivation or *Bildung*; the spirit of Weimar; the Olympian tolerant, cosmopolitan spirit of Goethe, Schiller, and Wilhelm von Humboldt. There are also the drill sergeant of the barracks, the austere Prussian discipline, and the spirit of Potsdam. Both mental patterns will be considered.

Perhaps the fact that the Germans had been without a recognized fatherland for so long explains both their earlier national inferiority complex and their aggressive nationalism between 1870 and 1945. It was probably not by chance that Germany and Italy, the two Euro-pean nations that achieved political unity so late and at the same time, were more prone to the virus of fascist regimentation than the older and relatively more "democratic" nations. Today the world is much more interrelated and interdependent than it was sixty or a hundred years ago, when the man in the street rarely looked beyond his nation's frontiers. Before 1914 few Germans had any first-hand experience of foreign countries. They were generally contemptuous of the "decadent" French and the "inferior" Poles; they had scant knowledge of the Anglo-Saxon world and particularly of the trends and institutions of the United States. Their position did not change noticeably during the years of the Weimar Republic, when traveling abroad (apart from a honeymoon in Italy) was regarded by the great majority of Germans as a luxury that few people other than poli-ticians, businessmen, and a few journalists could afford. It is true that during Hitler's Third Reich the party organization *Kraft durch Freude*

---

[1] The prominence of these figures does not imply that the more idealistic or introverted type of German had disappeared altogether by 1914. The story of the German Youth Movement before and after World War I provides evi-dence for his survival.

(Strength Through Joy) offered manual and white-collar workers cheap trips abroad to Norway or to the Mediterranean; yet they had little chance of making informal contacts or seeing foreign countries for themselves. It was only in 1945 when the spell of mass intoxication and mass conformity was broken and Hitler and Goebbels had ended in suicide that the German windows to the outside world, so long closed or distorted, were reopened. The Four-Power occupation of Germany not only added a number of words to the German vocabulary, but also exposed the German people for some years to the impact of American, British, Russian, and French institutions and *mores* in their respective zones. New cultural and institutional ties developed between West Germany and America, Britain, and France, and between East Germany and the Soviet Union. English in West Germany, Russian in the Soviet Zone took preeminence among foreign languages and literatures. When the two rival German republics were established in the summer of 1949, each continued to look toward its sponsor. The impact of these foreign influences (little controlled in West Germany, but under tighter political and ideological supervision in East Germany) contributed to the growing separation and alienation between the two Germanies. Although at the end of 1969 Chancellor Brandt said, "even though two states exist in Germany they are not foreign countries to each other," it has been argued that today West Germany has less in common with East Germany than with the German-speaking part of Switzerland.

To understand the German situation today it is therefore necessary to understand the common past as well as the different developments of the two present Germanies. The internal story of the two German republics will be outlined in the rest of this chapter, while their involvement in foreign affairs forms the theme of the last. Nineteen forty-five has been called the Zero Year of contemporary German history. Let us first consider the character and meaning of this fateful incision in the long and complex course of German history before we consider the earlier centuries and the evolution of the First, Second, and Third Empires.

GERMANY UNDER FOUR-POWER CONTROL (1945–1949)

The utter defeat of Hitler in the spring of 1945 ended a ruthless regime and at the same time destroyed the German Reich and its government. The four foreign powers that jointly occupied Germany, an event unique in the annals of history, were confronted with large

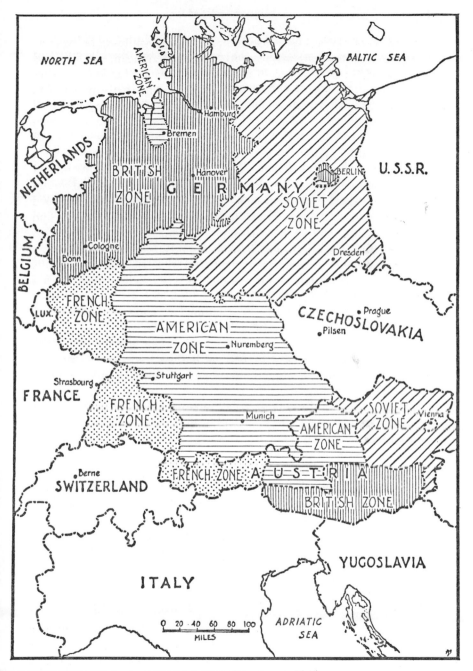

GERMANY AND AUSTRIA IN 1945

5

areas of utter chaos and a bewildered and disillusioned nation. In 1945, the three major victors, the Americans, the British, and the Russians, were prepared to allow an administrative unity of Germany. The original zoning of the country by the Big Three, which the French were later grudgingly allowed to join, was not intended to preclude an overall administration of the country.

The word "Germany" simply meant the territories held by the four occupation powers in July, 1945. These territories did not include the areas of the former Reich east of the Oder-Neisse Line such as parts of Pomerania, West Prussia, Silesia, and East Prussia, now administered by Poland and, in the case of northern East Prussia, by the Soviet Union. The former city of Breslau in Silesia now appears on the map as Wrocklav, while the name Königsberg, the home of Immanuel Kant, has been changed to Kaliningrad. Officially the Western powers and the Federal Republic of Germany regard these territories as only being administered by Poland and Russia, respectively, pending a final settlement by peace treaty, an arrangement that was accepted by the original four victorious powers of 1945; however, twenty-five years afterward, no such Peace treaty has been signed or is likely to be signed in the foreseeable future. These former German areas have in fact been integrated into Poland or Russia and remain outside the jurisdiction of the two rival German states that were founded in 1949.

The minutes of the Potsdam Conference of August, 1945, stated explicitly that "during the period of occupation, Germany shall be treated as a single economic unit." They specified areas of economic activity for which common policies should be pursued by the four powers represented in the Allied Control Council. If the concept of economic administrative unity did not work out in practice, it was not primarily the fault of the defeated Germans. It seemed, in 1945, that for years to come, they would not be the determinants in their country's affairs. Their fate and the responsibility for preventing utter chaos in a country badly hit by the impact of war was now in the hands of the conquerors, who were soon plagued by serious dissensions and differences in policy among themselves. Disagreement was probably inevitable between the Western capitalist democracies and the Communist Soviet Union. The first serious bone of contention over the question of reparations seemed largely technical. According to the economic provisions of the Potsdam Agreement, Russia and Poland, whose economies had suffered badly under Nazi domination, should receive reparations from the Soviet Zone. In addition, 15 percent of the usable industrial equipment of the Western Zones would be made available to the Russians in exchange for food and raw materials from their zone, and a further 10 percent would be delivered to them from the Western Zones at once without payment or exchange of any kind in return. However, nothing had been said in the Potsdam Agreement of the amount the German economy was to produce, and there was no reference to the possibility of taking reparations from current production. A decision on these tricky points might have been expected from the Allied Control Council; but the Russians lost no time and immediately began to dismantle the German factories. The disgruntled French, who had not been allowed to send representatives either to the conference at Yalta or to Potsdam, refused to be bound by the decisions of the Potsdam Conference and opposed any move to treat Germany as a unit. After Germany's collapse they wanted to remove the Ruhr from German control and bring the Saar under the economic and political control of France.

During the first twelve to eighteen months of occupation, the Allied troops and their civilian advisors were too busy restoring a modicum of "normality"; providing a minimum of housing, transport, and food for the Germans; ferreting out major Nazi criminals; and inquiring into the past of others under Hitler to realize the ideological and practical differences that existed between them. It was still a major objective for the Allies to prevent the resurgence of Nazism and militarism. In the first "Directive of the United States Joint Chiefs of Staff to the Commander-in-Chief of the United States Forces of Occupation Regarding the Military Government of Germany," issued in April, 1945, a few weeks before the end of hostilities, Article Two declared that "the rights, power, and status of the military government in Germany" were "based on the unconditional surrender or total defeat of Germany." Germany was "not to be occupied for the purpose of liberation, but as a defeated enemy nation," the principal of which was "to prevent Germany from ever again becoming a threat to the peace of the world."

Basic German living standards should not be "higher than those existing in any of the neighboring nations." The "Directive" was obviously influenced by the earlier views of Henry Morgenthau, secretary of the U.S. treasury, on the pastoralization of post-Nazi Germany, which he put forward in 1944. The Morgenthau Plan had "aimed at the creation of a new, peace-oriented Germany without heavy industry, but with a well-established agriculture. By implication this policy aimed at building an economically strong Europe with a weak Germany." [2] Gradually the Americans discovered that such an objective was utopian and even perilous to their own interests. The British, incidentally, never pursued such a drastic policy. Direct contact with the German population enabled both the Americans and the British to see the practical problems they had to face as occupying powers and modified their earlier views. When, by the autumn of 1946, the U.S. authorities in Germany felt it necessary to restore reasonable conditions in their zone, they did so not only because the resentment and hatred of the Nazi plague was gradually receding, but also owing to a growing fear of the Russians and of the advance of Communism. Although ostensibly the divergency of views on the reparation question led to the growing alienation between the U.S. and Britain and Soviet Russia, its deeper roots lay in the recognition of the incompatability of Western democracy and Stalinist "people's democracy."

In a major speech delivered in Stuttgart on September 6, 1946, James F. Byrnes, the American Secretary of State, announced that no further reparations from the American Zone would be delivered to the Russians. "The Allied Control Council had failed to take the necessary steps to enable the German economy to function as an economic unit," and the "essential German administration," visualized at Potsdam, had not been established. The Americans, Byrnes pointed out, still favored the economic unity of Germany; but if this seemed untenable for the time being, at least partial unification was practicable. In the future, the Americans would do everything in their power "to secure the maximum possible unification." The speech revealed a notable change in American policy towards the Germans. Under proper safeguards, Mr. Byrnes declared, the German people should be given the primary responsibility for running their own affairs. There was a subtle but unmistakable change in emphasis from the war crimes of the Nazi regime to protective measures for the post-Nazi Germans to survive economically. They should be given the chance to work their own passage back to a civilized existence. Byrnes's momentous statement foreshadowed the path on which, a few years later, Konrad Adenauer was to proceed so successfully. At first the pawns of Allied control, the Germans would gradually become the rulers of their own destiny. The American people were prepared to "return the government of Germany to the German

[2] Nicholas Balabkins, *Germany Under Direct Controls: Economic Aspects of Industrial Disarmament 1945–1948* (New Brunswick, N.J., 1964), p. 207.

people" and to help them "to win their way back to an honorable place among the free and peace-loving nations of the world."

A month later, the Byrnes line was supported by the British Foreign Secretary, Ernest Bevin. In a speech in the House of Commons on October 22, 1946, the vigorous former trade-union leader expressed "almost complete agreement" with the words of his American colleague. He welcomed the continuance of American interest in Europe, calling it "vital to the peace of Europe and particularly to the future of Germany." Bevin felt it was "extremely distasteful to see victorious nations courting a defeated enemy for ideological reasons." It was in England's interest, he declared, that Germany not become "a permanent distressed area in the center of Europe and that the Germans . . . have a proper and reasonable standard of living."

When they realized that the German economic situation was rapidly deteriorating, the Americans issued a new directive in July, 1947, that stressed the need for economic rehabilitation of Germany and the integration of Germany into the economic community of Western Europe. Both economic insights and political reasons were behind their change of attitude. Black market conditions in Germany and the appearance of a rather primitive barter economy between town and country contributed as much to it as the onset of the Cold War. "The inability or unwillingness of the Western occupation powers to provide food rations for the Germans before the currency reform in mid-June, 1948, held in check even 'permissible' industrial production and was thus partly responsible for the breakdown of the monetary currency." [3]

The fact that the American Marshall Plan of 1948 was extended to the American and British Zones of Germany proved of great significance. It meant with these two zones, and eventually the French Zone, the whole of West Germany would come under the American Economic Cooperation Act of 1948; as the American Secretary of State George Marshall put it in Moscow on March 31, 1947, the United States was "opposed to policies which will continue Germany as a congested slum or an economic poorhouse in the center of Europe."

Help under the Marshall Plan for West Germany, together with a currency reform in 1948, met fierce opposition from Soviet Russia. The Marshall Plan was generally interpreted by Stalin as an American

[3] Nicholas Balabkins, op. cit., p. 209.

attempt to subjugate the economies of European countries. Early in 1948, Russian control over Eastern Europe had been strengthened by the Communist coup d'etat in Czechoslovakia and by the creation of the *Cominform*. There is little evidence in 1945 or early 1946 that either the Russians or the Allies had expected the partition of Germany into two rival states; but it had become a fact by the autumn of 1949. The estrangement between the Western powers and Soviet Russia as a result of the Soviet policy in East Germany, the transformation of the East European states into Communist-controlled "people's democracies," and the conflict over Berlin in the summer of 1948 that led to a sharp dividing line between East and West Berlin—all contributed to the birth of two German states, one sponsored by the United States, Great Britain, and France, the other by the Soviet Union. Without the Cold War the demarcation line between the three Western Zones and the Soviet Zone would never have hardened into the frontier between two rival republics. West Germany took the lead in the process of forming a state. In the apt words of a French observer: "The Federal Republic was born in 1949 as a twin sister of the Atlantic Alliance. Its father was the Cold War. It happened in 1949 and not in 1945." [4] At least the Federal Republic started under a luckier star than the one under which the Weimar Republic had begun in 1919. One could not easily blame the new state for the chaos and misery of the immediate postwar years; many Germans held the Nazi regime responsible, and some the occupation powers. On the other hand, the quick economic recovery, the *Wirtschaftswunder*, and its gradual rise in prestige on the international scene appeared to the credit of the Federal German Republic. To a lesser extent and only many years later, the German Democratic Republic also gained in economic strength and political prestige.

WEST GERMANY: THE FEDERAL REPUBLIC

Economic Recovery and Political Foundations

The economic recovery of West Germany after the currency reform of 1948 was due to the interplay of a number of factors. The enforced exchange of the new Deutsche Mark for the devalued old Reichsmark (on the general basis of 1 to 6.5 and the more favorable one of 1 to 1.10 for the repayment of debts) led to the end of the

---

[4] Alfred Grosser, *Die Bundesrepublik Deutschland, Bilanz einer Entwicklung* (Tübingen, 1967), p. 12.

obnoxious black market. The subsequent shortage of money brought many goods withheld by their owners onto the market and was, with the stabilization, an incentive to hard work. The bold, concommitant, large-scale abolition of controls over wages, prices, and supplies proclaimed by Dr. Ludwig Erhard, then German director of the Joint Economic Administration Office for the American and British Zones, encouraged free enterprise, an attitude particularly welcomed by the Americans. At a time when world demand was high, German industry found itself with spare capacity, the right products, and relatively low costs, so that exporting was easy and profitable, and hence popular.[5] West German exports particularly boomed from 1950 onwards, owing to the Korean War. There was a high rate of saving; and for the first two or three years, the large number of unemployed supplied a large and flexible labor force, which included many refugees from the East. During the second half of 1948, industrial production increased by 50 percent and in 1949 by another 25 percent. Four years later, by 1953, the living standard in West Germany was higher than it had been under Hitler in 1938. It was fortunate for the new republic that during its first few years it became the fourth largest recipient of the Marshall Plan and obtained about a tenth of its funds. "Without these dollars to draw on for vital purchases, the German balance of payments would have caused even more anxiety than it did. Moreover Marshall aid meant that Germany was recovering in the middle of a continent doing the same; each stimulated the other." [6] Because of the political stability and the relative price stability from 1949 onward, there was a surprisingly high rate of investment.[7] The index of overall industrial productivity, based on the figure 100 in 1936 for the output per manhour worked, was at 82.3 in 1949, which was still under the earlier figure, but it was surpassed in 1951 with 102.6 and in 1953 with 113.3. The growth in individual branches was striking, particularly in the iron and steel industry, and in chemicals, vehicles, and food processing.[8]

German manual and white-collar workers were less demanding than their colleagues in other countries; the trade-union leaders proved

[5] M. Balfour, West Germany (London, 1968), p. 180.
[6] M. Balfour, op. cit., p. 175.
[7] Henry C. Wallich, Main Springs of the German Revival (New Haven: Yale University Press, 1955), p. 154.
[8] See the table "Index of Industrial Productivity" in Wallich, op. cit., p. 208.

to be sensible and cooperative; and there were no strikes. This and the rapidly soaring export prices of foreign countries proved favorable to German competition. Dr. Erhard, minister of economics in the Adenauer cabinets for the first fourteen years of the Federal Republic, proclaimed a "socially conscious free market economy"; but in the words of Henry C. Wallich, the economy had "perhaps not been altogether free nor especially outstanding for its social consciousness." [9] The government continued to "play a preponderant role through its large budget, through the indirect control exercised over investment, by means of the taxation system, through ownership and operation of important industries and through its somewhat paternalistic habits." In spite of some faults, "by design of accident a balance of freedom and control" was achieved that proved successful. Yet few German and foreign observers expected at the end of the 1940s that West Germany would become the world's second largest exporter by 1958, and its third largest producer by 1961.

The "Basic Law" (in fact, though not in name, the constitution of the Federal Republic) was conceived in 1948–49 by a parliamentary council of sixty-five members drawn from the parliaments of the eleven *Länder* (states) in the three Western zones with the two major parties, the Christian Democrats and the Social Democrats, about evenly represented.[10] The draft of the Basic Law was accepted with some minor modifications in May, 1949, by the Western occupation powers, and was later ratified by the legislatures of the eleven *Länder*, with the exception of the Bavarian Diet. The fathers of the Basic Law clearly regarded it as provisional, a stepping-stone to a future constitution for the whole of Germany.

It has been rightly said in retrospect that the Basic Law was "not the reflection of a positive enthusiasm for a better future," but rather "the expression of a deep revulsion against a distasteful past." [11] It is certainly a more sober and practical document than the Constitution of the Weimar Republic of 1919 and gives less prominence to ideology, although the first chapter, "Basic Rights," speaks of "the inviolable and inalienable human rights as the basis of any human community, of peace and justice in the world." Similar to the Consti-

[9] Henry C. Wallich, op. cit., p. 147.

[10] Dr. Konrad Adenauer, the chairman of the Christian Democratic Union in the British Zone and Lord Mayor of Cologne under the Weimar Republic, was elected chairman of the parliamentary council.

[11] Peter Merkl, *The Origin of the West German Republic* (New York, 1963), p. 176.

tution of the Weimar Republic, which had been in force from 1919 to 1933, there was to be a parliament with two chambers—the Federal Diet and the Federal Council; the federal government was to be headed by a chancellor and a president.[12] Yet the makers of the Basic Law tried to avoid the pitfalls of the Weimar system, and several lessons they learned from it are clearly discernible in its clauses. The federal president, for instance, was not to be chosen by popular vote as before 1933, but jointly by the deputies of the federal and state parliaments. A chancellor in office could only be overthrown if a majority of deputies in the federal diet agreed on the nomination of his successor (Article Sixty-seven). This is the so-called "constructive vote of no-confidence" that was intended to prevent a repetition of the chaotic situation of the early thirties when a majority of right- and left-wing opponents in the Reichstag could overthrow the chancellor without agreeing on a successor.

The Federal Republic, as set up by the Basic Law, differed greatly in structure from any of its predecessors (see the map on p. ii). Prussia, the largest of the individual German states, was the main pillar of the country under Bismarck and later under the Weimar Republic; but it had disappeared from the map. Out of the eleven *Länder* of which the new West German state was composed, only two were made up of the old provinces of Prussia, Schleswig–Holstein, and Hanover, now named Lower Saxony. The former Prussian province of Westphalia was allied to the northern half of the Rhineland, forming the state of North Rhine–Westphalia, the most populated *Land* in the Federal Republic. It borders on the state of Rhineland–Palatinate, a combination of the southern part of the old Rhine province with the former Bavarian province of the Palatinate. The state of Hesse was enlarged. Bavaria retained its traditional territory, apart from the loss of the Palatinate. Baden and Württemberg formed three different states in 1949, but have since been amalgamated into the one state of Baden–Württemberg. Hamburg and Bremen remained city-states, as they had been between 1871 and 1933. At present the Saar also forms part of the Federal Republic and so does West Berlin, up to a point. Today it looks as if Bonn, once a sleepy university town, is going to remain the "permanent provisional" capital of the larger part of Germany and the focal point of its political life; yet the role of the capitals of the individual states such as Munich, Stuttgart, Hanover, Mainz, Wiesbaden, Saarbrücken,

[12] See Chapter 8, pp. 172–73.

Düsseldorf, Kiel, Hamburg, and Bremen should not be overlooked. Other towns of major importance are Frankfurt am Main and Karlsruhe (the seat of the Federal Constitutional Court), with West Berlin in a category of its own. Each of the *Länder* has its own parliament and administration. Bavaria has the most territory, but North Rhine–Westphalia, which includes the Ruhr, the greatest number of people. Hamburg and North Rhine–Westphalia are outstandingly prosperous, whereas Schleswig–Holstein, the Saar, and Rhineland–Palatinate are comparatively poor. Although provision has been made for the richer states to help the poorer ones financially, this has not always worked out satisfactorily.

Under the Basic Law the *Länder* are represented in the upper house, the Federal Council in Bonn. It consists of forty-five members, and the number of delegates from each state varies according to the strength of its population—between three, four, or five. The post of President of the Council rotates annually between the member states. On the other hand the Federal Diet alone, elected by the people on the basis of party politics, is able to pass laws, though most of them are drafted by civil servants and submitted by the government. Its members, who can also initiate bills, keep a close watch on the government's budget and may pass or reject it. The cabinet ministers are chosen from the ranks of the Federal Diet, although the Basic Law does not make this obligatory. In the first twenty years of its existence the Bonn Diet has modeled itself largely on the Western type of parliament.

Not only is the approval of the Federal Diet required and necessary in all cases for a wide range of legislation, but also that of the Federal Council, because the laws concerned affect the *Länder*. There are clearly limited areas in which the federal authorities have jurisdiction and can administer alone—for instance, in matters of federal finance, railways, and postal services. There are others where federal legislation is, in fact, administered by the *Länder*, following a tradition going back to the days of Bismarck. Finally, to a considerable extent the *Länder* follow their own legislative policies and have autonomy. In recent years there has been a good deal of criticism to the effect that the limited powers of the federal government are inadequate and inefficient in such important fields as education or fighting crime. Admittedly, the entire organization of education from kindergarten to the university has its traditional roots in the *Länder*, each of which possesses its own minister of education with all the relevant laws being drafted in his ministry.[13] Attempts have been made to mitigate this lopsided situation, for in Germany, as elsewhere, the existing institutions and ways of learning have to adjust to changing conditions in an age of student unrest. There is now a Standing Conference of the Ministers of Education in Bonn which "aims at finding a common denominator in educational policy while preserving the justified interest of the respective *Länder*." [14] It is also significant that in October, 1969, for the first time the Federal Minister of Education and Scientific Research, Professor Hans Leussink, was appointed in place of the former Minister for Scientific Research only. Many new ideas have come to the fore with the reform of universities and secondary schools. Some comprehensive schools have been established in Hamburg and Berlin; and at the Free University in West Berlin an assistant lecturer has been elected president for seven years, thus breaking the time-honored privilege of full professors to head the university for one or two years. Sooner or later, the pressures for educational reform will require an extension of the power of the federal government at the expense of the *Länder*.

From Adenauer to Brandt: Parties and Voters

The political situation in 1945 differed greatly from the one in 1918. The old parties of the monarchy at that time had continued in the new republic, although in some cases they operated under a new name. After the Second World War all parties had to be licensed by the occupation powers, which at first appeared to favor reestablishing some of the old pre-1933 parties rather than founding entirely new ones. There was at first "a marked dislike among the general public for party-political obligations and activities—a reaction to totalitarian party politics [of the Third Reich] with their consequences for each and all." [15] Many people were afraid to commit themselves by joining a party. Of the former major parties, only the Social Democrats were able to continue on from the past and even retain the traditional structure of their organization. The Communist Party never counted for much, as it was tainted by its affinity with Soviet

[13] The Bonn government has, however, joint legislative powers with the *Länder* in the field of scientific research and subsidizes it jointly.

[14] Joachim H. Knoll, *The German Educational System* (Bad Godesberg: Inter Nationes, 1967), p. 10.

[15] Theodor Schieder, *The State and Society in Our Times* (London, 1962), p. 130.

Russia and the German Democratic Republic. The old right had been completely wiped out because of the support the German Nationalists had given to the Hitler regime in 1933, only to be stifled quickly by it. Later, the conservative groups who had opposed Hitler were mostly destroyed after July 20, 1944. An attempt was made to revive the old Catholic Center Party, but it soon proved out of date. Instead there rose a new man's party for Catholics and Protestants alike, the Christian Democratic Union (CDU), similar to the new Christian Democrats in France and Italy. The liberals established the Free Democratic Party (FDP) with a platform designed to combine the former South West German Democrats with others who had formerly sympathized with Dr. Stresemann's German People's Party. Political regionalism also made itself felt. In Bavaria the Christian Democrats, more conservative than elsewhere, called themselves the "Christian Social Union" (CSU), but they combined under this label with the CDU in the Bonn Diet and also in Adenauer's coalition government. A much fiercer regional note was struck by the Bavarian Party. Of little importance on a federal level, it exercised some influence in Bavarian state politics. There was also a regional conservative party in Lower Saxony that later tried, not very successfully, to expand in Northern Germany under the name of "German Party." Among the ranks of the six million refugees and expellees from Sudetenland and the former East German provinces now under Polish or Russian control, there emerged a new supraregional refugee party, the B.H.E. For some years it played a role in Bonn and was also represented in the *Land* governments of Bavaria, Hesse, and Lower Saxony.

Yet the main trend in the political situation in West Germany after 1949 lies towards two or three parties only. In the Reichstag of the Weimar Republic there were up to a dozen parties; however, no single party ever obtained an absolute majority. In the first Federal Diet in Bonn in 1949 ten parties were still to be found, but their number declined steadily to six in 1953 and to four in 1957. Since 1961 only three parties have had deputies in the federal parliament. In 1949, 72 percent of all the voters already supported the three major parties; by 1957 89 percent of them did so, and by 1969 no less than 95 percent.[16] Because two of these three parties (the CDU–CSU, the SPD, and the FDP) usually form the government, and the third the opposition, a fairly stable situation has developed in which

[16] K. D. Bracher, ed., *Nach 25 Jahren: Eine Bilanz* (Munich, 1970), p. 255.

government and opposition have become rather institutionalized and are now taken for granted.

The Electoral System and the Parties

Of the three major parties, the Christian Democrats (CDU–CSU), the Social Democrats (SPD), and the Free Democrats (FDP), only the Social Democrats retained their traditional features. Again, as before 1933, the SPD, a semi-Marxist party, began in 1949 as the spokesman of the working class and of international socialism.[17] Its leader, Kurt Schumacher, emphasized the national line more than earlier Social Democratic politicians. For some years no serious effort was made to interest groups other than manual and white-collar workers. Instead the need for a planned economy and for large-scale nationalization of industry was emphasized.

The CDU–CSU stressed its ideological background and general outlook as a Christian party, which for the first time comprised both Catholics and Protestants. Its interdenominational character was largely the outcome of the Nazi persecution of both churches. However, apart from its basic Christian views, the CDU presented facets in different regions. As a French press correspondent observed in September, 1946: "This party is socialist and radical in Berlin, clerical and conservative in Cologne, capitalist and reactionary in Hamburg, and counterrevolutionary and particularist in Munich." But in spite of its pluralist character, it became fairly integrated as a modern conservative party under the firm and skillful hand of Dr. Konrad Adenauer. With the "social market economy" of Dr. Ludwig Erhard, it could claim much of the credit for West Germany's economic revival.

The Social Democrats wanted the new republic to be kept free at its inception from strong ties with the West in order to avoid alienating the Germans under Soviet control. On the other hand, the CDU–CSU emphasized the need for making the Federal Republic a model state that would attract their fellow countrymen in East Germany.

In the first election of the Federal Diet in August, 1949, Adenauer's CDU–CSU emerged as the strongest party, polling 34.5 percent of the total vote, followed by the SPD, with 29.2 percent. The Free Democrats obtained third place with 11.9 percent. In September,

[17] For the earlier history of the Social Democratic Party see Chapters 7 and 8.

1949, the new Federal Diet elected Dr. Konrad Adenauer chancellor with a bare majority of one (his own vote). Securing 202 out of 402 votes, he formed a broad antisocialist coalition that comprised the Christian Democrats (CDU–CSU), the Free Democrats (FDP), and the tiny German Party (DP). Adenauer made much of the incompatibility of the socialist ideas of planning with those of a "free social economy." The Free Democrats had succeeded in electing their liberal party leader, the urbane and spirited Dr. Theodor Heuss, as federal president.[18] With some variations in South West Germany and the Rhineland, the Free Democrats were both anticlerical and anti-Marxist.

West Germany's growing economic prosperity strengthened Dr. Adenauer's adroit hand in gradually removing the last fetters and ties of the occupation and in gaining gradual recognition abroad for the new Germany.[19] His success was reflected in the increasing vote of his own party, where his tough leadership remained unchallenged. At the elections to the second Federal Diet in 1953 it rose by over 10 percent to 45 percent of the total vote. Though the CDU–CSU obtained a slight majority with 244 seats in the diet, Adenauer was shrewd enough to continue to include the smaller nonsocialist parties in his cabinet. Four years later in 1957, the CDU–CSU secured an absolute majority of votes and seats in the election (270 seats out of a total of 497). The success of the CDU can be explained by the continued economic prosperity of the country, which enabled her to compete favorably in the export trade with France and Great Britain, and also by the aversion of most Germans for experiments both at home and abroad.

On the other hand, the failure of the Adenauer government to make any headway on the question of German reunification strengthened the chances of the Social Democratic opposition. By 1957, the smaller parties had practically become irrelevant in federal politics. In the elections to the fourth and fifth diets of 1961 and 1965, all the small parties missed out. In 1961, the share of the vote for the CDU–CSU fell from 50.2 percent to 45.4 percent; but combined with the Free Democrats as junior partner (which had polled 12.8 percent), the Adenauer government had a comfortable majority. However, the Social Democrats, now under the dynamic leadership of

[18] He remained in office for ten years until 1959 and was followed by the Christian Democrat Heinrich Lübke (1959–69) and by the present president, Gustav Heinemann, a Social Democrat, elected in 1969.

[19] For Adenauer's foreign policy see Chapter 11.

Willy Brandt, who had become a national figure as Lord Mayor of West Berlin, had increased their strength to 36.2 percent of the vote. The retirement of the aged Dr. Adenauer in October, 1963, and the replacement of his successor, Dr. Erhard, by Kurt Georg Kiesinger in December, 1966, did not seriously impair the strength of the CDU. In the general elections of 1965 both the CDU–CSU and the SPD managed to increase their number of seats, the CDU–CSU by three and SPD by twelve. The Free Democrats lost and their mandate declined by eighteen seats. For a while Dr. Erhard, who lacked Adenauer's tactical acumen, managed to keep the Free Democrats in the cabinet; but by October, 1965, there were serious disagreements between the two over plans for higher taxation, and the FDP members resigned from the cabinet. In both the CDU and the SPD, powerful voices were heard in favor of a "great coalition" between these major parties.

The rapprochement had been facilitated by the Socialists' Godesberg Program of 1959, which clearly indicated the road it had traversed from a class party to a people's party, a kind of progressive and human type of populism. Its ideology stressed "a democratic socialism, rooted in Europe in Christian ethics, in humanism and the classic [German] philosophy." Marxist socialism, while declaring religion a private matter, had formerly claimed that it replaced the old-fashioned Christian creed. Now the Godesberg Program clearly stated that socialism was "no substitute for religion." The SPD not only expressed its respect for the churches and religious communities, but also its readiness to cooperate with them. The Social Democratic Party claimed to have "developed from a party of the working class to a party of the people." While rejecting totalitarian Communist planning, the SPD favored an economic policy that secured full employment and increased economic productivity in the nation.

The Godesberg Program sharply criticized big business for preventing free competition, but private property would be protected as long as it did not prevent the building of a just social order. Efficient medium- and small-scale enterprises were to be strengthened in order to compete with big business. "Competition—as far as possible; planning—as far as necessary" was the new motto of modernized social democracy in the technological age.

The Great Coalition (1966–1969)

Although in December, 1966, many Social Democrats would have preferred a "little coalition" with the Free Democrats, the Great

Coalition emerged in the end with the CDU–CSU having twelve members in the cabinet and the SPD nine. The new chancellor, Kurt Georg Kiesinger, had built his reputation as an able and balanced premier of the *Land* Baden–Württemberg. In contrast to Kiesinger, who in the Third Reich had been a member of the Nazi Party for some years and an employee of the foreign ministry, the new vice-chancellor and minister of foreign affairs, Willy Brandt, had spent the years of the Second World War abroad as an emigré in Scandinavia. Both were agreed on a middle-of-the-road course in domestic and economic policy, in the continuation of West Germany's integration in Western Europe, and in a possible rapprochement with some of the states in Eastern Europe. Professor Karl Schiller, as minister of economics, and Dr. Gustav Heinemann, as minister of justice, were other prominent socialists in the government. The forceful leader of the Bavarian CSU, Franz Joseph Strauss had been obliged to resign as minister of defense in December, 1962, over his questionable role in the arrest of the publisher and a contributor to the magazine *Der Spiegel*; but he returned as minister of finance, while Gerhard Schroeder exchanged the ministry of foreign affairs, which he had held for the last five years under Adenauer and Erhard, for that of defense.

Looking back on the overall development in West Germany under the Great Coalition government, a number of major trends became evident:

1. "The extension of the sphere of influence of the state and particularly of the Federal Republic in the social and economic spheres."
2. In the age of a more permissive society, a "retreat of the state from the position of moral judge."
3. More central planning and guidance—partly at the expense of the federalist forces—and assistance in orientation to an environment that is becoming more difficult to grasp.
4. "An extension of the welfare state." [20]

In the last instance, the coalition of Christian Democrats and Social Democrats of 1966 was helped into being by a general trend in Western Europe that made itself felt particularly in West Germany. This trend has been marked by the decline of ideology and the em-

[20] Rudolf Zundel, *Die Zeit* (July 11, 1968).

phasis on equality in a modern mass-consumer society. To win the masses, individual concerns and grievances must neither be ignored nor overstressed. A political platform with a common denominator counts for more than one that acknowledges the specific demands of political and social groups, although they can by no means be overlooked. Class differentiation, though still in existence, matters less in an age where the industrial workers are no longer depressed. The dividing line between employers and employees, bank managers and bank clerks, newspaper owners and journalists, has lost a good deal of its former significance. On the other hand, in a highly industrialized society new attitudes have developed with reduced working hours and more leisure. Everywhere the role of the bureaucracy has grown. It is no longer confined to government bureaucracy, which in Germany operates on the federal, state, district, and municipal levels. The bureaucracy of the trade unions is a powerful factor. Trade unions are one sector of the so-called *Verbände* (economic interest associations), the others consisting of employers' federations and farmers' associations. Their influence on the political decision-makers has grown at a time when the exclusive appeal of the parties to a specific social stratum (workers, middle classes, peasants, Catholics, refugees, or Bavarians) has decreased. The political program must be sufficiently concrete and nonsectarian to appeal to a wide group of people. Apart from two extremist political parties on the right and left, the National Democrats and the German Communists, which were only readmitted in 1968, all the West German parties today "affirm Christianity, are liberal, social-minded, and democratic, but each of them wants to outdo the others by its emphasis on at least one of these values." [21]

Looking back on the short history of the Federal Republic as a whole, the democratic institutions of the new state have stood the test of the first twenty years. However, when one considers the degree to which people actually participate in the affairs of the country, the picture is less satisfactory. Admittedly, in most countries with a democratic constitution the role of the voter in deciding political issues is confined to voting at regular intervals. However, the democratic position is less perilous in countries with a long parliamentary tradition such as Switzerland or England. In West Germany a dangerous trend towards party oligarchy, on the one hand, and mass po-

[21] Heino Kaak, *Die Parteien in der Verfassungswirklichkeit der Bundesrepublik*, 2d ed. (Bonn, 1964), p. 77.

litical apathy, on the other, has been seen by a number of observers. The eminent philosopher Karl Jaspers has complained that "most people are frighteningly uninformed. The parties tell them nothing, teach them nothing, and do not spur them to think. At election times they operate with advertising techniques, and between election times they consider the material interest of groups whose votes they are after." [22] The picture is indeed very different from the days of Bismarck when "the State was everything, the party little." Today, Karl Jaspers claims, "the parties are the state. The state leadership rests with the oligarchy of the parties."

The Federal Elections of 1969—A "Minicoalition"

Experienced foreign observers who toured West Germany during the election campaign in September, 1969, were struck by the intense interest people took in the election. This was evident not only in the high percentage of votes cast—86.6 percent of all registered voters appeared at the poll—but even more in an interesting and novel feature; in the streets of many towns groups of people, mostly under 40, discussed and argued about the controversial issues during the evening. This lively new popular commitment was one of the reasons why the extremist groups fared badly in the elections. The extreme left-wing "Action for Democratic Progress" managed to obtain only 0.6 percent of the total vote and gained no seats. More serious was the challenge from the extreme right, the National Democratic Party (NPD), which had made considerable progress in state elections in 1966 and 1967 under the leadership of Adolf von Thadden. This party, in spite of its denial, has some points in common with Hitler's NSDAP, and there are many formerly active National Socialists in its leadership. Many expected that it would poll more than the required minimum of 5 percent of the total vote and thus enter the Bonn Parliament with between twenty-five and forty deputies.[23] However, at the federal election the NPD missed out altogether, gaining only 4.3 percent of the total vote.[24]

Another major feature of the 1969 elections was the high percentage of votes (88.8 percent) that went to the two major parties, the CDU–CSU and the SPD, which until then had formed the gov-

[22] Karl Jaspers, *The Future of Germany* (Chicago and London, 1967), p. 4.
[23] For the structure and rise of the National Socialist Party, see Chapters 8 and 9.
[24] The trend continued in 1970 when the National Democrats lost all their previous seats in the elections to the diets of Hesse and Bavaria.

ernment of the Great Coalition. Yet the Great Coalition was not renewed. The difference in the domestic, financial, and foreign policies of the two partners had proved too great an obstacle for them. In spite of slight losses, the Christian Democrats (CDU–CSU), who had been in the government for twenty years, still remained the strongest party with 46.1 percent of the vote.[25] The Social Democrats on the other hand, increased their votes to a total of 42.7 percent, a figure they had never reached before.

The major losers in the elections were unquestionably the Free Democrats, whose strength fell from 9.5 percent to a mere 5.8 percent of the total vote. They retained only thirty out of their former forty-nine seats.[26] The leadership of the party had aimed at an alliance with the SPD for some time. This move was foreshadowed by the fact that in the spring of 1969, the FDP declared itself for the socialist, Gustav Heinemann, as federal president rather than for the CDU opponent, Gerhard Schroeder. Without the FDP support, Heinemann would not have been elected. After the general election in September, 1969, the irony of the situation was that, in spite of its severe mauling, the FDP tipped the political scales; for without its support neither of the two major parties could form a government. The FDP decided to become the junior partner to the SPD. While a few of its deputies, including the former leader of the party, Erich Mende, did not favor this step, the overwhelming majority of thirty deputies did. The "minicoalition" of the SPD and FDP holds a small majority of six seats in the federal diet. The leader of the Free Democrats, Walter Scheel, is vice-chancellor and minister for foreign affairs in the government of which Willy Brandt, as chairman of the SPD, is chancellor.[27] Two other Free Democrats have seats in the cabinet. There have been coalition governments between these two parties before in some of the *Länder*; a conspicuous example is the coalition, renewed in 1970, of many years standing between Social Democrats and Free Democrats in North Rhine–Westphalia, the largest single state in the Federal Republic. By 1969 the Social Democrats had become respectable. They were no longer in the political ghetto where they had found themselves in the days of Adenauer and Kurt Schumacher. Like the British Labour Party, they had ceased

---

[25] However, in the *Land* with the largest population, North Rhine–Westphalia, they lost their previous preponderance to the Social Democrats.

[26] The Free Democrats failed to retain any seats in the June 1970 state elections in Lower Saxony and the Saar.

[27] For the foreign policy of the Brandt–Scheel government see Chapter 11.

to be a mere class party. In the election campaign of 1969, they had appealed effectively to people from all generations and from many social strata.

After twenty years of predominance in the government, the Christian Democrats were in opposition for the first time. The CDU and CSU together are still numerically the strongest party in the West German parliament. In opposition, they are able to give less consideration to the older and middle-aged generations and more to the young. Although at the age of sixty-five Mr. Kiesinger was reelected chairman of the CDU at its party congress at Mainz in November, 1969, it is quite possible that he will be replaced before the next federal election by a younger and more dynamic man. Rather than continuing to be a party of elderly notables, the Christian Democrats still have an opportunity to become a representative mass party once more.

EAST GERMANY: FROM THE SOVIET ZONE (1945–1949)
TO THE GERMAN DEMOCRATIC REPUBLIC (1949 TO THE PRESENT)

> Seen in historical perspective, Germany is a very variable political and geographical concept. I will not go back as far as the map of Germany during the times of the Holy Roman Empire or that of the Napoleonic Wars. Already since 1914 Germany has considerably changed her shape several times.
> WALTER ULBRICHT, CHAIRMAN OF THE STATE COUNCIL
> OF THE GERMAN DEMOCRATIC REPUBLIC
>
> From an address to the Central Committee of the Communist Party on December 13, 1969.

From the beginning in 1945, the attitude of the Soviet Military Administration (SMA) to political life in the Soviet Zone differed from that of the Western occupation authorities in their zones. The only point that all four powers had in common was the determination to prevent a revival of National Socialism and nationalist organizations. Apart from this, the main interest of the Soviet administration was to exact the highest amount of reparations possible. During the immediate postwar years, the idea of a united democratized Germany was by no means a mere fiction in the eyes of Stalin and the Russian powerholders in East Germany. It was hoped that the "antifascist democratic front," to which all the legal parties in the zone belonged, would become a spearhead for the formation of a reorganized united Germany at a later date. The first four parties admitted in the Soviet Zone were: the Communist (KPD), the Social Democratic

(SPD), the Liberal (LPD), and the Christian Democratic (CDU). To all appearances there was, as in the West, competition between recognized parties that offered different programs and represented different social strata. Party leaders were screened by the SMA, but otherwise few obstacles were put in their path at first.

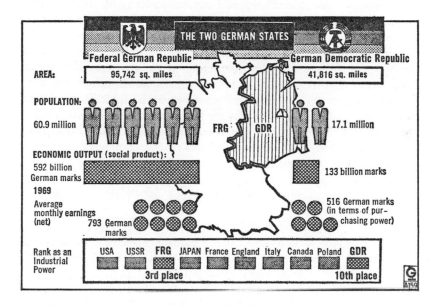

However, the situation changed in April, 1946, when a merger of the Social Democrats and the Communists into a United Socialist Party, the SED, was announced. The idea of such an amalgamation had been rejected by the Social Democrats in the three Western Zones and also by the overwhelming majority of the members of the SPD in West Berlin. The merger ended the SPD in the Soviet Zone, and most of its former members accepted the new SED. On the other hand, the occupation authorities did not allow the SED to operate in the other zones. Differing from the Russians, the occupation powers in the West did not identify themselves with one party.

In accordance with economic policy of redistribution of land and industrial property, the Soviet administration soon considered the SED as the only party that represented the Communist masses. After the first year, the SED grew into a mass party with a membership of 1.8 million by May, 1949; the original parity between Communist Party and former Social Democrats had eroded to the point that nearly all the leading positions were filled by reliable, orthodox Communists. The two "bourgeois" parties, the CDU and the LPD, found themselves in an increasingly precarious position. To make things more difficult for these nonsocialist parties, in 1948 the Soviet authorities arranged the formation of two further parties, the Peasants Party and the National Democratic Party. Controlled by Communists, they appealed to specific interests and were calculated to attract distinct groups; the Peasants Party turned to the peasants, and officials of the farmers cooperatives occupied the top positions; the National Democratic Party appealed to nationalists and former minor Nazis who were to be reorientated along pro-Communist lines.

However, the SED dominated what was soon officially called the "National Front." This term suggested the integration of all parties and vital mass organizations under the leadership of the SED. The SED included the Trade Union Federation, the Democratic Federation of German Women, the Free German Youth, all of which were led by SED members and sympathizers and were represented in parliament by seats on the National Front list. These separate organizations acted as channels through which the slogans and directives of the state could reach the man in the street. The SED could soon openly claim that it controlled the administrative apparatus; in the words of a party writer in 1956, ten years after its foundation, "not a single decision is taken without reference to the guiding directions worked out by the Party." The public had no alternative to the list submitted by National Front. In the October, 1963, elections for instance, out of 11,621,000 registered voters in East Germany, no less than 11,533,000 voters went to the polling stations. The list of the National Front received 99.95 percent, and 0.05 percent "adverse votes" and 0.04 percent votes were declared invalid.

Towards "Democratic Centralism"

The Soviet Zone was composed of three former *Länder*: Saxony, Thuringia, and Mecklenburg–Pomerania, and two *Länder* provinces, Saxony–Anhalt and Brandenburg. All had their own diets that were elected in October, 1946; *Land* governments were formed soon afterwards. Though the Communist SED, with 47.5 percent of the total vote, proved to be by far the strongest party, the two nonsocialist parties, the CDU and the LPD, gained a slightly higher share (49.1 percent). Different from the situation in West Germany, these five *Land* diets did not prepare the way for drafting a constitution. This was done in a more indirect manner. A self-appointed "German People's Congress for the Unity of Germany and a Just Peace," first formed for the entire Soviet Zone at the end of 1947, elected a People's Council (*Volksrat*) in the following year. Its 400 members, declaring themselves the only representative body of the German people, drafted a constitution for the "German Democratic Republic" (GDR) that was later approved in a plebiscite by a slight majority. There was no general election. Instead, the People's Council turned itself into a provisional "Lower House" of the *Volkskammer*, provided by the constitution. Its executive committee appointed a government in which all permitted parties were represented by men who had been previously approved by the Soviet Control Commission. (After the proclamation of the German Democratic Republic in October, 1949, this commission had replaced the SMA.) There were no elections to the Lower House until October, 1950. The first prime minister was Otto Grotewohl, and the first and only president of the republic was Wilhelm Pieck.[28] In 1952, the sharp trend towards centralization of power led to the abolition of the *Länder*, which were replaced by fourteen (with East Berlin, fifteen) districts, and six years later to the abolition of the Upper Chamber, although its existence was anchored in the constitution.

The 1949 constitution of the GDR was drafted at a time when the Communists of the SED still hoped to obtain power in a future all-German parliament. It was therefore based on the model of a parliamentary multiparty system; and in some ways it followed the pattern of the Weimar Constitution of 1919 more than the West German Basic Law. The later practice of voting on the basis of only one list of candidates was contrary to the spirit of the constitution, which clearly intended the voter to have a choice. Here and in other aspects, the discrepancy between the humanistic theory of the constitution and the harsh practice of the one-party state soon became evident. "The regime flouted its constitution by openly refusing higher education to most children of middle-class parents and pressuring farmers to give up their property without bothering to pass a coercive law, while the privileges of the churches [expressly acknowledged in the constitution] were increasingly disregarded." [29]

As in other Communist states, the political structure of the German Democratic Republic is one of "Democratic Centralism," and

---

[28] After Pieck's death in 1960 the office of the president was abolished.
[29] Arnold J. Heidenheimer, *The Governments of Germany* (New York, 1961), p. 101.

the top positions in the government and the Communist Party are closely interrelated. The most important decision-making organs are not the Central Committee of the Socialist Unity Party (ZK), which consists of 100 members and 50 candidates, but the powerful Politbureau of the party and the Secretariat of the ZK. The Secretariat of the ZK consists of six professional functionaries, with a large apparatus of experts in twenty departments under them. The ministers of the Politbureau include not only the prime minister (now Willi Stoph) and his first deputy, but also the chairman of the planning commission, the chairman of the economic council, and the chairman of the council for agriculture. The Politbureau comprises the seven secretaries of the ZK, with the first secretary as chairman, his deputy,[30] and the secretaries for industry, agriculture, consumer policies, and for ideology and agitation.

In this top-heavy bureaucracy, the main task of the Politbureau is to formulate policy statements on all-German questions and ideological issues, including those relating to art, literature, mass culture, and on the speed of nationalization. Finally, the Politbureau controls the instruments of power: the armed forces, the various branches of the police, and the secret service (SSI).

The Council of Ministers comprises thirty-five ministers; but its inner circle, the *Präsiduum*, only fifteen, of whom four or six are also members of the Politbureau. While the Council of Ministers decides all questions of economic policy and practice, including agriculture, foreign trade, and consumer supplies, the task of the *Präsiduum* is to coordinate the policies. The highest power in the GDR, however, probably lies with the Council of State, which was elected by the People's Chamber in September, 1960. This council consists of a chairman, six deputy chairmen, sixteen members, and a secretary. Walter Ulbricht has been chairman since its foundation, and the position seems to have been specially tailored for him. As the chairman is authorized to issue decrees with the force of law and to interpret existing laws, he is in fact, if not in name, head of the state above the legislative and the executive branches.

In Ulbricht, a life-long Communist and once a carpenter, Stalin had found a ruthless party leader and an able organizer, whom he and his associates felt they could trust. Like Pieck, he had spent many years of exile in Moscow before 1945. When the tide of the

---

[30] Walter Ulbricht was the first secretary and Erich Honecker his deputy until May 3, 1971, when Honecker took Ulbricht's place.

war turned against the Nazis, Ulbricht assisted in the "reorientation" of German prisoners of war and in translating Soviet policy into guidelines for German Communists.

Soon after his return to Germany, Ulbricht became a power behind the official façade of the reconstituted German Communist Party by acting as deputy to the more friendly and congenial Wilhelm Pieck. In 1950, Ulbricht advanced to the position of general secretary of the party's important Central Committee (ZK), a position he held until May 1971 (though later under the title of First Secretary). He continued to accumulate power. In the words of Carola Stern, Ulbricht's critical biographer: "To be sure, he was particularly responsible for certain spheres—the economy and government administration; there were others he took special pleasure in supervising—the youth movement, sports, the armed forces; but, unlike the other SED leaders, he concerned himself with everything. Stalin had found an ideal deputy." [31]

Economic planning worked hand-in-hand with political planning to transform the new state into "a people's democracy." From the beginning, East Germany's rulers had introduced far-reaching changes in the ownership of the means of production. In 1945–46, agricultural holdings of over 100 hectars (247 acres), mainly estates owned by the *Junker*, the Prussian landed aristocracy, were expropriated without compensation and distributed to rural workers, small peasants, and expellees from the former German territories east of the Oder–Neisse Line. Soon, heavy industry and other key industries were taken over by the state. To justify these measures, the large landowners and industrialists were blamed for their assistance in Hitler's rise and for opposing democratic development in Germany. By early 1948, 99 percent of the coal-mining industry in the Soviet Zone, half of its metallurgic production, and the entire production of electric power were in the hands of the state. "To learn from the Soviet Union is to learn how to win," ran a slogan of the SED.

At the second SED Party Conference in July, 1952, Ulbricht and his lieutenants made two important decisions: first, the collectivization of agriculture and the artisans and the socialization of industry and commerce; second, the establishment of the armed forces. These drastic measures made it practically impossible for representatives of the bourgeois parties to continue to be politically active.

[31] Carola Stern, *Ulbricht: A Political Biography* (New York and London, 1965), p. 127.

Many leading bourgeois personalities lost their jobs in public service, were arrested, or escaped to the West. The flight was, however, by no means confined to politicians. Farmers, shopkeepers, clerical workers, doctors, writers, and university teachers felt that they had lost all chance for a worthwhile existence, and many of them were afraid of the secret police and the internment camps of the SSD.

The end of the Stalinist era in Russia also brought some changes in the GDR. It speaks for Ulbricht's tactical skill that he who had always backed Stalinism survived as a ruler after Stalin's death. In June, 1953, new directives were received in East Berlin from Moscow that ran severely counter to Ulbricht's rigid policies. With the "Declaration of the New Course," which was published in the East German press as a GDR Politbureau resolution, the rigorous general campaign against private property, inaugurated at the second SED Party Conference, came to an end. Hundreds of farmers and artisans had been forced into "producer cooperatives," industrialists and businessmen had been expropriated, and any resistance met with instant arrest. The expropriations and confiscations were stopped, and property was returned to its owners. Manufacturers and individual farmers were to be encouraged and given credits from the state.

A short time afterward the government, backed by a resolution of the Central Committee of the party, decreed that the work quotas of state-owned factories had to be increased by at least 10 percent. Vladimir Semjonov, the new Soviet High Commissioner for Germany, who explained Moscow's "New Course" to the comrades in East Berlin, seems to have agreed that these increased work quotas should stand. On the other hand, the opponents of Ulbricht in the Politbureau and in the Central Committee, Minister for State Security, Wilhelm Zaisser, and editor of the main party organ *Neues Deutschland*, Rudolf Herrnstadt, regarded Ulbricht's stubborn course as disastrous and favored a new economic policy and far-reaching changes in the SED. The details of the in-fighting need not concern us here; in the end, the issue was decided in Berlin by workers of the building trade and others. Under their pressure at a meeting of selected party activists on June 16, 1953, Ulbricht and Prime Minister Grotewohl announced the cancellation of the 10 percent increase in work quotas. Ulbricht declared that "the Party is abandoning an admittedly mistaken road and is taking the right one."

A week earlier, such a concession might have silenced the incensed workers; but by the next morning, the uprising of the workers in East Berlin had spread all over East Germany and exploded in other large cities. At noon, the commander of the Soviet troops in Berlin proclaimed a state of emergency. The occupation forces established martial law, Soviet tanks appeared in the streets of East Berlin, and Russian troops fired on demonstrators who refused to follow their orders to disperse. Military tribunals sentenced some demonstrators to death, and the sentences were carried out immediately. By the evening of June 17, 1953, the revolt had been crushed in Berlin and elsewhere

Afterwards, the two factions in the GDR Politbureau blamed each other for what had happened. After Moscow had decided to back Ulbricht, Herrnstadt and Zaisser were dismissed from their posts and from the Politbureau. Thus, in the end, the workers' revolt did not overthrow Ulbricht; on the contrary, it saved him, although the Soviet leaders insisted that he should engage in self-criticism and support the post-Stalinist New Course.

In 1956, Ulbricht's position was challenged once more by the "thaw" in the Soviet Union. Liberalization trends seemed to carry the day in Poland under Gomulka, and even more so in Hungary during the October Revolution. After Krushchev's revelations on the errors of Stalin at the Twentieth Congress of the Soviet Communist Party, a good many prominent East Germans, particularly the party intellectuals, expected the problem of de-Stalinization to be discussed at a conference of the SED. Many East German communists felt that Ulbricht had applied Stalinist methods and had flouted the new "principle of collective leadership" by his dictatorial methods. According to Carola Stern, at an informal meeting of writers and intellectuals in the summer of 1956, shortly before his death, the writer Bertolt Brecht described Ulbricht "as an orthodox dictator, alienated from the people, whose policies had completely destroyed the humanist content of socialism and had created an intolerable situation in the GDR." [32]

What the opposition inside the SED wanted was reform after the Polish model of an anti-Stalinist "revolution from above." But Ulbricht saw to it that the Polish example was not followed in East Germany. The abortive October Revolution in Hungary played right into his hands. It was not difficult for him to eliminate some hostile and incautious university intellectuals. Ulbricht also knew how to play off one group in the SED against another, and how to involve members of the Politbureau as much as possible in his own positions

[32] Brecht is discussed in Chapter 10, pp. 292-97.

and actions. Although the men in the Kremlin were by no means blind to Ulbricht's faults and mistakes, they never failed to back him in the decisive moments. While Ulbricht did not refrain from resorting to methods of terror in critical moments, he was also quick to make concessions to disgruntled groups if it suited his purpose. His staying power has been no less remarkable than his versatility in meeting new situations.

Ulbricht even liked to formulate ideology for the masses, though he can hardly be classed as an intellectual. At the SED Party Congress in 1958, he proclaimed the "Ten Commandments of Socialist Ethics." They were to replace the Christian Ten Commandments which, in Ulbricht's opinion, merely served the ethics of slaveholders, capitalists, and imperialists. His new commandments stressed "international solidarity of the working class and of all workers, and the unshakeable links between all socialist [i.e. Communist] countries," the fight against exploitation of man by man, and regard for collective property. The collective idea became sacrosanct: "You shall respect the collective and take to heart its criticism." Though the citizen is asked to love his fatherland and always be prepared to use his "entire strength and ability for the Workers' and Peasants' Power," there is no reference to a specific German patriotism or to a desire for German unification. By 1958, the platform of the party had changed. In 1946, Ulbricht could still declare that "every German wants reunification. Our people cannot live without unity. Saxony cannot exist without the Ruhr." But this view had long been abandoned; uneasy coexistence now seemed the only possibility. As the National Program of the SED put it in 1962: "Two hostile German states confront each other on German soil today." [33]

A Change of Emphasis

There has been a considerable improvement in the economic position of the GDR since 1955. For many years the East German state had been simply a target for Russian reparations, which ceased only in 1953. In the end East Germany profited from the Cold War and from the integration of West German forces in NATO. The Soviet Union now agreed to the buildup of East German armed forces and to their complete integration in the East European Forces under the Warsaw Security Pact. The East German Diet passed laws to establish "a national people's army" and a defense ministry in 1956 (considerably later than the Bonn Diet's similar move). Since in-

[33] The problem of German coexistence is considered in Chapter 11.

dustry in the GDR has been rebuilt and reorganized, it has played at least as important a part in the Soviet-controlled COMECON as West Germany's has in the European Common Market. In COMECON one superpower is allied with eight satellite or semi-satellite states. Yet the GDR has made a considerable economic advance among them. During the first six years after the collapse of the Third Reich, the economy in the Soviet Zone (and afterwards in the GDR) suffered not only the huge amount of reparations extracted by the Russians, but also through the wastage and unmethodical manner in which the reparations were carried out. New production was often taken away by the Russians without any plan and survey. Until 1955, therefore it was only possible to have a "deficient economy" (*Mangelwirtschaft*) to provide the minimum essentials of food, clothing, and transportation. However, after 1955, East Germany's industrial production, subsidized to a considerable, though still unknown, degree by the Soviet Union, rose remarkably. Between 1955 and 1963, it increased by about 15 percent. Today in many branches of industry, East Germany ranks first among the countries in COMECON.

In 1964, N. W. Faddejev, the Russian secretary of COMECON could declare: "Today, the GDR is one of the strongest industrial states of Europe and the world. It has a highly developed industry, particularly in the fields of machine production, chemicals, and electric power. Her industrial production ranks her fifth in Europe and eighth in the world. With her per capita production of electric power, she takes third place in Europe; with her chemical products, second place in the world (behind the U.S.A.)." Even though these figures are not entirely correct, they indicate the importance of the East German economy in the eyes of its COMECON partners. It is true that the goals of the Seven-Year Plan (1959–65) were by no means reached, yet the actual increase in national income during that period—from seventeen billion dollars in 1959, to over 20 billion in 1965, and to 23 billion dollars in 1967—are remarkable. The goal set for 1970 was a further rise to 107 billion marks.

By the end of the 1960's, a younger generation had, to some extent, replaced the older in the East German administration and industry. The obsessed Marxist revolutionary who returned from exile abroad in 1945 has been supplanted by the technician and the expert who has grown up in the new state, and therefore takes its regime and structure for granted. The new generation is less inclined to blindly accept the Russian example, but it is equally averse to returning to an unplanned capitalist society. They pursue a line of pragmatic technology and planning, rather than Marxist faith and dogma. Since 1955–56, the GDR has produced goods not only for its own 17 million inhabitants, but also for the 320 million people in the member-states of the COMECON. Higher production has necessitated better training for the young, stronger emphasis on mathematics and science in the schools, and a general willingness to make work more varied and interesting for everyone involved.

The economic recovery and the relative rise of living standards have undoubtedly made it easier for East Germans of both generations to be more accommodating toward the regime. Many East German critics of the regime became resigned when the Western powers, particularly West Germany, did not seriously challenge the erection of the Berlin Wall in August, 1961. Moreover, the East German people have since become more attracted by industrial work because of the greater choice of consumer goods.

Although political pressure and victimization have not disappeared entirely, they play a lesser part in the economic life. Since 1956, the economy has been viewed in economic and not primarily political and ideological terms. Large nationalized industrial combines are now led by qualified experts rather than by party hacks. There is less reason for biting the hand that feeds one or for rejecting the leadership that proclaims a respect for all those who work in industry. Moreover, the greater need for qualified scientists, technicians, and economists has made it possible for middle-class youth to obtain places and study grants at the universities. The rigid social discrimination against them has lessened. Specially trained workers and academically trained engineers now have more prestige than their colleagues in West Germany. Qualified engineers, scientific technologists, and industrial economists (now officially described as "Allies of the Working Class") enjoy many privileges. "Even the peasants," Ernst Richert reports, "had, in the end, resigned themselves to their fate of collectivization and mechanization by 1965. Their sons, as well as the remaining 5 percent of the independent people, are moving towards industry and competition to qualify as masters and for academic degrees."

The Seven-Years Plan for 1959–65, with its demand for more academically trained persons, gave the children of middle-class parents their first chance to study at a university or a similar institution. At the same time, many more consumer goods, unavailable so far to the majority of the people, appeared in the shops. Motorcycles, washing machines, television sets, and sophisticated cameras, hitherto earmarked for export, appeared on the home market, though still in limited numbers. Between 1957 and 1960, there was also an increase in apartment construction and in furniture production. It is true that the actual production of houses fell short of the plan, but the new houses were welcome in that they made life easier for many housewives. By 1964, some types of modern furniture could be purchased, and the clothing styles had improved. There was still a considerable delay in the implementation of orders for new types of goods. This was particularly true of motor cars, the price of which in 1964 was three times that of the same car in West Germany.

The impact of the Berlin Wall, though hard for many people on both sides meant in the long run a greater stability for the GDR. In the first instance, it increased the work force; the eighty thousand workers from East Berlin and its environs who had crossed daily to work in West Berlin were now available to work in the factories of the GDR. Before the gates were closed, 50 percent of the refugees from East Germany were under the age of twenty-five whereas they made up only 35 percent of the population of the GDR. Many of these young people had fled with their parents or other relatives, but others had come alone and not always for political reasons. Some were driven by a desire for change or adventure.

In the 1960s, the 1953 spirit of revolt had given way to resignation among many men and women of the older generation and to accommodation by the great majority of the people. To the average citizen who takes his work seriously and is diligent but free from political ambitions and zeal for reform, life in the GDR has become bearable and acceptable. The number of nonconformists now seems small; and if there is little intellectual freedom, people are accustomed to it. All the available evidence points to the truth of an overall statement by Ernst Richert, one of the most balanced and sober experts on these matters. "The society of the GDR functions by and large quite well, much better than is thought in the West. However, it functions by no means in the way in which Ulbricht and his lieutenants, Honecker, Schumann, and others, would like to see it function. It is not a 'proletarian revolutionary society' but a society of arrangements, and it has reservations." [34]

[34] Ernst Richert, *Das Zweite Deutschland* (Gütersloh, 1964), p. 319. Walter Ulbricht resigned from his key position as first secretary of the Central Committee of the Socialist Unity Party on May 3, 1971, because of age. He was succeeded by Erich Honecker. Ulbricht continued in his other office as chairman of the State Council.

WEST BERLIN

N
W   E
S

Havel

Tegel

Reinickendorf

Spandau

Wedding

5

Spree

Tiergarten

6

Charlottenburg

Wilmersdorf

Grünewald

Autobahn

Schöneberg

Havel

Steglitz

Zehlendorf

Nedlitz

Potsdam

Autobahn

Outer boundary of East and West Berlin
The Berlin Wall separating East and West Berlin
Boundary between French-, British-, and U.S.-occupied sectors
Brandenburg Gate, at the city's geographical center

West Berlin checkpoints
Soviet Zone checkpoints
Checkpoint for control of Allied
   military missions and diplomats
   only
Main railways
Canals
Forests, parks, nature preserves

Border crossings between West
and East Berlin since August 1961:

1 Friedrichstrasse/ Zimmerstrasse
2 Prinzenstrasse/Heinrich-Heine-Strasse
3 Bahnhof Friedrichstrasse
4 Bornholmer Strasse
5 Chausseestrasse
6 Invalidenstrasse
7 Oberbaumbrücke
8 Sonnenallee

Weissensee

Pankow

Prenzlauer
Berg

Mitte

Friedrichs-
hain

Lichtenberg

EAST BERLIN

Kreuzberg

Neukölln

Treptow

Spree

Tempel-
hof

Köpenick

Schönefeld

0   2   4   6   8   10 km.
0   2   4   6 mi.

BERLIN: SYMBOL OF DISCORD

From the point of view of the Federal Republic, West Berlin is a *Land* and an integral part of its territory. However, this claim has been constantly challenged by the spokesmen of the German Democratic Republic in East Berlin, who would like to see West Berlin an unattached, demilitarized "free city." Twenty-five years after the end of World War II, divided Berlin has become a symbol of the latent conflict and discord between Germans as well as between the former Allied Powers; and the three Berlin crises of 1948, 1958, and 1961, which can be only briefly mentioned here, are thus part of both German and international history.

Berlin was conquered by the Russians after bitter fighting in April, 1945. Following an earlier agreement between the three Allied Powers, the United States, Britain, and the Soviet Union, the division of Germany into zones was paralleled in Berlin by the division of the city into sectors of control. The Russians were alloted northeast Berlin, the British the northwest, and the Americans the south. A short time later a sector was carved out for the French from the area originally earmarked for the British. This four-sector system came into operation in July, 1945, with the joint Allied *Kommandatura* as the supreme authority over a city largely in ruins. From the outset Berlin was entirely surrounded by territory under Russian control. The problem of regulating the access routes of the other Allies to Berlin was left to the Allied commanders. After the American General Lucius Clay experienced some difficulties with the Russians, they reached an agreement, confirmed by the Allied Control Council for Germany in November, 1945, that one main road, one railway line, as well as three air corridors from the Western Zones to the city could be used by the three Western Powers without advance notice. (See the map on pp. 36–37.) Although repeatedly challenged since by the Russians and by the East German government, this arrangement still continues.

The joint administration of Berlin by the Four Powers lasted until 1948. After a preliminary constitution for Greater Berlin had been proclaimed in August, 1946, the first and only elections for the entire city took place in October. The result was a big disappointment for the Communists because their Socialist Unity Party (SED) polled less than 20 percent. The Communists thus stood little chance of gaining control through elections. As the Cold War developed, cooperation in the Allied Control Council disintegrated, a situation that was finally symbolized when the Russian representative, Marshal Sokolovsky, walked out on March 20, 1948.

In the summer of 1948, this event turned out to be, in the words of President Truman, "the curtain-raiser for a major crisis" in Berlin. Gradually the Russians cut off all road, rail, and river traffic to and from West Berlin. Incensed by the plans of the Western powers to establish the new German Deutsche Mark in their zone, the Russians suddenly declared that the Western Allies never had any legal right to be in Berlin. The obvious attempts to force West Berlin into submission by starvation were countered by the remarkable enterprise of the British–American airlift, which eventually carried from 4,000 to 5,000 tons of food and coal daily to the stubborn Berliners. By the spring of 1949, Stalin must have realized that he had overplayed his hand and that the Western Allies were not going to be pushed out of Berlin. In May, the Russians signed a Four-Power communiqué that repermitted free civilian communication between Berlin and West Germany. But by then the division of the city with 2,200,000 people in West Berlin and 1,100,000 in East Berlin had hardened, and there were now two rival municipal administrations and two chief burgomasters.

For nine years (1949 to 1958), open conflict over Berlin between the two power blocs was avoided, and the municipal S-Bahn continued to connect the two halves of the city. But all this time the Communists tried to isolate West Berlin. In May, 1952, the East German authorities cut the telephone cable between the 32,500 telephone subscribers in East Berlin and the 132,000 in West Berlin. Gradually West Berlin established a reputation as "the window of the West." The wealth of its consumer goods and uncensored books and newspapers contrasted markedly with the poorer products of the collectivist economy and political conformity of East Berlin, which even the calculated brightness of the Stalin Allee (now renamed Karl Marx Allee) was unable to conceal.

The Western Allies still clung to the Four-Power status of the city because they felt that this abstract concept was the basis of Berlin's military security. For this reason they did not agree to a request from the Adenauer government that West Berlin be declared the twelfth member-state of the Federal Republic with full rights and duties. Although the West Berliners can elect a number of deputies to the diet in Bonn and are represented in the Federal Council, their deputies in the diet have no right to vote, as this would be contrary to the Four-Power arrangement and might give the Soviet Union a pretext for interference in West Berlin. Federal laws are therefore valid in West Berlin only after the West Berlin parliament has formally passed corresponding laws.

Although the economic position of West Berlin has improved over the years, there have been considerable difficulties because its primary produce can no longer be obtained from its natural hinterland, all of which is now part of the hostile German Democratic Republic. West Berlin remains largely dependent upon imports from West Germany and foreign countries. The city has developed important secondary industries, particularly electric power and chemical production, and with machine and garment manufacturing. The stream of refugees that poured incessantly into West Berlin during the fifties enabled new textile and glass factories to be established. Without large-scale financial assistance from Bonn, West Berlin could not have survived economically. During the last two decades, West Germans have been encouraged to open factories in Berlin and have been granted considerable fiscal consessions. About 70 percent of the goods produced in Berlin are marketed in West Germany, which in its turn is the principal supplier of goods imported by West Berlin.[35]

The second Berlin crisis came in November 1958, at a time when the rulers in the Kremlin had become increasingly self-confident from their intervention in Hungary two years earlier. The Russians wanted diplomatic recognition of the German Democratic Republic by the Western Powers as a basic condition for any German settlement. They resented the continued Western presence in Berlin, considering it an unwelcome anachronism. In their eyes West Berlin was a focal point of anti-Communist Western intelligence and propaganda, and was thus a menace to the security of the Warsaw Treaty Powers.

In a speech on November 19, 1958, Mr. Khrushchev attacked "the so-called Four-Power status of Berlin" as "a position in which the three Western Powers have the possibility of lording it in West Berlin, turning that part of the city, which is the capital of the German Democratic Republic, into some kind of State within a State." He fiercely demanded that the signatories of the Potsdam Agreement "renounce the remnants of the occupation regime in Berlin, and thereby make it possible to create a normal situation in

---

[35] In 1965 the value of goods supplied by West Berlin to West Germany totaled 10,100 million DM ($2.525 billion) and that of purchases made by West Berlin from West Germany 10,500 million DM ($2.625 billion).

the capital of the German Democratic Republic." In a note sent a fortnight later to the three Western Powers, the Russians insisted that "the occupation regime" in Berlin be ended and West Berlin made into a demilitarized free city. The sinister aspect of the note was the fixed deadline of six months.

In their replies the Western Powers refused to discuss the issue under threat, but otherwise declared themselves ready to consider it as part of the German problem and of European security. Mr. Khrushchev gradually retreated. In March, 1959, he publicly admitted that the Western Powers had a legal right to be in Berlin and added, somewhat cynically, that this was the reason for his proposing a German peace treaty that would make such rights invalid. Two years later at a meeting with President Kennedy in Vienna in June, 1961, Khrushchev repeated his earlier threat that the Soviet Union would conclude a separate peace treaty with the GDR unilaterally if the United States was not prepared to sign a joint peace treaty with the two Germanies. However, in the end the Soviet Union did not do so, but confined itself to a treaty of friendship with the GDR (June, 1964) without attempting to terminate the rights of the Western powers.

The East German authorities have tried from time to time to block the flow of the traffic to and from Berlin by road, railway, or through the air corridors. Such temporary interference, at the end of March, 1969, when the West German parliamentarians gathered in Berlin to elect a new federal president, and again on a similar occasion toward the end of January, 1970. On the other hand, in 1963, West Berliners were granted permission to visit relatives in East Berlin. Nearly a million people took advantage of the offer, which was repeated in 1964 and 1965. However, after friction between the West and East Berlin authorities it was dropped the following year.

In a way, the period since August, 1961, has been something of an anticlimax for West Berlin. The erection of a wall thirty miles long has brought tragedy, death, or injury to a defiant people who have occasionally tried to escape to West Berlin, in spite of barbed wire, booby traps, and savage police dogs. The fact that the daily crossing of thousands of people living in East Berlin to work in West Berlin was stopped resulted in a serious decline of the labor force available in West Berlin. Great efforts were made to induce young people from West Germany to live and work in the city, but few of them stayed for long. On the other hand, West Berliners tended to leave the city for the West, where they expected to find more openings and better jobs. To some extent, Berlin has become a city of elderly pensioners. In 1967, 21 percent of the West Berliners were over 65, compared with only 11 percent in Hamburg.

Meanwhile the hard facts of reality remain. Although protected by the three Western Powers, Berlin, one of the largest industrial cities in Europe, is handicapped by its geopolitical isolation. It is significant that Willy Brandt, for many years ruling burgomaster of West Berlin, has as chancellor of the Federal Republic stressed the need to find some accommodation with the rulers of East Germany, an attitude fully supported by his successors in the town hall of West Berlin. Yet none of them has been willing to see the integrity and independence of their city impaired. The Four Power Agreement on Berlin, initialled by the Ambassadors of the United States, the U.S.S.R., Great Britain, and France on September 3, 1971, was welcomed by Chancellor Brandt as an important move towards an improvement in the position of the city.[36]

Like most German cities, Berlin has had a long and varied history; and without taking this into consideration, her present situation cannot be fully understood. Founded in 1230 as an East German colonial town by two margraves of Brandenburg, it developed into the foremost city of the area during the fourteenth century because of its well-favored position on the important trade route from Central to East Germany. Accompanying the rise of the state of Brandenburg–Prussia from the fifteenth to the middle of the nineteenth century, Berlin largely centered around the court with its appendages of aristocrats, public servants, and military officers; compared with them, her hard-working artisans and peasants were of minor importance. Berlin's symbol was the Royal Castle of the Hohenzollern rulers, an immense baroque structure that was deliberately pulled down in 1950 by the East German regime. Berlin's population, which had sunk to a mere 7,500 at the end of the devastating Thirty Years War in 1648, grew considerably by the end of the seventeenth century, partly as a result of immigration for economic and religious reasons. A hundred years later, at the end of the reign of Frederick the Great in 1786, there were just under 150,000 Berliners. The influx swelled during the nineteenth century when Berlin developed into an industrial center, attracting many people from the country. Prussian traditions and modern industrialization set Berlin's character when it became the capital of Bismarck's Second Empire in 1871.

[36] *Bulletin*, No. 127 (Bonn: September 3, 1971), 1359.

Its population leaped from 932,000 in 1871 to 3.7 million in 1910. Many Berliners settled in the growing belt of suburbs, which were neatly divided between working-class and upper-class districts. Berlin became a stronghold of the socialist workers' movement, and in 1912 three-quarters of the voting Berliners opted in support of the Social Democratic Party. By 1925 it had become the third largest city in the world, after New York and London. While World War I left her untouched, Berlin suffered much destruction during and particularly at the end of World War II, when the Russians closed in on the capital in March and April, 1945. Over 500,000 of her apartments were destroyed, and the ruins of the town amounted to 15 percent of the total destruction in Germany.

Altogether this divided ex-capital today reflects a good deal of the long and complex course of German history during the First and Second Empires, to which we must now turn.

2

Aspects of the First Empire:
I. Medieval Germany

ORIGINS: THE CHANGING MEANING OF "GERMANY"

German history has always been complex and often complicated. One of the reasons for this is that the term "Germany" had different meanings at different times and by no means always referred to the same area. In the centuries immediately before and after the birth of Christ, it indicated the region southwest and west of present-day Germany. It was under Roman control; and the Roman Wall, or *Limes*, ran east from the lower and middle sections of the Rhine, along the Upper Neckar, and continued to the northern sector of the Danube. Roman Germany was an important part of the Roman Empire which carried many of its institutions and customs to the Germanic people. The first German cities sprang up as Roman settlements. It is still fascinating today to trace the Roman origins and study the Roman relics at sites in Cologne, Trier, Bonn, Mainz, Augsburg, and Regensburg.

By A.D. 800, when Rome's power had long been broken, this region belonged to the eastern part of the mighty Carolingian Empire of the Frankish king, Charlemagne (or Charles the Great), which covered most of Western Europe and most of Italy, though it did not include Britain, or Spain, or Scandinavia. As a champion of Christendom, Charlemagne went with his warriors and bishops into the uncultivated land east of the *Limes* and extended his realm far into what is now Central Germany. In some hard-fought campaigns he forced the proud, pagan Saxons, then living in the northwest between Westphalia and Holstein, to accept his rule and embrace Christianity. By subjugating and Christianizing the Saxons before and after 800, he brought the Teutonic tribes under a common rule and government. Instead of the Rhine, the Elbe and Saale rivers far to the east marked Germany's frontier. Many new towns were founded within these German lands, but none of them ever became a focal point as Rome had become in the history of the Roman Empire or as Paris was to become in the History of France. From the tenth century onwards, German kings and emperors of the Holy Roman Empire spent much time and energy south of the Alps in Italy as pioneers of a Christian crusade; and the center of gravity in Germany moved eastward once more, mainly during the period between 1150 and 1350. German immigrants went beyond the regions of Saxony into the eastern areas of Mecklenburg, Pomerania, Silesia, and what was then called "Prussia." Military and religious reasons had prompted Charlemagne to invade the lands of the Saxons; but the motives for this later expansion, carried out by princes, nobles, and townfolk, were the need for skilled labor, the desire for land of their own, and better living conditions. Not only did the Rhine and the Elbe now figure in German history, but also the Oder and Vistula, which ran through areas that saw both cooperation and clashes between German migrants and Slav natives. Austria had been Germanized in the tenth century after the Magyars had been defeated, and in the twelfth century became a separate political unit; together with Brandenburg–Prussia, these two states belonged not to the original German heartland, but rather to the eastern border region.

The first German king was elected in A.D. 911, and the first German emperor was proclaimed in Rome in 962. Technically, the First Holy Roman Empire of the German nation lasted until Napoleon I forced it off the map in 1806.[1]

To understand the development and the nature of Germany under the First Empire, we have to look back to that great early European ruler, Charlemagne (768–814). The Frankish kings had long regarded themselves as champions of Christendom by their missionary work and their protection of the Roman Church. Charlemagne believed it his mission, inspired by Christ, to convert the infidels. The mixed motives in Charlemagne's rule can be clearly

[1] The Second Empire, created by Bismarck, lasted from 1871 to 1918; the Third Empire, Hitler's Third Reich, from 1933 to 1945. See Chapters 6, 7, and 9.

discerned in his policy toward the Saxons. From his point of view, the pagan Saxons were a serious danger, for they had threatened the safety of the Rhineland since the beginning of the eighth century. When the Saxons under their Duke Widukind were defeated in the ruthless wars that lasted over thirty years (772–804), thousands of them were executed, while many others were deported to various parts of the Frankish kingdom. Given the alternative of death or conversion to Christianity, led by Widukind, they chose adherence to the new creed. In spite of all its harshness, the aim of the Frankish policy was not the annihilation but the integration of the Saxons into the Frankish state. In fact, their sense of mission and power politics were closely interrelated. As the contemporary chronicler Einhard commented on this savage war: "It was only ended under the condition that they [the Saxons] would reject the cult of the demons and accept the sacraments of the Christian creed and, now being asso-ciated with the Franks, would become one people with them." [2]

An event of great significance in Charlemagne's life was his un-expected coronation as emperor by Pope Leo III at St. Peter's in Rome on Christmas Day, A.D. 800. The Romans then hailed him as "Charles Augustus, crowned by God, the great and peace-giving Emperor of the Romans, life and victory!" Charlemagne was as much King of the Franks (since 768) as King of the Lombards in Upper Italy (since 774), and it was necessary for the weak Pope to rely on his protection. Nevertheless, the fact that Leo III could crown Charlemagne created a precedent. It was "a resounding success for the Pope," but "it failed to establish a Rome-orientated Empire." [3] In spite of its Roman features Charlemagne's empire was basically Germanic as well as Christian, and was motivated by realistic and idealistic factors. Another success came shortly before Charlemagne's death with his recognition after protracted negotiations, as the ruler of the West by the ruler of the Eastern Roman Empire in Byzan-tium. This meant that there were two successors to the Roman Em-pire of the past, the Empire of the East with its seat in Constanti-nople, and the Empire of the West, which included Rome as an imperial city, but was centered in an area marked by the Rhine, Moselle, and Meuse rivers.

The divisions of the Carolingian Empire in which a European

[2] Peter Rassow, ed., *Deutsche Geschichte im Überblick* (Stuttgart, 1962), p. 80.
[3] Peter Munz, *The Origins of the Carolingian Empire* (Leicester, 1960), p. 31.

of the 1970s could in some ways see an early forerunner of the six Common Market countries were greater than its power. The further idea of one empire, one church, one Christianity was never fully realized. Impressive as the Carolingian Empire was, its existence depended upon the strength of the Frankish kingdom and on the personality and skill of its ruler. The social and cultural disparities in its various parts were too great, and after Charlemagne's death internal quarrels and inadequate government led to its decline. The various Frankish tribes, spread as they were from the Loire to the Elbe and from the Alps to the North Sea, had little in common and developed different languages. When in 842 the two brother-rulers, Louis and Charles, met in Strasbourg, their armies could no longer understand each other's language. Whereas the East Frankish tribes had clung to the old Germanic dialects, the language of the West Frankish tribes had, under the influence of Gallo–Latin, turned into the Romance tongue, a forerunner of French. When the two rulers took an oath of continuous loyalty to each other, it had to be read in Romance as well as in what was called "German" (*theodisca lingua*). The Carolingian Empire was divided into three parts by the Treaty of Verdun (843). The oldest brother, Lothar, was given the imperial title, the two imperial cities of Aachen and Rome, and a territory comprising the central area around the Meuse and Moselle, as well as Burgundy and Italy. Charles became king of the Romanic West, and Louis the "German" king of the Germanic East.[4] In a further arrangement, after the extinction of Lothar's line Louis received some additional territory in the west under the Treaty of Mersen (870). By then the division into what was later known as Germany and France had begun.

It can be argued that German history proper began in 911 after the death of the last East Frankish ruler of the Carolingian Dynasty. The dukes elected Henry of Saxony "German King," as ruler of what was then called "Regnum Teutonicum," or "Kingdom of the Germans." By then there had emerged five "tribal duchies" (*Stammesherzogtümer*)—Saxony, Franconia, Bavaria, Swabia, and Lorraine. The people in each duchy shared common customs and languages. The political importance of the duchies was played out by the thirteenth century, when they were replaced by other, mostly smaller, regional units; but their dialects and folklore have continued, and even today make for variety in German life and manners.

[4] His realm included Franconia east of the Rhine, Bavaria, Swabia, Thuringia, and Saxony.

In the tenth century tribal dukes like Konrad in Franconia, Otto in Saxony, and Arnulf in Bavaria created a new type of political rule based on unquestioned authority over their nobility, on military achievements, and on control of numerous vassals. These dukes elected one of themselves as primary duke, or king, and were prepared to fight under his leadership. Nevertheless they watched assiduously over their own positions. "No matter what his title, whether that of 'German King,' 'King of the Romans,' 'Emperor,' or 'Roman Emperor Elect,' the supreme head of the Empire which was created in the tenth century was never acknowledged by its members as their monarch." [5]

The power of the dukes was broken by the end of the twelfth century. It became customary for the monarch to consult the high nobility, first at regular court meetings and later at special imperial meetings, which developed into the Reichstag. First only the secular and ecclesiastical princes appeared at these meetings; later they included the counts and barons. After 1489 representatives of the imperial cities and bishoprics were also admitted. The corporate system of the high clergy, the nobility, and the towns was known as the Estates. After 1200, the Reichstag acquired a joint power of legal decision-making, imperial military undertakings, and tax-raising.

EMPEROR AND POPE

Henry I ruled from 919 to 936. His successor, Otto I the Great (936–973) was, like Charlemagne, crowned in 962 at St. Peter's in Rome as "Imperator Augustus" after he had restored law and order in Italy. The Pope and the people of Rome took an oath of loyalty to him. But whereas to be "Emperor of the Romans" meant little to Otto, he did regard himself as "Sword of the Church" and was deeply conscious of his mission to protect the Church at a time when the Church dignitaries in Germany were the main support of his power. The emperor appointed bishops and abbots who either belonged to his family or were trained as public servants in the service of his administration. Otto I owed his prestige as a ruler largely to his success in 955 at the Battle of Lechfeld near Augsburg when, heading a royal army of Franks, Swabians, Bavarians, and Bohemians, he beat the invading forces of the heathen Hungarians. The close alliance between Church and state is illustrated by that fact that Udalrich,

[5] Friedrich Heer, *The Holy Roman Empire* (London, 1968), pp. 23–24.

the bishop of Augsburg, played a major role in the ferocious battle. Otto's successors began as soon as they were crowned to regard themselves worthy of the dignity of being emperor, but often postponed for years the formal act of imperial coronation by the Pope in Rome. Otto II (973–983) called himself "Emperor of the Romans" in order to emphasize the universal nature of his position and his close nexus with the Church to his rival, the East Roman emperor in Byzantium. His son, Otto III (983–1002), who had a Greek mother and came of age only in 995, went even further by making Rome his seat of residence. Otto III was serious in his desire to renew the ancient Roman Empire on a Christian basis. Yet understandably, the transfer of the political center to Rome met with opposition in Germany, particularly in Saxony. It is therefore significant that Otto III's Bavarian successor, Henry II (1002–1024), the first of the Salio–Frankish emperors, felt obliged to stress the German foundations of the empire and to proclaim "the renovation of the kingdom of the Franks." When the frontier in the east of Germany was pushed forward by the formation of a new Church See in Bamberg, the step had religious as well as political motives. Henry II wanted to protect the eastern frontier of his kingdom and to encourage missionary work among the pagan Slavs at the same time. Under these feudal rulers there was a close identification between monarchy and church. The Ottonian ruler regarded himself as set by divine order above state and Church. On the other hand, the German bishops and abbots influenced the emperor's policy and also formed a welcome counterbalance to the power of the dukes.

During the reign of the Salian dynasty (1024–1125), the two swords that were to safeguard the unity of Christendom, the Papal and the imperial, turned against each other. The details of this momentous clash between empire and Papacy under Emperor Henry IV and Pope Gregory VII during the last quarter of the twelfth century need not occupy us here. Obviously the emperor's claim for control over the Church could not be final, but the severe political earthquake suffered by the German Empire in the quarrel might have been avoided. Pope Gregory VII, a man of extreme religious passion, was imbued with the idea of the universal power of the Papacy in its succession from Saint Peter. In his eyes, the assertion of the primacy of clerical power was a fight for "justice," "for the liberty of the Church" as ordained by God. In a statement in 1075, this Pope insisted on the primacy and infallibility of the Roman Church, founded by God. The ecclesiastical rights and powers, he asserted, exalted the

Pope high above everyone, including secular rulers. Gregory VII
challenged "the ideas of legitimacy, divine right, and paramount
overlordship on which the claim of the Salians to rule the German
Church was founded. . . . The theocracy of the Salians had to be
eradicated because it was so mighty that it endangered the supremacy
of Rome over the other churches of Christian Europe." [6]

Although the quarrel between Gregory VII and Henry IV occurred primarily over the procedure of investiture of German bishops,
which was different from that practiced in France and England, it
did not remain confined to this issue, but immediately developed
into a bitter fight over the basic principles of the ranks and duties of
the imperial and ecclesiastical forces within the German Empire. This
furious struggle dominated history in Germany to an extent unknown
in the West. At the age of twenty-five, Henry sided with the twenty-
six German bishops, who in January, 1076, had sharply protested
against the arbitrary actions of the Pope. He ordered the Pope to
vacate the Holy See. Gregory answered by excommunicating Henry
and deposing him as emperor. In political terms this not only put
the emperor beyond the pale of the Church, but also encouraged
opposition to him from the German princes. In consequence, Henry
was obliged to appear in the garments of a repentant sinner before
the Pope's castle at Canossa in Upper Italy in January, 1077. When
on the third day of his ordeal he promised to accept the arbitration
and the verdict of the Pope in his quarrel with the German princes,
he was freed from the Church ban denying him the sacraments.
German liberal historians of the nineteenth century, particularly
during Bismarck's feud with the Roman Catholic Church, were inclined to regard Henry's submissiveness only as the humiliation of a
German emperor before the sinister ultramontanism of the Pope.
The view held by historians today is less one-sided. First, it is wrong
to see Gregory VII only as a power-ridden politician. In fact, the
priest in him scored over the politician when faced with Henry's
dramatic gesture of repentance. Secondly, this act has been viewed
as "a decisive political success" for the king, as by this step he "prevented further cooperation between the Pope and the [German]
princes and thus saved his crown." [7] In a second contest a few years
afterward, Gregory used the weapons of banning and deposing Henry
again, and this time went further by recognizing Rudolph, Duke of

---

[6] G. Barraclough, *The Origins of Modern Germany* (London, 1947), p. 113.
[7] Theodor Schieffer in *Deutsche Geschichte im Überblick*, ed. Peter Rassow
(Stuttgart, 1962), p. 150.

Swabia, as king. Henry IV retaliated by deposing Gregory and nominating the Archbishop of Ravenna as his pope. The death of Rudolph in a battle against Henry severely weakened Gregory's German supporters; and a few years later, Henry was crowned in Rome by his pope, Clement III, under the eyes of the unhappy Gregory who was confined in a building opposite. Before Gregory died in exile in Southern Italy in 1085, he bitterly complained that he had been defeated in a just cause.

Yet the fate of his adversary was no less poignant. Not only did the schism continue, but the emperor's own son, Henry V, allied himself with the papacy, imprisoned his father, and forced him to abdicate. Though Henry IV escaped, he died soon afterwards shorn of his power. After the death of the two principal adversaries, the struggle continued, although on a more restricted issue—the question of the rights of investiture of bishops by the emperor or the Pope. In 1122 a compromise was reached between Henry V and Pope Calixtus II with the Concordate of Worms. As the emperor was represented at the elections of these church dignitaries, he retained some control over the appointments and over the German clergy as a whole. However, filling the high offices remained largely an internal matter of the Church. In the end, neither the imperial nor the Papal power could implement its claim to supremacy over the other. Their future relationship was one of uneasy coexistence.

The power of the emperor reasserted itself under Frederick I (1152–1190), the second ruler of the House of Hohenstaufen. Frederick, commonly called Barbarossa on account of his auburn beard, managed to maintain the imperial prestige partly through his skill in handling the German dukes, especially his formidable cousin, Henry the Lion, Duke of Saxony. He granted him not only important royal rights in Saxony, but also the Duchy of Bavaria, though not before part of it had been made into the separate Duchy of Austria under the Babenbergs. Frederick also gained the support of the German bishops. However, he clashed later with Pope Alexander III, who found allies in the cities of Lombardy and in Venice. It took the emperor fifteen years to separate his opponents and to assert his authority in Germany as well as in Italy. Frederick regarded himself as the recognized head of Christendom; and its unity, he argued, was as much his task as that of the Pope. By fulfilling it he "also satisfied the national pride of the Germans as they proved themselves the first, i.e. the strongest nation in Christendom." [8] In spite of some

[8] Peter Rassow, op. cit., pp. 190–91.

setbacks and defeats, he made sure by the Peace of Venice in 1177 that Alexander III recognized his control over the German Church, while in return he acknowledged Alexander as Pope. When the power of the ambitious and unscrupulous Guelph, Henry the Lion, in North Germany reached dangerous proportions and the minor German princes complained about him, Frederick deprived the Guelph of all his fiefs. In 1190 the emperor drowned in a river in Asia Minor during his third crusade, which he headed with some three thousand knights in order to rescue Jerusalem from the Muslims. Frederick's death on a Christian enterprise against heavy odds increased his posthumous prestige.

German historians have differed in their views on the advantages and disadvantages of the close connection between the German kingdom and Italy by way of the "Roman Empire," but there can be little doubt that in the eleventh and twelfth centuries it had a twofold effect. On the one hand, it increased the authority of the crown; on the other, it furthered the trend towards greater independence of the German princes. Frederick's strong-minded son, Henry VI (1190–1197), had also acquired through his wife Constance the crown of the Norman kingdom in Sicily and was, at least nominally, ruler of a super-empire comprising the whole of Italy, Germany, and Burgundy. Yet his efforts to make the position of German king and Roman emperor hereditary were cut short by his untimely death. There was a chaotic twenty-year interval with two rival princes bidding for the German crown and the intervention of Innocent III, who was perhaps the strongest personality among the medieval Popes. The Pope supported one of them, Otto the Guelph, who was to rule as Otto IV from 1208–1215. Then the young son of Henry VI and Constance came at last to the throne. Frederick II (1215–1250) was through education and inclination a Sicilian. Though he never became a German, he soon took to the idea of the universal power of the empire. Keeping an eye on Germany, imperial Italy, and Sicily, he tried to gain time to establish a centralized bureaucratic state in Sicily by making many concessions to the German princes. When Innocent III deposed him at the Council of Lyons in 1246 and the Rhenish archbishops elected another king, the cause of Frederick II seemed lost. Yet he managed to reassert himself and constantly came to terms with the changing situation. He was obliged to acknowledge the privileges of the German princes and make more concessions to them. A pact he concluded with the German ecclesiastical rulers in 1220 gave them virtually full territorial freedom in the lands they held from the empire. Even more far-reaching was the statute "In favor of the Princes" in 1231 that increased their territorial power at the expense of the growing cities. Whereas in Italy he created a highly modern centralized administration with public servants and favored the creation of new towns, in Germany he recognized the existing feudal system, the oligarchy of the secular and ecclesiastical princes, and opposed the rising power of the towns. Frederick II's intense preoccupation with Italy forced him to make his son Konrad IV king and governor of Germany. The growing independence of the German princes became even more evident when Konrad IV came to the throne after the death of his father in 1250. Konrad IV's own early death in 1254 ended the Staufer Dynasty. There was a tragic epilogue when his son Konradin, aged sixteen, was beheaded at Naples in 1268 by order of the French Charles of Anjou, by then King of Sicily.

The empire continued on an elective basis, and there was a new distribution of power. Since 1257 the College of Great Electors evolved, which ultimately consisted of three ecclesiastical rulers, the Archbishops of Mainz, Cologne, and Trier, and four secular rulers, the Duke of Saxony, the Count of the Palatinate, the Margrave of Brandenburg, and the King of Bohemia. These electors tended to vote only four measures that increased their power, and they secured considerable influence in the affairs of the empire. Large Reich fiefs could now be bestowed by the emperor only with their consent. Besides the Great Electors there were other important ruling houses such as the Dukes of Brunswick and Lüneburg, the Landgraves of Thuringia and the Dukes of Bavaria and Austria who ruled over a large territory and were eager to expand their power. In addition, there were a great many smaller, medium-rank territorial rulers, both ecclesiastical and lay, including the Counts of Hapsburg, Württemberg, and Tyrol, all with not insignificant landed properties. In this welter of territories the continual rivalry and friction forced the king to act as referee, mediator, and ultimate judge. Violent feuds were frequent, and the various attempts by the kings to proclaim a *Landfrieden,* or pacification of the realm, often proved unsuccessful. Peace was maintained or restored less by the power of the king than by the impact of the leagues formed by some of the territorial rulers.

After the chaotic interregnum of "the emperorless, the terrible time" (1256–73), during which several foreign rulers tried to secure the imperial crown, Count Rudolf von Hapsburg was elected German king in 1273, the first of a succession from different dynasties.

By 1338 the "Electors Union" (*Kurverein*) established the validity of imperial elections without Papal approval. Twenty years later, the "Golden Bull," issued by Charles IV of the House of Luxembourg, Emperor of Germany and King of Bohemia, laid down the principles of imperial elections and increased the privileges of the Great Electors (1356). To prevent the appearance of rival voters, all emperors were to be elected through a majority vote. The territorial power of the four secular electors was increased, and their territories were declared indivisible and hereditary on the basis of the right of primogeniture.

By that time, this embarrassing multitude of territories and political factors was as characteristic of the "Holy Roman Empire" as the trend towards centralization and bureaucracy was of contemporary England and France. The *Landfrieden* decree, issued at Mainz in 1235, "by implication defined the Empire as a league of princes within the framework of a monarchy." [9] It continued to be a "commonwealth of nations, an association which embraced bodies of greatly varying legal status, and which in the narrower sense comprised the federation of the electors under the emperor." Altogether, during the middle ages the empire was, at least in theory, a supernational symbol of Western Christendom that had primacy over all other kings and princes and was the guarantor of peace and of law. Even in the fourteenth century this ideology still prevailed, while two centuries later the rule of Emperor Charles V came close at times to worldwide hegemony. By the end of the middle ages, Germany had not yet emerged as a compact nation-state, as had England and France. The specific authority of the German king was submerged too much under the international sovereignty of the emperor. From the fourteenth century on, the distinction between empire (*imperium*) and kingdom (*regnum*) gradually lost its significance. Only toward the end of the fifteenth century were the words "of the German Nation" added to the official title "Holy Roman Empire," and this was done more to restrict than to amplify the meaning of the term.

From 1348 to the end of the Holy Roman Empire in 1806, the position of the emperor was almost always filled by a Hapsburg; yet as it remained based on the elective and not the hereditary principle, every emperor felt obliged to promote the power of his dynasty, even at the expense of the empire, if necessary. This con-

[9] F. Heer, op. cit., p. 82.

frontation between the interests of the empire and those of his own dynasty continuously threatened and weakened the central authority. In addition, the College of the Great Electors was severely divided; and the vested interests of its members prevented it from acting as a compact body and carrying out an effective central policy. The Imperial Diet or Reichstag was equally ineffective. Its composition and competency were never clearly defined. The Estates in the diet lacked a common aim and were more often than not disunited. They only combined to oppose the emperor.

THE RISE OF THE TERRITORIAL STATE

After the fifteenth century, the territorial states became the actual focal points of German politics. Their princely rulers increased their territorial rights vis à vis the emperor. On the other hand, they had to reckon with their own Estates, which had developed since the latter half of the Middle Ages. These Estates, the corporate representatives of the nobility, the higher clergy, and the towns, gathered regularly in the diet where they acted as a counterweight to the power of the ruler. Diets had sprung up in nearly all the principalities, both ecclesiastical and secular. They appeared first in the Tyrol—the only instance where the peasants were also represented—then in Austria, the Archbishopric of Magdeburg, and later in Bavaria. The constitution of the territorial states was based on the right of custom and not on a written document. This made the prince financially dependent upon his Estates in the *Diet*, the knights and the towns usually exercised the greatest influence. The power of the ruler and the customary rights of the Estates therefore coexisted uneasily. After the Reformation, the clergy, who had until then formed the First Estate in most lay principalities, disappeared from the diets. With few exceptions only two Estates remained: the nobility and the towns. Although the nobility was sometimes divided into higher and lower sections in the diet, they both enjoyed high prestige in a society where the line between aristocrats and commoners was sharply drawn.

It has been recently argued that there were two main reasons for the development of territorial Estates in the fourteenth and fifteenth centuries. First, the princes were forced by wars, economic hardships, and the reduced value of money to ask the nobility and burghers in the towns for financial aid. Gradually the diet became so powerful that the prince could not do without its financial support. Second, the prince was often troubled by quarrels in his family, by territorial partitions, and, last but not least, by wars and could not face these difficulties without backing from the country, as represented in the diet. Not infrequently in such cases the Estates were able to act as arbitrators just as they functioned as guarantors of treaties or dynastic settlements. They were much opposed to princes who viewed their territory as private property. On the other hand, "it was to the advantage of the prince to have a working institution that could come to his aid, rather than to have to negotiate with individual groups. Through the diet, moreover, the prince could associate the country with his policy, gain its backing for new laws and decrees, for innovation in religion, for an alliance or a policy of expansion." [10] As the princes and their councillors often proved inept in financial matters, the Estates took control in many principalities, even the actual conduct of the financial administration (it is significant that they were able to borrow money at a much lower rate than their rulers). However, the pivot of their power was their indispensable consent to any taxation. Although the Estates had no power to legislate outside financial matters, drafts of laws and decrees on many topics were, in fact, frequently submitted to them.

GERMAN TOWNS

German towns became an important economic, if not a political factor during the middle ages. By the end of the period, the financial depression of the peasantry was accompanied by the astonishing social and economic rise of the towns. It is estimated that in the late middle ages the total population of Germany ran to about 12 million, of whom 80 percent lived in the country and worked in agriculture. Only 10 to 15 percent lived in the cities. In the fifteenth century, there were about 3,000 towns with between 1,200,000 and 1,600,000 people, all told. Twelve to fifteen towns each had more than 10,000 inhabitants and were regarded as "large." Another twelve to fifteen medium-sized towns had populations between 2,000 and 10,000. There were 150 towns each with between 1,000 to 2,000 people, while the great majority of them had only between 200 and 1,000.

These towns varied a good deal in their origins. As has been seen, some of them in the south and west had been founded inside

[10] F. L. Carsten, *Princes and Parliaments in Germany from the 15th to the 18th Century* (London, 1957), p. 428.

the *Limes* by the Romans. They often developed later into seats of Sees of the Church and became "Bishop's Cities." Others, like Bamberg and Magdeburg, sprang up in the wake of eastern colonization. Behind the protective walls of these cities people from the country took refuge in times of war. In the tenth and eleventh centuries new towns grew up, often outside the walls or beside "Bishop's Cities," and protected themselves with walls of their own. Artisans and burghers involved in small-scale farming were characteristic of these towns, rather than merchants. However, it was in the towns that commerce and trade developed into independent occupations, and where the first steps toward capitalism were taken. The land was controlled in some towns by the nobles, and was cultivated by peasants who were burdened with many services and dues; these towns were far different from those which the burghers were ready to defend by force, if necessary. During the second half of the middle ages some cities strove for independence and pursued policies of their own. They desired to become "Imperial Cities," a status that carried many privileges. All major cities tried hard to acquire land outside their walls in order to keep the territorial princes at bay. The principle that "city air makes you free" attracted many outsiders into the towns or on the adjoining land owned by them. The cities remained outside feudal control, which made them attractive to people who felt all too dependent in the country. But town life was also strictly regulated, partly on the basis of occupational groups and associations, and partly because of the unquestioned rule of Church doctrine. Prices were based on the doctrine of "a just price" and controlled by the town councillors and guilds. The function of the trade guild, or *Zunft*, was many-sided. It was also an occupational association that regulated prices and wages and laid down working conditions, a community of worship with Church altars of its own, and a military unit for the defense of the town. The entire life of the artisans and trades people was determined by it. Each guild had its own patron saint, whose picture appeared on its banners and shields and whose annual festival day was duly celebrated. First created in the twelfth century as an "open" association, the guild developed into a "closed shop" with a monopoly which precluded nonmembers from pursuing that trade in the town. Membership in the guild became compulsory, and outsiders were not allowed to buy or sell at retail prices in the city. While at first the artisans had only worked for wages and for a limited number of clientele, after the fourteenth century they produced for a wider market, facilitated by the great trade routes in South and West Germany. More and more, job work replaced work for a wage. The interests of masters and journeymen, previously unified, began to clash. The master often developed into a small-scale entrepreneur, while the journeymen, who frequently changed masters and traveled widely, formed fraternities of their own. From the thirteenth century onward, there were special guilds for all branches of industry, each of which laid down rules for manufacture, quality of material, and wages and prices, and allowed only a fixed number of masters, journeymen, and apprentices in the town. These strict regulations were salutary in many ways because they prevented excessive individual profits and provided a reasonable living standard for all concerned.

Medieval society in the Holy Empire was based on feudal law (*Lehnrecht*). Secular and ecclesiastical princes were, in theory, vassals of the crown; counts and free lords below them were considered subvassals, as they did not receive their fiefs direct from the king. Unlike France and England, Germany had no broad stratum of royal subjects. In addition to the original nobility, there was also another kind of fief-holder, the so-called *Ministeriales*, who did not become servants of the empire or form the nucleus of an imperial civil service. They gradually joined the knights and shared with them the ideals and life style of the nobility; together they formed a united front against the parvenues from the ranks of city burghers and peasants. The knights developed their own norms of nobility, with customs like *Schwertleite* (bestowing the right to a sword on their descendants) and tournaments. Only the knights participated in the life of the court and in the crusades. Despite the clear demarcation line between the lower nobility and the higher nobility, which included only imperial princes and counts, the tie between them should not be underestimated. Although imperial knights were immediately under the emperor, they nevertheless belonged to the lower nobility. They enjoyed many privileges, including freedom from imperial taxation. Many lower nobles desired to become imperial knights because they would be free from obligation to their territorial ruler.

EXPANSION AND COLONIZATION IN THE EAST

While the Hohenstaufen were involved in bitter struggles in Italy, a significant development occurred along the frontiers in the east and north in which, however, the emperors took little part. As already indicated, from the eleventh to the thirteenth centuries German colonization in the east advanced beyond the Elbe River to the Vistula and along the Baltic Sea to the Gulf of Finland. Altogether Germany acquired an area corresponding in extent to two-thirds of its original territory. It was not only a question of conquest, but also of peaceful settlement and colonization. Although racial antagonism between Slav and Teuton and religious friction between Christian missionaries and heathen natives played their part, the desire for land and the peasants' dissatisfaction with their conditions inside the old Reich led to the gradual large-scale emigration to the virgin soil east of the Elbe. Undoubtedly part of the Slav resistance to Christian–Germanic rule was due to the cruelty and lack of consideration of some of the colonizers, who were motivated by greed rather than genuine missionary spirit. As the contemporary chronicler Helmold wrote of Henry the Lion: "In all his various expeditions there was no mention of Christianity, but only of money." On the other hand, Albrecht the Bear, Margrave of Brandenburg, cooperated with the Church and granted it vast areas for colonization. However, he foiled a clerical attempt to impose a heavier tithe on Slavs than on German settlers. From the middle of the twelfth century, large numbers of Dutch and Flemish settlers worked the marshlands bordering the Havel River, until then unpopulated and uncultivated. In the thirteenth century the first towns in that area developed, including Spandau and Berlin. By 1300, thirty-eight towns had been founded in Pomerania on both sides of the mouth of the Oder River. As in Mecklenburg, German knights were given tracts of land as fiefs in order to arrange for the settlement of peasants from the empire. In Silesia, too, 120 towns and over 1,200 villages were founded in 150 years; and nearly all of them were populated by German settlers. The Slav nobility and the native princes favored the German settlers, and soon German and Slav lords vied for them. Colonization was looked upon by the well-to-do as a means of investment. To attract German settlers they made use of a special type of agent or "promoter," the "locator," without whose activities the development of new villages or towns was unthinkable. Settlers from the west formed their own villages and had their own village magistrate, often the locator who had called them; and apart from paying hereditary interest on their land, they were free from any services or burdens. As the position of farmers in the old empire had deteriorated and peasants in Saxony had lost a good deal of their freedom, the situation in the colonial areas seemed attractive to the emigrating peasants and artisans. After 1250, there was a good deal of systematic planning of villages and towns. The markets of the towns "were a stabilizing factor in the economic sphere, their walls a protection, and their legal system a means of cohesion. . . . The immigrants were not isolated, but took their place in a comprehensive scheme, and were strengthened by a sense of solidarity in a communal undertaking." [11] They were free from burdensome obligations to the lord of the manor; they enjoyed personal freedom and freedom of movement, which was also later extended to many of the Slav natives.

Conditions were different in the lands between Poland and the Baltic beyond the Vistula. Poles had run into trouble with the fierce and warlike natives, the Prussians, and were unable to overcome them. They called on the Order of the Teutonic Knights, which had been founded in 1190 in the Near East during the Third Crusade. The work of the Order was not confined to looking after the poor, the sick, and the wounded; it was also pledged to fight the infidels. The poles promised them full control of all the territories they could conquer, and Frederick II had confirmed this privilege in 1236. The knights set out on a ruthless military undertaking that "regarded baptism simply as a token of subjection." They erected towns like Thorn, Kulm, and Marienwerder largely as fortified centers from which to conduct their military operations. They founded Memel in 1252 and the important city of Königsberg in 1255. Several waves of rebellion were ruthlessly suppressed, and this continued until the native Prussian chieftain laid waste his land and fled to pagan Lithuania. It was only then that mass immigration of German peasants began. Most of the remaining Prussians were forced into serfdom, and the best land went to the new German settlers. By 1410 the Order had founded 1,400 villages and 93 towns. The seat of its Grand Master was Marienburg—half monastery, half castle, monumentaal and solemn, reflecting more the determination of a warrior race than the spiritual depth of Christianity. The strength of the Order—strict centralization and rigid submission to the authority of the Grand Master—also proved to be its weakness, as it was incapable of adapting to changing circumstances. The knights never came to terms with the indigenous population and were unable to secure their cooperation. The Order was decisively beaten in the Battle of Tannenberg in 1410 by the Poles, who had

[11] G. Barraclough, op. cit., p. 274.

grown in strength in the fourteenth century, because of desertions by the burghers and nobles under its control. The Baltic lands were never fully colonized or subjected to the will of the German masters. Yet it should be mentioned that Lübeck, founded in 1143 at the gateway between East and West, became the model for a number of daughter-cities such as Wismar, Stralsund, and Rostock.

Alliances or leagues between some cities that were fighting for their autonomy from princes and nobles emerged in Germany during the thirteenth and fourteenth centuries. The Rhenish League was founded in 1254–55, and the Swabian League in 1331. The Hanseatic League, which gradually developed during the second half of the thirteenth century, was to become much more significant. It was the only alliance of German cities that was "outward-looking" and operated on an international basis. The term "Hanse" was first applied to the settlement of Rhenish and Westphalian merchants in London who had joined together to secure legal protection and freedom of commerce abroad. It was later used to describe a league of German towns, led by such major North German cities as Lübeck, Danzig, Brunswick, and Cologne. By the end of the thirteenth century, the members of the Hanse enjoyed trading privileges and controlled foreign markets from London to Bergen in Norway and from Novgorod in Russia to Bruges, then in the Netherlands. The Hanseatic traders bought raw wool, cloth, and minerals at Bruges and London and exchanged them for furs, amber, wood, grain, and flax from Russia, Sweden, Prussia, and Poland. The Hanseatic League became powerful by controlling the mouths of the Elbe, Weser, Oder, and Vistula, and by maintaining a fleet of its own that safe guarded its trading in the North Sea and the Baltic. This league established a monopoly for Baltic trade, particularly in the herring and cod industries. Bruges became a center of West European sea trade, controlling the export of the highly valued Flanders cloth. At its peak the league was a political and an economic power, and its fleet could be used for warfare as well as for trade.

In the fifteenth century, over 160 German cities were members of the Hanse, including such places outside the old empire as Breslau, Cracow, Wisby, and Stockholm. From the beginning of the sixteenth century, however, the fortunes of this once-powerful confederation declined for a number of reasons. One was the change of European focus as a result of the great geographical discoveries in North and South America with the subsequent change of emphasis from the Mediterranean to the Atlantic diminishing the importance of Venice

and the Baltic Sea. Another reason was the growing strength of
the territorial states in Germany, which imposed their will on an
increasing number of cities and forced them to leave the Hanseatic
League. In the end, princely power had won out over the medieval
idea of the political independence of large cities.

3

Aspects of the First Empire:
II. Early Modern Germany

REFORMATION AND COUNTER-REFORMATION

Germany on the Eve of the Reformation

Some historians have maintained that by 1500 the Holy Roman Empire was an anachronism. This is an exaggeration, but if it existed it was certainly not very effective. The authority and power of the emperor did not in fact rest on his imperial prestige or property, but on his own possessions and strength as a territorial ruler. Emperor Maximilian I (1493–1519), "the last knight," was little inclined to share his power with the electors, led by the able Berthold von Henneberg, Prince–Archbishop of Mainz, but had to make concessions to the imperial diet. He granted a reform of the imperial court of law and agreed that the diet could appoint a committee to govern during his absence from Germany. Chivalrous, ambitious, unstable, and irresponsible, Maximilian later withdrew these concessions. He was more interested in obtaining money from the Estates for his wars and his passion for hunting than in reforming the institutions of the empire. There was a growing political crisis in Germany. The empire had long become "one political structure beside others that wanted equal rights"; yet in the later medieval period, the imperial idea had neither been discarded by the emperors themselves nor by the political theorists in the country. In fact, since the thirteenth century the German king was "the primus inter pares, the first prince of the realm among the territorial princes." [1] The only real progress made under Maximilian was a law accepted at the Diet of 1495 that proclaimed internal peace. From then on the feud as the traditional mode of settling conflicts was no longer recognized. However, the emperor lacked an imperial public service that could implement decrees issued at the diet. With its multiplicity of rulers, Germany suffered from disorganization. At the same time the territorial princes tried to consolidate their own position through self-aggrandizement and by reducing the power of the feudal nobility and the status of peasants and towns.

While in the fifteenth century nationalism in Spain, France, and England led to a centralized monarchy, in Germany particularism prevailed instead. Whereas in the Western countries a national church developed, this did not happen in Germany. It is true the German princes secured privileges from the Church by special concordates, but they had to pay for them by agreeing to most of the financial claims of the Roman Curia, claims that often served the malpractices of the Papal officials and emissaries. The first major protest demanding reform was laid down in the "Grievances of the German Nation," formulated in 1456 and since repeated at all meetings of the Diet and assemblies of the Estates until they were finally taken over by Luther in his "Address to the German Nobility" of 1520. The German bishops themselves often expressed dissatisfaction with the Curia's demands for dues. A good deal of German nationalist feeling was anticlerical, and it deplored the self-indulgent ways of the Italian prelates and other high clergy. Critics compared the priests' conduct with the ideals of priesthood, and their conduct was frequently found wanting. They overlooked the fact that there were also priests of high and low rank who took their vows seriously. However, much ethical indignation was vented in anticlerical outbursts, and "most of this antagonism towards the clergy was inspired by national and local feeling against the drain of money from Germany to Rome." [2] The literature on Church abuses in Germany in the fifteenth century germinated in all the Estates and groups. The economic privileges of the clergy and the acquisitive activities of the monasteries and the tradesmen connected with them were bitterly criticized by the town burghers.

[1] Erich Hassinger, *Das Werden des Neuzeitlichen Europa 1300–1600* (Braunschweig, 1959), p. 107.
[2] R. Pascal, *The Social Basis of the German Reformation: Martin Luther and His Times* (London, 1933), p. 7.

On the eve of the Reformation the cities were more important economically than politically. While in the era of the city leagues of the fourteenth century, they had been a political factor to be reckoned with, they were now checked by the growing power of the territorial princes. Although the imperial cities had been regularly admitted since 1489 to the Diets in which they ranked third after the electors and the princes, they did not achieve full equality in voting and deliberation with the "Upper Estates," which never acknowledged the full political autonomy of the towns. However, the town rulers and the princes feared a mass revolt, "which often led to a hardening of the authoritarian regime of the town rulers towards the community of the citizens." [3] Yet the citizens did not regard the town rulers with the awe displayed by the subjects toward princes. However, the political decline of the imperial cities, which never became city-states after the Italian pattern, was accompanied by economic growth. There were two types of German towns; first, the self-contained towns of farmer-burghers who produced for their own market and a limited vicinity; second, the big export and trade centers involved in long-distance transactions. It was in the trade centers that a new type of relationship developed between commerce and finance. The members of the Hanse still carried out an immense trade in foreign goods, with wide-ranging contacts and a large number of transactions. On the other hand, the towns in South Germany relied much more on their own products, particularly on textiles. An early entrepreneur like Jakob Fugger, "the Rich" (1459–1525), had risen from weaver to merchant and had then, in an age of discovery and worldwide communication, raised his family to a first-rank financial power. Jakob Fugger became the financier of the emperor and lent large amounts of money, first to Maximilian and then to his grandson Charles V. Indeed in the campaign for the election of Charles as German Emperor, the subsidies provided by Fugger, considered immense by his contemporaries, played a decisive role. Over two thirds of the bribes paid to the greedy electors and their lackeys came from Fugger's funds.

Fugger had invested in copper mines and soon possessed the very rich mines in Hungary; he controlled practically the entire European market in that commodity. His firm developed into a family company, as did some of its rivals in Augsburg and Nuremberg. Restless and ambitious, Jakob Fugger was the very essence of the capitalist entre-

[3] Stephan Skalweit, *Reich und Reformation* (Berlin, 1968), pp. 25–26.

preneur, but he retained his rather profound religious ties. In the spirit of the Church's teachings, he acknowledged the need of the rich to provide for the poor by building a little welfare community within the town of Augsburg. This foundation, the *Fuggerei*, still exists today. Perhaps Fugger's conscience was sensitive at a time when taking interest on money lent was still regarded by the Church as usury. The new family companies were far from being popular; and their apparently easy gains seemed to run counter to the ethics of the Church. The popular outcry against the sharp practices of these "monopolists" was discussed at various diets after 1500, and restrictions were imposed on the trading companies. But as Charles V needed credit and as he had become financially dependent on the Fuggers, he saw to it that the activities of the companies were in fact not much interfered with.

There was a good deal of peasant unrest in Germany some decades before the "Peasants War," and this was one of the main features of the age of the Reformation in the empire. However the position of peasants varied a good deal in different parts of Germany, and they were by no means uniformly depressed. In most of the empire little servitude was to be found; and most peasants owned their land, although the services they had to render to the nobility increased. Generally speaking, there was no economic crisis. The peasant unrest of the fifteenth century and at the beginning of the sixteenth often had diverse and local causes. But all territorial princes desired to create a uniform stratum of subjects, to increase their dues and services, and to reduce their autonomy and common land. This was often done with the help of trained lawyers who dug up forgotten or not fully utilized legal claims. The peasants, for their part, based their claims on the power of tradition, the "Ancient Rights." The political clash between the growing territorial state and the peasants' associations who found their rights reduced exploded in riots.[4] Protesting peasants in Württemberg unanimously decried new consumer taxes and the deterioration of weights and coins instigated by the authorities.

A demand for "divine justice" was put forward by the *Bundschuh* rebellion in the Upper Rhine area in 1502, 1513, and 1517. Its symbol was a peasant's lace boot, which was carried by the demonstrators on a stick or painted on a flag. The peasant leaders challenged the

[4] W. P. Fuchs, in Bruno Gebhardt, *Handbuch der Deutschen Geschichte*, ed. Herbert Grundmann, 8th ed. (Stuttgart, 1962), p. 57.

political authorities, who were themselves divided. Their criticism appeared in a fresh light with Luther's movement against malpractices in the Church. When they learned that this rebellious monk had attacked the Church's authority as anti-Christian, they felt justified in trying to improve their lot in the Peasants' War of 1525. Yet they were to be bitterly disappointed in their hopes that Luther and the Reformation would back their cause.

The demands of the rebels were summarized in the "Twelve Articles of the Peasants in Swabia," a pamphlet by Sebastian Lotzer from Memmingen that quickly became a best-seller. The "Articles" included the demand for a reduction of the tithe, abolition of servitude, freedom of hunting and fishing, reduction of arbitrarily increased services, restitution of communal meadows, and reduction of excessive fines. Although these demands were moderate, in many places the peasants got out of hand and began to plunder and destroy castles and monasteries. Some of the territorial rulers made concessions for a while, but their real aim was to gain time to crush the rebellion and subject the peasants completely. They succeeded in South as well as in Central Germany; the peasants showed little fighting spirit and lacked competent leaders. It was easy for the troops of the Swabian League (under the efficient command of Georg Truchsess von Waldburg) to destroy the rebellion in the South, and for the combined forces of Hesse, Brunswick, and Saxony to put an end to the ill-founded theocracy of the radical priest Thomas Munzer in Thuringia. Many thousands of peasants were killed, and the fugitives were hunted down like rabbits. Others were heavily fined, and all peasants were deprived of the right to bear arms. Although the economic position of the peasants did not deteriorate, they were now eliminated as a political factor. Luther alienated many of the survivors in his harsh tract, "Against the Robbing and Murderous Gangs of Peasants," condemning their cause as the work of the devil and asking the authorities to put an end to the terror of the rebels. They fell back on the old creed or turned to sects like the Anabaptists. The voice of the German peasant had been crushed and was to remain silent for more than two centuries.

Martin Luther and Charles V

So far as Germany was concerned, the great antagonists in the Reformation were not so much Luther and the Pope, but Luther (1438–1546) and Charles V (1500–1558). Their confrontations at the Diet of Worms marked the end of the first phase of Luther's attempts to reform the Church from within. It also revealed the attitude of an emperor whose worldwide possessions were kept together only by dynastic unity. Charles regarded himself as the heir of Charlemagne and, equal with the Pope, as the secular head of a united Christendom. Ruler over the Austrian lands, Burgundy (which included the Netherlands), and the various kingdoms in Spain and their astonishing extensions in the recently discovered New World, Charles could rightly boast that the sun never set upon his realm. But his worldwide possessions also contributed to his weakness as ruler of the German Empire; for he was able to be only intermittently present in Germany and had many other problems and issues to worry about. He moved constantly from one of his dominions to another and was forever involved in wars and crusades, many of which were not directly relevant to the German Estates. There was the traditional friction betwen the German Empire and France over Alsace and Lorraine and a sharp Spanish-French confrontation in the prolonged Italian wars. War was "the keynote of Charles V's reign, war and the expenditure it demanded." [5] However, Charles knew how to handle people. He made skillful use of his rights of patronage, which to many nobles became in the end a substitute for loyalty. On principle the emperor regarded it as his duty to stand by the Pope, though he had no great love for him and was well aware of some of the questionable ways in which the Curia secured money. When he gave Luther a safe-conduct permit to and from the Diet of Worms, his sense of honor compelled him to keep his word. But as a good Catholic he was bound to oppose any doctrine that challenged the spiritual claims of the Pope and the clergy. When Luther appeared before Charles V at Worms, the Church regarded him as a dangerous heretic who aimed at splitting it. The "very reluctant revolutionary" did not think at that time of forming a new church, but "hoped to appeal from a deluded pope to a reforming emperor." Before Worms, Luther was confident that the abuses he pointed out in such vivid and popular language would be abolished and the spirit of true religion based on the scripture would permeate the Church.

The son of a miner, Martin Luther had at the age of twenty-two become a monk and was soon afterwards appointed professor of theology at the Saxon University of Wittenberg. He entered on the path of the reformer by nailing his *Ninety-Five Theses* to the door of the castle church in that town on October 31, 1517. In them he

[5] G. R. Elton, *Reformation Europe: 1517–1559* (London, 1963), p. 39.

attacked the Church practice of selling indulgences, and the system by which the Church secured money from the faithful by promising commutation of penance to the repentant sinners. The new theology behind the *Theses* was conceived through much mortification, doubt, and self-examination. Luther was convinced that man could not achieve salvation by relying on his own works, no matter whether they consisted of prayer, fasting, self-degeneration, purchasing indulgences, or in giving money for charity. Luther's belief that man cannot be justified by his works but by his faith alone became the fundament of the Reformation.

Luther, the theologian, was also a formidable pamphleteer and writer who expressed himself vividly and in language the man in the street could understand. His translation of the Bible into German became a literary as well as a religious landmark. In the three treatises of 1520, Luther put forward his criticism of the Church and his ideas for reforming it. "Only one thing" was necessary for the Christian life, righteousness, and liberty: "the most Holy Word of God, the gospel of Christ." Equally important was Luther's doctrine of universal priesthood. He maintained that those who exercise what he called "the ministry of the word" were nothing but the first among equals and "should serve the rest by teaching them the freedom of believers." What mattered was that all "share one baptism, one gospel, one faith and are equally Christians: for baptism, gospel, and faith alone make spiritual and Christian people."

It was one thing for Luther to write his challenging treatises that reached a wide public, but quite another to display the courage and determination before fierce opposition at the Diet of Worms in 1521, which was presided over by the enigmatic young emperor. According to tradition, Luther then uttered his final words of resistance: "Here I stand; I can do no other, God help me. Amen." At the end, when most of the delegates had left the Diet, the emperor issued his "Edict against Luther." It condemned him completely, put the imperial ban on him, and forbade the Estates to protect him. However, most of the Estates ignored the edict.

What was first largely a one-man crusade developed during the next eight years, between the two Diets of Worms (1521) and Speyer (1529), into a mass movement with a number of rival factions and centers challenging the old theological order. Some princes and cities accepted the new creed and set the trend toward territorial state churches, which became a characteristic feature of the political structure of Protestant Germany until 1918. This development occurred first in Saxony under Elector John. Soon territorial rulers who adhered to Luther's creed began to secularize Church land. The canonic law of the Church was no longer considered valid, only secular law. However "secular authority" was still viewed in the framework of a Christian order. Its task was not to be the enjoyment of power, but a benevolent paternalism that included a duty to assist in the eternal salvation of the subjects by providing Christian doctrine and discipline. Luther's appeal to the secular authorities to protect religious teaching and discipline substantially strengthened their hands. His concept of the state by no means suggested that it be religiously neutral. In his view the princes had been given their office by God not only in order to feed their subjects and to look after their physical welfare, but mainly to educate them "to the glory and honor of God." The authorities could not permit false religious doctrines to be taught and the wrong type of service to be carried out. Yet, conversely, when the secular authority supported a false creed and persecuted true believers, or even had them killed, Luther insisted upon absolute obedience because he considered them to be an institution ordained by God.

Luther did not confine his idea of "false" religious views to the Roman Curia. He also turned against other reformers, Zwingli in Switzerland and the radicals Karlstadt and Thomas Müntzer in North Germany. Huldrych Zwingli (1484–1531), a preacher at the cathedral in Zurich, shared Luther's conviction of the direct relationship between man and God. He, too, belittled the significance of good works and rejected many ceremonies and observances as detrimental to man's salvation. Like the humanist Erasmus of Rotterdam, he felt strongly about the contrast between Christ's Sermon on the Mount and selfish, unjust, and violent attitudes of the nominal Christians. However, Zwingli stressed the oneness of religious and political activity much more than Luther. While Luther was deeply convinced of the impossibility of changing the sinful world, Zwingli regarded it possible to make the commonwealth of citizens totally Christian. To him "A Christian City" was "nothing but a Christian Church, and a Christian nothing but a loyal and good citizen." Different from Luther, Zwingli in Zurich and Bucer in Strassburg "thought in terms of towns, and their ideas proved more congenial to people cherishing traditions of urban communalism and independence. Zwinglians were strong among the guilds." [6]

[6] G. R. Elton, op. cit., p. 71.

The Radical Element

In addition to the Lutherans and the Zwinglians there were the radicals, who combined extreme religious enthusiasm and belief in direct contact with God with a concern for the downtrodden and suppressed in the social order. Apocalyptic visions of a coming City of God on earth went hand in hand with an anarchist attitude against all existing authority, against an establishment deemed sinful and corrupt. This radicalism with its variety of modes that ranged from the parish priest Thomas Müntzer to the Anabaptists had its centers in Saxony and Switzerland, the areas where the more conservative reformers Luther and Zwingli operated. Some recent historians have put more emphasis on the religious enthusiasm, the *Schwärmerei* of these radicals, others on their unmistakable note of social protest. With all the confusion of an unstable mind, Müntzer was sincere in his concern for the oppressed and sympathetic with the poor and exploited; and he proved it by his active participation in the Peasants' War, in which he eventually perished miserably. Yet the core of his sermons that incited to rebellion was religious. His main aim was "not to provide a better life for the poor and the oppressed, but to eliminate the obstacle that diverted the 'man in the street' from his inner life and from God."

There were other itinerant preachers of similar passion in Germany, Switzerland, and the Netherlands who obscurely prophecied the forthcoming arrival of God's rule on earth. Some of the Anabaptists waited for that arrival quietly and passively; others felt they should establish God's Kingdom on Earth here and now, and should not shirk from violence in doing so. In Münster, traditionally the seat of a powerful prince-bishop, a group of fanatical Anabaptists, some of them Dutch, tried in their own way to transform the city into the New Jerusalem. Mass baptisms and prayer meetings were held, all faithful Catholics and Protestants driven out, and communal ownership of property and polygamy proclaimed. When the Catholic bishop of Münster, supported by the Lutheran ruler of Hesse, reconquered the city, their troops took a frightful revenge on the rebels of both sexes.

The Emergence of Protestantism

Luther did not intend to leave the Church when he defended his views at the Diet of Worms in 1521. He wanted to establish the true

Christian creed which, as he saw it, had been adandoned by the Papacy during the last few centuries. Luther still regarded himself as a reformer within the Church. However when the Pope threatened Luther with the Church Ban in 1520 and Luther replied by publicly burning the Papal Bull and some books of canon law, the break with Rome seemed complete. Both truly religious and very worldly motives played a part in the progress of the Lutheran movement during the next two decades. Tucked away in the safety of the Wartburg in Thuringia for a year, Luther was asked for advice from many people in many countries. The extent of his correspondence shows that he was regarded as a unique leader against the Roman Curia. Yet it is rather doubtful whether the Lutheran movement would have survived "had not a great many Estates realized their substantial interest in it." [7] By 1525, in addition to numerous towns, John, Elector of Saxony, and Philip, Landgrave of Hesse, were among the rulers who accepted the new creed. Albrecht von Brandenburg, the High Master of the Order of the Teutonic Knights in the territory east of the Elbe, transformed his order into a secular duchy and, advised by Luther, introduced the new doctrines.

Charles V was absent from Germany for eight years owing to his involvement in the wars with France for control of Italy which ended in triumph for him in the Peace of Madrid (1529) and the Peace of Cambria (1529). The emperor's military and political successes abroad were counterbalanced by the increased prestige of the German princes following their victory over the peasants. Affairs in Germany were looked after meanwhile by the Imperial Governing Council (*Reichsregiment*), over which the emperor's brother Ferdinand presided. The growing cooperation between the French and the Turks against the Hapsburgs weakened the emperor's power in German affairs. Ferdinand therefore did not dare to take a firm stand against the forces adhering to the new creed at the First Diet of Speyer (1526), but accepted a compromise resolution.

However, at the Second Diet of Speyer three years later (1529), when the emperor's wars with France and the Pope were about to end, Ferdinand became more intransigent and insisted that Catholics should be able to continue their services in territories that had accepted Luther's doctrine. Five princes, including the Elector of Saxony and the Landgrave of Hesse, and fourteen South German cities pro-

[7] P. Rassow, *Deutsche Geschichte im Überblick* (Stuttgart, 1962), pp. 260–61.

tested against this; and the supporters of the new creed were from then on called "Protestants." By the withdrawal of the protesters from the Diet, a situation was created that could easily lead to a religious war. There were, however, considerable dissensions within both the Catholic and the Protestant camps, as is evident from the controversies between Luther and Zwingli at Marburg, and between Charles V and Pope Clement VII at Bologna. These controversies and the appearance of the Turks on the outskirts of Vienna formed the background to the important Diet of Augsburg in 1530. In the absence of Luther, his friend Melanchton, a much milder and less emotional academic, advised the Elector of Saxony and drafted the moderate "Confession of Augsburg" as a Protestant platform to which the Catholics replied with a sharp counter declaration. The emperor still hoped for a compromise and worked to convene a Church council. Yet he finally refuted the Protestant "Confession." The fronts hardened; in 1531 representatives of eight Protestant territorial princes formed a political alliance against the emperor, the League of Schmalkalden. Even the conservative Luther reluctantly agreed that a common resistance to the emperor was permissible, should he provoke a religious war, a view by no means shared by all Protestant authorities.

By 1546 almost all of Germany had turned Protestant; but internal discord among the Protestant rulers played into the hands of the emperor, who in the Battle of Mühlberg won a major victory over the Elector of Saxony and made him prisoner in 1547. Another key figure among the Protestant princes, the unsaintly Landgrave of Hesse also fell into the emperor's hands. Yet eight years later, the position of the emperor and of the adherents of the old creed had deteriorated with changing circumstances. The Agreement of Passau of 1552, reached between the rebellious princes and King Ferdinand, meant that Charles V had failed in his policies. He had been unable to prevent the pact between Protestantism and some major German princes and to preserve the unity of the creed. He realized at last that the Edict of Worms could no longer be maintained. At last the "Religious Peace of Augsburg" was concluded at another Diet in 1555, presided over by Ferdinand. Its main point was the important admission that members of the Diet could be either Catholic or evangelical (Lutheran). In each territory, however, there could be only one faith—the faith of the ruler. Religious minorities had the right to emigrate. Ecclesiastical princes could, if they wished, accept the Lutheran creed, but in doing so would have to give up their territories. Adherents of both creeds were allowed to coexist only in the imperial cities.

Many questions remained unsolved, and the decisions were soon interpreted in different ways by the opposing parties; yet the great achievement on this tortuous path was that the Peace of Augsburg allowed for the principle of tolerance at least in the Estates, although it did not yet apply to individuals. "With the establishment of the right of two creeds, the concept of the one Christian church was given up and the avenue was opened not only for a second church but for many churches and thus for a new age." [8] Germany was no longer in the forefront of events, but it remained peaceful for sixty-three years, during which time Western Europe was badly shaken by serious religious and political conflicts.

From the Religious Peace of Augsburg to the Thirty Years War

The Reichstag of Augsburg in 1555 represented a double defeat for Emperor Charles. He had not managed to restore religious unity in Germany, nor had he succeeded in imposing his will on the Estates. So long as he ruled and Luther lived (Luther died in 1546), Germany was the center of great religious and political controversies. After that period the decisive political and religious impulses no longer originated within the empire. Germany became a backwater of obscure theological controversies and politico-religious groupings. The two new religious movements that were to complicate the issues came from outside: Calvinism from Geneva, and the Counter-Reformation from Spain and Rome. Both, however, had important repercussions in Germany. Calvinism, the proud and fierce doctrine of absolute predestination developed systematically by John Calvin in his *Institutes of the Christian Religion* (1534), did not allow for Luther's careful separation between the mundane and the ecclesiastical spheres, but proclaimed a theocracy. Although Calvinism made its biggest impact in France, the Netherlands, and later in Scotland, it nevertheless established itself as a second Protestant creed in the southwest and other parts of Germany. It gained a foothold in the Palatinate, where in 1559 the Elector Frederick III declared himself in favor of Calvin and against Luther on the doctrine of the Eucharist. He inaugurated the Heidelberg Catechism of 1563 on moderately Calvin-

---

[8] Peter Rassow, op. cit., p. 283.

ist lines, which was also introduced in some other German principalities. The split between Lutheran and Calvinist, or "Reformed," princes also had political repercussions. The Elector of Saxony, a staunch Lutheran, continued to largely support the policies of the Catholic emperor for dynastic reasons, while the Elector of the Palatinate headed the anti-imperial party.

There was no love lost between Lutherans and Calvinists. However, battles just as fierce raged after Luther's death in his own camp between the extreme fundamentalists and the moderates, of whom Philip Melanchton, that gentle humanist don, was the often unhappy leader.[9] Although the Calvinist conquests were small compared with those of the Lutherans, they were to gain additional strength in the seventeenth century when the Elector of Brandenburg accepted the Reformed Creed. It was perhaps the weakness of German Lutheranism that after the death of its founder it "became introverted, absorbed in its controversial efforts to understand itself; it could not easily be a missionary religion." [10]

The Catholic Counter-Reformation advanced meanwhile. The long and weary sessions of the Council of Trent (1545–1563) under four successive Popes were eventually brought to a successful conclusion. The Council had not achieved the purpose for which Charles V had supported it, to end the heresy of Protestantism and to restore unity of creed; but it had led to internal reform and restitution, to a redefinition of the Church's doctrines, and to the abolition of abuses and outdated practices.

It has been rightly said that at the time of the Peace of Augsburg the German masses had only vague ideas of what the actual difference between Catholicism and Protestantism was. The earlier champions of the old doctrine such as John Eck (1486–1543) and Thomas Murner (1475–1537) were more concerned with eloquent and biting attacks on heresy than with renewing the Catholic creed and practice. However, it was only when a branch of the Society of Jesus, founded by Ignatius of Loyola in 1534, was established in South Germany by Peter Canisius (1521–1577) that the restoration of the Catholic Church progressed. Canisius, a Dutchman by birth, was zealous in

[9] After the publication of the Lutheran "Formula of Concord" in 1580, sponsored by the Lutheran Elector of Saxony, Augustus I, German Protestantism was in fact divided into three groups: the supporters of the "Formula," its opponents in the Lutheran camp, and the Calvinists.

[10] T. M. Parker in the *New Cambridge Modern History* (Cambridge, 1968), III, p. 84.

preaching and spreading the true faith; but being deeply religious, he eschewed all polemics. He had been called to Rome by Loyola himself and was commissioned to set up the first Jesuit settlement in Germany. Canisius gained the confidence of some South German princes, preached for a while at the cathedral in Augsburg, and tried to improve the religious education of the masses. It is characteristic of the dialectics of history that when one of two opponents makes progress in a field, the other feels obliged to follow suit in his own fashion. As the Protestant schools, under state control and devised by Melanchton, had achieved a good level of learning, Canisius soon tried to match his achievement for the Catholics. Much greater care was taken with the training and the discipline of Catholic priests.

By 1610 the political balance between Catholic and Protestant territories had changed in favor of the Catholics, who had succeeded in regaining some of the big ecclesiastical states in northwest Germany that were lost earlier to the Catholic cause. Religion and politics still remained closely intertwined, and all religious parties maintained contacts abroad. For the time being however, there was a precarious balance of power within the empire "between emperor and estates, between princes great and small, between Protestant and Catholic, even between law and disorder." [11] At the beginning of the seventeenth century, a population of some 21 million was ruled by some 2,000 authorities, out of which 200 might have become involved in clashes of dissension.

The right of the Reichstag to grant revenue to the emperor made him more inclined to listen to the grievances of its members, particularly when the Turkish forces threatened. For the first two decades after the Peace of Augsburg, the Reichstag worked rather constructively; but after 1576 a widening split between its Catholic and Protestant members became visible. Having retrieved some of their previous losses in territory and prestige in 1594, the Catholics succeeded by a majority vote with their demands; and consequently the emperor obtained his desired subsidy. But three years later, the Calvinist Elector of the Palatinate and his associates refused to agree to the payment of a subsidy that had been accepted by the majority. It was obviously an act of planned sabotage and clearly indicated the deteriorating state of affairs between the two camps. Though the settlement of 1555 had, as we have seen, provided for the peaceful coexistence of Catholics and Lutherans in the free cities, in many

[11] G. D. Ramsay, *New Cambridge Modern History*, III, 331.

cases the minority position proved hazardous and full of tribulations. There were confessional squabbles in all towns, but the quarrel between the Protestant council and the well-organized Catholic minority in the free city of Donauwörth near Augsburg led to an imperial crisis, and an incident of national significance. When the Catholic minority of Donauwörth asked the emperor for support, he appointed the fiercely Catholic Duke Maximilian of Bavaria as his official agent. His troops occupied the town in December, 1607, and soon afterwards he reimbursed himself for the expenses he had contracted in his intervention by simply annexing Donauwörth, which thus lost its independence, and, due to the faith of her new master, became a Catholic town. It was a striking example of the helplessness of the free cities, "as neat a piece of power politics veiled by religious principles as could be found in Europe." [12]

THE THIRTY YEARS WAR AND ITS AFTERMATH

The intervention in Donauwörth contributed to the open break between the Catholics and most of the Protestant princes, which occurred at the Reichstag at Regensburg in 1608. The previously often discussed idea of forming political alliances on confessional lines was now translated into action. In May, 1608, Lutheran and Reformed princes in South Germany, headed by the Elector of the Palatinate, formed the Protestant *Union*, which was joined by some smaller territorial rulers, the free cities of Ulm, Nuremberg, and Strassburg, and by the Elector of Brandenburg in 1610. Duke Maximilian of Bavaria and some ecclesiastical princes in South Germany responded by founding the Catholic *League*. Both alliances were defense pacts, but each set up an army and formed connections abroad; the Union with France and the League with Spain.

It is not possible to discuss the issues and events of the Thirty Years War in detail here. Yet to understand its impact and significance, it is imperative to realize that during its later phases, Germany largely became a battlefield for foreign troops sent by Spain, Sweden, and France. From a predominantly "internal" affair during its first twelve years (1618–30), when the conflict involved mainly Bohemia, the Palatinate, and Lower Saxony, the war reached truly European proportions during its last eighteen years (1630–48), with France and Sweden joining against the Spanish and Hapsburg claim to

[12] C. D. Ramsay, op. cit., p. 343.

hegemony. The conflict began on the fringe of the empire in Bohemia, where the Protestant nobility ignored the claims of Archduke
Ferdinand, a staunch Catholic. In August, 1619, they chose instead
the young and inexperienced Calvinist Elector of the Palatinate,
Frederick V as their king. Earlier in that year, the Bohemian Protestants had protested against the destruction of their churches on
ecclesiastical grounds and submitted their grievances to the imperial
governors. A group of radical nobles used violence, throwing the
two governors, Martiniz and Slawata, out of the window of Prague
Castle. They survived, but the rebels formed a government of their
own and an army. Meanwhile, after the death of Emperor Mathias,
brother and successor of Rudolf II, Archduke Ferdinand had become
emperor. He had also inherited the Hapsburg lands. The new emperor was supported by the head of the League, the formidable
Duke Maximilian of Bavaria. The Union, on the other hand, held
back; and the Lutheran Elector of Saxony sided with the emperor
because he was opposed to the Calvinist reforms carried out in
Bohemia. The combined troops of Ferdinand and the League under
General Tilly soon invaded Bohemia and, in November, 1620, decisively defeated the inexperienced rebels in the Battle of the White
Mountain, west of Prague. Unhappy Frederick, the "Winter King,"
fled while the rebels were subjected to savage revenge. Their leaders
were executed, and all the possessions of the Protestant nobility confiscated. The religious issue flared up once more. In conjunction
with Spanish troops, the army of the League occupied the Palatinate
in 1622. A year later, the emperor made Duke Maximilian of Bavaria, Elector Palatine in place of Frederick V.

The advance of the Catholic party shocked the Protestants in
North Germany, for the Catholics might threaten the compact area
east of the lower Rhine and the formerly Catholic parts of Westphalia, that were in the hands of Protestant territorial princes or
Protestant administrators of former ecclesiastical territories. The appearance of Tilly's troops in Lower Saxony alarmed King Christian
of Denmark who, as overlord of Holstein, had an important foothold
in Lower Germany. In February, 1625, the Estates of the empire in
Lower Saxony appointed the king of Denmark as their military
commander (*Kreisoberst*). He advanced into Westphalia and was
soon supported by the troops of such adventurers as Ernst Mansfeld
and Christian von Halberstadt.

A new factor in the game of power politics came into play.
Albrecht von Wallenstein (1559–1632) is one of the most enigmatic

and interesting figures in modern history. Springing from an old Bohemian aristocratic family of modest means, he had soon managed to rise, partly through his acumen in army affairs and partly through a rich marriage. His support of King, and later, Emperor Ferdinand II paid good dividends. After he had acquired an immense complex of confiscated lands in northeast Bohemia, the emperor made him Duke of Friedland and granted him special rights by which he almost became a territorial prince. He developed a large armament industry on his estate that helped to set up and maintain his armies. Wallenstein had an impatient, restless mind. He liked to test new ways and methods; but he was secretive, suspicious, changeable, egotistical, and commanding. He was not without a streak of cruelty, and he lacked the gift of making friends. He was also indifferent to anything not conducive to his own profit. Wallenstein marched into North Germany with a large army and, in April, 1626, inflicted a decisive defeat on Mansfeld near Dessau. Three months later, Tilly managed to do equally well against the army of King Christian of Denmark in the Battle of Lutter. Things looked black for the anti-Hapsburg camp, and for the Protestant cause altogether.

Fortunately for them, Wallenstein's ruthless exploitation of the occupied territories in North Germany, his ambitions as a "General of the Baltic and Atlantic Seas," and his insistence on being made Duke of Mecklenburg after conquering the country were viewed with envy and suspicion, even in the imperial camp. When Emperor Ferdinand II, at a meeting with the Electors in Regensburg in 1630, heard complaints from both Catholics and Protestants about the conduct of the imperial army under Wallenstein, he decided to dismiss the self-willed general. Ferdinand was forced to make this concession after he had antagonized many princes by the Edict of Restitution of March, 1629. This decreed that all imperial religious endowments (*Stifter*) and all ecclesiastical property that had been taken over since the settlements of 1552 and 1555 must be handed back to the Catholic bishops.

The Edict of Restitution and the threatening presence of Wallenstein on the shores of the Baltic were among the reasons for the intervention of the dynamic King of Sweden, Gustavus Adolphus. His motives for entering the German war were complex. Sympathy for the threatened cause of German Protestantism was one, the desire for political aggrandizement was another. The Swedish king proved as hard a taskmaster as Wallenstein. After landing in Pomerania in June, 1630, he forced her duke into an alliance that put the entire military and financial resources of the state at his disposal. Though most of the Protestant princes were reluctant to join him, they were encouraged to at least protest at a meeting in Leipzig against the Edict of Restitution and the financial burden imposed on them by the imperial party. Meanwhile, Sweden had concluded a pact with France and Holland that granted the Swedish King subsidies with which to pay his army.

At the confrontation between the armies of Tilly and Gustavus Adolphus near Leipzig in September, 1631, Tilly was beaten, and his troops had to leave North Germany, only to be defeated a second time, six months later, in South Germany. King Gustavus advanced into Bavaria and occupied Munich, the residential city of Elector Maximilian, the head of the League. When the hereditary lands of the Hapsburgs seemed threatened, the emperor reappointed Wallenstein, who, resentful of the slight he had suffered, had earlier from his Bohemian estates made secret contacts with Protestant princes, Bohemian emigrés, and even the King of Sweden. He was now given unlimited power as commander of the army and also the right to negotiate with the Elector of Saxony, who had concluded a pact with Sweden after his country had been invaded by Tilly's troops. In November, the imperial armies under Wallenstein, and the Swedes under their king faced each other at Luetzen, fifteen miles west of Leipzig. Wallenstein, the condottieri, and Gustavus Adolphus (who prayed before the whole army, asking the blessing of God on the Protestant cause) showed great courage in adversity. In the end, Wallenstein lost the battle, but the fierce king from the north lost his life. "That night, over his whole camp, among Swedes and Germans, Scots, Irish, Poles, French, and Dutch, among mercenaries as among his subjects, there hung the silence of unutterable sorrow." [13] By his dramatic death, Gustavus Adolphus appeared afterwards to many as the gallant savior of German Protestantism. However, had he lived on, his plans to control the German Protestant princes might well have alienated their sympathy. While Swedish policy in Germany was now ably conducted by Chancellor Axel Oxenstjerna, Wallenstein remained the sphinx in the political game. Although Wallenstein, now aged and ailing, also realized the need for peace, he was preoccupied with his own egotistical plans and the desire for revenge. Both the Spaniards and Maximilian of Bavaria distrusted him, and finally the court at Vienna shared their suspicion of this

[13] C. V. Wedgwood, *The Thirty Years War* (London, 1964), p. 327.

double-faced soldier-politician. When, at the beginning of 1634, an imperial decree declared him deposed and a second one accused him of treachery, the army deserted him. Accompanied by a few troops, Wallenstein withdrew to Eger to join the Swedes, only to be murdered in cold blood by some of his own officers.

Far from destroying the imperial army, Wallenstein's removal made it a reliable instrument in the hands of the emperor. A severe defeat inflicted by imperial troops on the Swedes near Nördlingen turned the tables, and soon the whole of South Germany was regained by the imperial forces. The course was clear for the Peace of Prague, concluded between the emperor, the electors of Saxony and Brandenburg, and most of the other German princes. It seemed that the emperor and the Catholic and Protestant members of the diet would join forces against Spain, France, and Sweden. However, these powers were determined to continue the fearful war on German soil. After 1635, the confessional factor receded, while that of international power politics gathered momentum. The emperor and the German princes allied with him fought against the foreign invaders —the Catholic French and the Protestant Swedes. Under the Machiavellian leadership of Cardinal Richelieu, France had become involved in an intense struggle with Spain and wanted to secure Lorraine and possibly Alsace. From 1640 onward, French cooperation with the Swedes enabled the anti-imperial forces to gain the upper hand. In the autumn of 1646, Bavaria suffered grievous devastation by the French and Swedish troops. The religious issue had become obliterated when French Catholic and Swedish Protestant soldiers ravaged and pillaged Catholic Bavaria. One after the other of the emperor's allies were obliged to negotiate for peace with the enemy. Even the adamant Elector of Bavaria was forced to agree to an armistice. The Peace Congress of Westphalia began as early as 1644. Delaying tactics were employed in the hope of a military turn of the tide; disagreements arose between the German princes, and between the French and Swedish delegations—all these developments complicated matters, along with the fact that the emperor and the German Catholics negotiated with France at Münster and with the Swedes and German Protestants at Osnabrück. At last, in October, 1648, peace was concluded both at Münster and Osnabrück. Most belligerent parties had long realized that the survival of what was left of the country was more important than religious discord and foreign alliances. The desire for peace had probably been strongest with the mute peasants and the townsfolk from whom the war had taken manpower, food, and sustenance while they had been entirely unable to prevent or to end it.

Significantly, France and Sweden, the two powers who had been largely responsible for the continuation of the war for another eighteen years, became guarantors of the peace. There were, in fact, three different settlement treaties concluded at Münster and Osnabrück: the first concerned the relations between the emperor, Germany, and the outside powers; the second determined the pluralism of Christian creeds and territories within the empire; and the third revised the relations between the emperor and the territorial powers of Germany.

The empire as a whole lost territories and states. The declaration of independence of Switzerland and the United Provinces of the Netherlands only confirmed the actual situation. The loss of parts of Alsace to France and of Western Pomerania to Sweden was more serious. Foreign powers now controlled the mouths of four great rivers; the delta of the Rhine was in the hands of the Spaniards and the Dutch; the Elbe was controlled by the Danes; the Oder by the Swedes; and the Vistula by the Poles. Sweden also received a large compensation for her troops, while French control over Metz, Toul, and Verdun was confirmed in the peace treaty.

In the settlement of the religious issue, the legal and property position was based on that of 1555. All the rights and benefits granted earlier to the Catholics and Lutherans were now expressly extended to the supporters of Calvinism. Thus the peace treaty meant a further step towards tolerance, but only one step, as an article of the Treaty of Osnabrück declared: "Beyond the religions mentions above, none shall be received or tolerated in the Holy Empire." However, within the Christian camp no future decisions on religious questions could be enforced by a majority or a minority. The principle of "he who rules the land, determines the religion" remained intact; but religious minorities enjoyed the rights they possessed in January, 1624—at the very least, they had the right to emigrate with their possessions.

Within all the German states the power of the ruler had increased and, apart from the independent cities, often turned towards absolutism. Yet with so many impoverished medium-rank and petty states, the empire now took a back seat in Europe and did not participate in the forceful overseas expansion of countries like Holland, England, and France. For another two centuries Germany was to remain outside the scramble for naval power and colonial territories.

The granting of amnesty and the restitution of secular territories according to the status of 1618 and of ecclesiastical territories to that of 1624 were reasonable and constructive. However, the Peace of Westphalia was significant mainly because it weakened the power and authority of the emperor. The declared principle of "German Liberty" (*Libertät*) within the empire gave the territorial princes power and influence they had never possessed before. From then on the empire was to mean nothing more than a traditional convenience, a geographical term, or in the words of a leading contemporary jurist, Samuel Pufendorf: "an irregular structure similar to that of a monster." Insofar as Germany had any political life at all, it lay with the nearly three hundred sovereign principalities and states and, above all, with Austria, Bavaria, Saxony, and Brandenburg–Prussia. The fragmentation of Germany suited the foreign powers who were guarantors of the peace. However, the Hapsburg monarchy functioned as a great European power, and none of the German dynasties could match it for many years. The duel between the Bourbons and the Hapsburg–Spanish alliance continued, but it was France and not Austria or Spain that set the tone. Inside the empire the major territorial princes consolidated their positions and saw to it that the emperor abided by the fateful decisions at Münster and Osnabrück. There was a good deal of anti-Hapsburg sentiment, and North and South Germany drifted apart more and more. Neither the universal power of the Papacy nor that of the emperor was recognized, and special clauses were inserted as safeguards against such claims. The acknowledgment of the right of different religious creeds and political forces to coexist was as rational as it was opportunistic. Whatever its faults, the settlement helped to cement a badly needed peace that was to be valid for many decades to come.[14]

The Impact

To assess the effect of that long war on German society is difficult because our estimates have to be based on incomplete and fragmentary evidence. For some time there was a tendency among historians to exaggerate the economic, social, and human consequences, but it seems equally unjustified to understate them. The areas of

[14] For a recent analysis of the Peace Congress of Westphalia and its results, see Fritz Dickmann, *Der Westfälische Frieden* (Münster, 1959).

the empire were affected in various degrees: some in the southwest like the Palatinate and Hesse, and Pomerania in the north suffered much, while Silesia or Bohemia were less affected. In all regions the people who had to put up with occupation troops were subjected to heavy financial impositions, loans, and billeting of soldiers, in addition to costly presents to generals and statesmen. It is reliably estimated that whereas in 1618 the German Empire, including Alsace but not the Netherlands and Bohemia, probably had a population of 21 million people, by 1648 it had dropped by over a third to less than 13.5 million. In any case, life was highly insecure and expendable during those frightful thirty years. In fact, the losses from the immediate impact of war, violence, and starvation were less than those caused afterward by the waves of epidemics. Recently a German historian cautiously calculated "that during these thirty emergency years about 40 percent of the German rural population were victims of the war and the epidemics. In the towns the loss may be estimated as only 33 percent." [15] The endless tribulations through loss of life and property made for pessimism and anxiety. "I would not have believed a land could have been so despoiled had I not seen it with my own eyes," said a French general in Nassau. Moreover, "there is evidence enough of such wasting in the drastic efforts of the rulers to revive cultivation." [16]

Most cities suffered from the war, but some improved their position. Ulm and Nuremberg gained through the influx of well-to-do Protestant refugees from Austria. Würzburg's population rose steadily, while Hamburg outdid its rivals in the sugar and spice trade and was able to hold its own in competition with Sweden and Holland in the Baltic. Although the war was a great destroyer, it also brought about new kinds of economic organization. In West Germany it "unmistakeably formed a stimulus for capitalist forms of economy." This is evident in the production and logistics of army supplies and in the role of men like Wallenstein, who was as much a large-scale army entrepreneur as a general. While large amounts of money were lost through theft and robbery and flight of capital, considerable sums were pumped into Germany in the form of subsidies from Spain, France, the Dutch United Provinces, and the Pope. It is safe to say that altogether German "society was dislocated rather than

[15] Günther Franz, *Der Dreissigjährige Krieg und das Deutsche Volk* (Stuttgart, 1961), p. 47.
[16] C. V. Wedgwood, op. cit., p. 513.

destroyed," and the wounds inflicted on it did not heal for a long time.[17] Germany had become a victim of international power politics. She found it difficult to establish a clear identity for the next two hundred years.

As we have seen, the outcome of the war immensely strengthened the territorial rulers; and with it came that kind of *"Obrigkeit,"* or the authoritarian regime of princes and nobles, and a gradually emerging bureaucracy, largely conditioned popular attitudes. The commercial middle classes declined sharply. The dependent official became typical, while the independent merchant did not reappear before the second half of the eighteenth century. "By becoming satellites of the governing class and identifying their interests with those of the rulers, the townsfolk virtually destroyed the buffer state between nobility and peasantry." [18]

In the erstwhile colonial areas east of the Elbe the deterioration in the position of the peasants contributed much to the development of *Grundherrschaft,* the economy of the big farming estates of the noble, into *Gutsherrschaft,* which gave the aristocracy control over the life of the peasants who were now entirely dependent upon them. "A steadily declining number of peasants had to manage an ever-growing area of land in servitude." [19] This development marks an important dividing line between the peasants in most of Germany and those in the lands east of the Elbe. It is true that in the older German territories during the war many farms had been destroyed; many cattle had been killed; and the peasants had fallen into debt; but their social position had not basically changed. In Eastern Germany, on the other hand, the once free peasants became troubled subjects of large-scale noble farmers without any rights.

THE SPIRIT OF POTSDAM: PRUSSIA, 1660–1786

In the seventeenth century the standard of life in Germany, political and cultural, was low compared with the impressive development and extending power of France, England, and the Netherlands. People had no chance and little desire for mass emigration overseas; on the other hand, there was, at least for a considerable period after 1648, hardly any involvement in foreign wars. Absolutism, which

[17] *Ibid.*, p. 515.
[18] *Ibid.*, p. 519.
[19] G. Franz, *op. cit.*, p. 104.

reached a peak in France during the reign of Louis XIV, also made its entry east of the Rhine, though on a very much smaller scale; in a sense, it was invited there rather than being allowed to evolve as a genuine development. Its success varied widely in different German states, but everywhere the prince and his council had to make substantial social and economic concessions to the nobility. The noble enjoyed considerable privileges over the commoner and kept him in his place. In Mecklenburg, Pomerania, Brandenburg, and Prussia and in East European countries such as Poland, Bohemia, Moravia, Hungary, and Russia, "the nobility remained the ruling class, and an urban middle class did not come into being until the later nineteenth century." [20] The majority of the people served the nobility as serfs; the nobility filled the major offices in the army and the public service and prevented any social and economic reforms that might have reduced its power and influence. The nobles formed the ruling class as a recognized part of a divine order under the absolutist ruler. "The remainder of the inhabitants had to obey and to pay, without being able to influence the course of events." [21]

As with the possessions of other princes and dynasties, the territories of Brandenburg–Prussia had been joined by accident under special circumstances, rather than by unifying design. At the beginning of the seventeenth century, Brandenburg was not an impressive country. The "sandbox of the Holy Empire"—as her neighbors disdainfully called her—had negligible towns and industries, a nobility with a rather parochial outlook, and a military force of little value, consisting entirely of mercenaries. However, by a fluke of luck on the eve of the Thirty Years War, the Hohenzollern rulers inherited two isolated and far-flung outposts, one in the West and one in the East. In the area of the lower Rhine the Duchy of Cleves and the counties of Mark and Ravensberg came to Brandenburg, which thus secured her first foothold in West Germany. In the East the Duchy of Prussia, formerly under the Order of the Teutonic Knights, was inherited by the Hohenzollerns, though it still remained a Polish fief during the Thirty Years War. Brandenburg was invaded by conflicting armies, yet in the end she did well in the Peace of Westphalia, adding Eastern Pomerania and important former ecclesiastical territories in North Germany to her lands. What was more, by careful diplomatic maneuvering in the war between Poland and Sweden (1655–1660)

[20] F. L. Carsten, *The Origins of Prussia* (Oxford, 1954), p. 276.
[21] *Ibid.*, p. 276.

the Great Elector Frederick William of Brandenburg (1640–1688) managed to obtain full recognition of his sovereignty over Prussia, a land that was soon to become a cornerstone in the rise of Brandenburg–Prussia as an absolutist state.

The Great Elector Frederick William, who broke the power of the Estates in his disjointed territories, was "a highly talented and imaginative political entrepreneur." [22] By the end of his reign, he dominated politics in North Germany, and Brandenburg–Prussia had become a factor in the power game of Europe. He laid the foundations for the rise of Prussia as a major land power by establishing his own standing army. To supervise it he appointed army commissaries who later became public servants under the dynasty. They not only had to maintain the troops and organize their billeting in the towns, but also to finance the army by taxing the peasants with a so-called "contribution." The son of the Great Elector was less interested in military display than in imitating the style and splendor of Versailles. In 1701 he managed to obtain the consent of the Emperor Leopold to crown himself King Frederick I in Prussia at Königsberg.

However, his son, Frederick William I (1714–1740) did not share his father's cultural interests; indeed, he transformed the country into a modern Sparta with a trained army commanded by officers from the nobility and a hard-working bureaucracy, both constantly watched by the autocratic king. It was mainly under him and his successor Frederick II that the behavior patterns and the overemphasis on certain qualities at the expense of others developed, which conditioned successive generations of Prussians and later spread to other parts of Germany. The spirit of Potsdam, the garrison town close to Berlin, was symbolized by Frederick William himself. He always went about in uniform; and he loved to personally drill his own regiment of "tall fellows," many of whom had been recruited abroad by none-too-scrupulous methods. The atmosphere of the barracks prevailed, and officials watched and supervised all the activities of the peasants and the burghers with a careful eye and an often harsh and demanding manner. Under this system the interest of the citizens, though not entirely ignored, counted for little compared with that of the state. The Prussian virtues of hard work, thrift, discipline and devotion to duty were exemplified by the irascible "military bully," Frederick William, and his son, the much more complex but no less

[22] Hans Rosenberg, *Bureaucracy, Aristocracy, and Autocracy* (Cambridge: Harvard University Press, 1950), p. 31.

determined Frederick II (1740–1786), whom his contemporaries were later to call "Frederick the Great." Many-sided and versatile, steeped in French culture, Frederick II was for some years a friend of Voltaire, who once said of the king that his life was "Sparta in the morning, Athens in the afternoon." Something of an Epicurean in his youth, the King developed more and more into a stoic and cynic, a hard taskmaster on himself and his subordinates and a lonely figure without family or personal ties.

The privileged position of the nobility was enhanced by the King's practice of reserving nearly all official positions to nobles and preferring them to commoners for the top posts in the civil service. On the other hand, many of the peasant-serfs of the aristocratic landowners were conscripted into the army as "cantonists" of which they formed one-half, the other being recruited from the dregs of foreign countries, including other German states. In this streamlined society taxation was a heavy burden on peasants and townspeople, while the nobility was exempt from it in most provinces. The administration of the state was centralized in 1723 by establishing the General (Financial and Domestic) Directory in Berlin with subordinate offices for the army and domestic affairs in the provinces. In addition, special departments for foreign affairs and for justice were founded. But there was no cabinet in the modern sense; it was the supreme authority of the King alone that held everything together. Frederick II told his officials that two things were conducive to the welfare of the country: "(1) To bring money in from foreign countries. This is the function of commerce. (2) To prevent money from leaving the country unnecessarily. This is the function of manufacture." Although Frederick did not favor state factories but rather encouraged private enterprise, "he directed the plans for industrialisation like a campaign, acting as his own Minister of Commerce after 1749." [23] When King Frederick William died in 1740, he left a trained army of 80,000 soldiers out of a population of 2.5 million and a state treasury of 7 million Thalers, neatly packed in barrels in the Royal Castle in Berlin. His military budget amounted to five-sevenths of the total state budget. Frederick William had drastically augmented his weaponry, but he had never actually used it.

During his reign Frederick the Great increased the army to 195,000 men and the war treasury to 50 million Thalers. Nearly two-thirds of the state revenue went to the army's upkeep. Frederick

[23] W. H. Bruford, "The Organisation and Rise of Prussia," *New Cambridge Modern History*, VII, p. 314.

William had admonished his son in the testament of 1722 "never to begin an unjust war." Yet Frederick II had his own ideas on the distinctions between "just" and "unjust" wars. When in December, 1740, the Prussian army invaded the Austrian province of Silesia with lightening speed, he cooly left it to his ministers and their lawyers to find arguments to justify this act of aggression. A year earlier in his book *Anti-Machiavel* he had still emphasized a moral point of view as well as the icily realistic one that was to become increasingly characteristic of him. A few years afterward in the foreword to his book *The History of My Times* (1742), he expressed the hope that "posterity would distinguish the philosopher in me from the ruler, and the respectable man from the politician." He confessed that it was "very hard to maintain purity and uprightness if one is caught up in the great political maelstrom of Europe," and he went on to draw a fairly accurate picture of the jungle of European power politics in which "one sees oneself continually in danger of being betrayed by one's allies, forsaken by one's friends, brought low by envy and jealousy."

In the three wars that Frederick fought with Austria and her allies over the possession of the Austrian province of Silesia, he was entirely guided by the reasons of state and, when necessary, even let his allies down. During the first and second Silesian wars the aggressor was never defeated. Austria had to acknowledge the loss of Silesia when both wars ended. During these wars Prussia had been supported mostly by the French, the traditional enemy of the Hapsburgs. Yet in 1756, Maria Theresa's outstanding foreign minister, Count Kaunitz, succeeded in bringing about a reversal of the alliance system. Frederick did not believe that the Bourbons and Hapsburgs could ever cooperate; but the unexpected happened after he had concluded the Convention of Westminster with England, then the deadly enemy of France in India and Canada. Austria and France joined in a defense pact that was soon transformed into an active alliance against Prussia. Again, Frederick anticipated his enemies by striking the first blow in invading Saxony. This time the Machiavellian soldier-king fought against three great powers; Austria, France, and Russia. Frederick faced a coalition superior in manpower, if not in military ingenuity. He lost as well as won battles, and repeatedly found himself in tight corners. East Prussia was invaded by Russian troops; and Berlin, Frederick's capital, was occupied by them in October, 1760. After the superior Russian and Austrian army had routed the Prussian troops at Kunersdorf in 1759, the King was in despair and toyed with the idea of finishing it all by taking poison. Yet he did not give in, and Prussia survived. Frederick "owed his survival more to the lack of co-ordination among his enemies than to his own daring leadership and the valour of his troops. The light-hearted aggressor of 1740 was now suffering from persecution mania, but there was never a thought of compromise." [24]

By 1761 Prussian troops were hopelessly outnumbered; and after the fall of William Pitt, the English statesmen were disinclined to subsidize Prussia. A fortunate incident suddenly came to his rescue. Empress Elizabeth of Russia died early in January, 1762 and was succeeded by the unpopular husband of Catherine the Great, Peter III, who saw in Frederick his hero. He promptly recalled all Russian troops from Prussian territory and did not ask for any compensation. The Seven Years War (1756–1763), which had worldwide repercussions, ended in a military draw for Prussia and Austria. But Frederick retained Silesia in the Peace of Hubertusburg with Austria in February, 1763. Prussia had suffered badly from devastation and loss of life, but the spirit of Potsdam had won the day for her, and from now on she counted as a power in Europe.

There were now two major powers in the German Empire, Austria and Prussia; and their cooperation or enmity became vital for German history from Frederick the Great to Bismarck. But whatever the change in the balance of power, the cynical power politics continued. They were displayed in the three partitions of Poland, which was carved up between the rival states of Prussia, Austria, and Russia in 1772, 1793, and 1795. Through the first partition Frederick secured West Prussia, which he had coveted for forty years as a vital bridge between Pomerania and East Prussia. It was Frederick's mediocre nephew and successor, Frederick William II, who in addition to the town of Thorn acquired the city and port of Danzig, which was to remain with Prussia until 1919. It then became a free city under the League of Nations and a convenient bone of contention used by Hitler in declaring war on the new Poland in September, 1939.

Frederick the Great, who died a lonely misanthrope in 1786, little mourned by his people, had found a royal pupil in Joseph II (1780–1790), the son of Maria Theresa. As an enlightened despot, Joseph was both more sincere and more doctrinaire than his model in his goal of modernizing the state. Singlehandedly he forced the

[24] G. P. Gooch, *Frederick the Great: The Ruler, the Writer, the Man* (London, 1947), p. 44.

process towards the formation of a unified, rationalized state in which there would be religious tolerance and equality of all before the law and the authoritarian ruler. Joseph would not brook interference by the Estates, and had no patience with the various characteristics and constitutions of different provinces and countries. By abolishing serfdom in Austria, he went further than Frederick II, who dared not touch the vested interest of the landowning nobility.[25]

Under the system of "enlightened absolutism" much could be done for the people but nothing by the people. "Their only right was to be governed well." In France the mighty revolution from below in 1789 enforced the participation in government of the third estate, the bourgeoisie, and for a while even the urban masses; and it posed a challenge to the old order in Europe. Frederick the Great's and Joseph II's historical achievements are undeniable; but by 1790 it had become abundantly clear that with them the age of absolutism, both enlightened and unenlightened, had come to a close.

Napoleon Changes the Map

The French Revolution was a European event. One may well ask: why then was there no revolution in the Germanies? One reason was obviously the nonexistence of an integrated German state. The moribund Holy Roman Empire formally came to an end at last in 1806 when the Hapsburg Francis II laid down the imperial crown. Second, different from the situation in France, the middle classes in Germany and Austria were still economically and politically weak. Third, the failings and abuses of the old regime east of the Rhine were less glaring and the position of the citizens before the law certainly less arbitrary and prejudiced than in France. Finally, Germany lacked a central capital from which the flames of revolution could spread over the entire country.

In vain did the conservative monarchs of Prussia and Austria send troops into France in the hope of laying the ghost of the Revolution. These armies proved no match for the well-organized and enthusiastic troops of the French revolution and later of General Bonaparte. Prussia left the anti-French coalition in 1795, while Austria desperately continued to oppose the French advance without success for another ten years. By the Peace of Basel in 1795, Prussia agreed to give up her possessions on the left bank of the Rhine, to be compen-

[25] However serfdom was restored by Joseph's successor, Leopold II, and disappeared for good only in 1848.

sated later by territory in the hinterland of Germany. Similar provisions were made with Austria in the Peace of Campo Formio of
1797, which however did not last long. By these treaties "the two
big German powers acknowledged the advance of France to the
Rhine, transferred the center of their realms farther to the east, and
reserved the right of compensation through future secularization
[of ecclesiastical lands]. They thus began a redistribution of territories
by which France was to gain a preponderant influence in German
internal affairs." [26]

After France had formally secured the left bank of the Rhine
by the Peace of Luneville in 1801, the final arrangements effected by
a committee of the dying Reichstag in 1803 became "a decisive document in German history." With one stroke, the map of Germany
was greatly simplified. The ecclesiastical princes, imperial knights, and
all but six of the imperial cities lost their independence and power.
It was Napoleon's policy to build up some medium-sized states in
South and Southwest Germany to compensate for the fading grandeur
of Austria and Prussia. Thus Bavaria, Württemberg, Baden, and
Hesse gained substantially in territory and status, the former two
states being raised to kingdoms, the latter two to grand duchies. Their
alliance with France was, however, not confined to territorial aggrandizement. It also signified the take-over of French ideas and institutions. The French legal code, the Code Napoleon, was adopted in
South and West Germany, either wholly or in part, and remained in
force until 1900. France also served as a model for a centralized and
modernized administration. The South German kings and princes
gradually introduced new political and administrative practices from
above, which in France had been the result of pressure from below.
In the South German states, equality of the citizens before the law
and equality of taxation were introduced; and the privileges of the
nobility were severely curtailed, though not entirely abandoned.
Serfdom was done away with, although peasants were still obliged to
give dues and services to their landlords until 1848. These reforms
constituted a break with the habits and patterns of a semifeudal
society.

The occupation of large areas of Germany and Austria by French
troops and the humiliating defeats of Austria at Austerlitz in 1805
and Prussia at Jena and Auerstädt in 1806 created a strong anti-

[26] K. D. Erdmann, *Deutsche Geschichte im Überblick*, ed. P. Rassow, 2nd ed.
(Stuttgart, 1962), pp. 370–71.

French resentment and kindled a new German patriotism that transcended any loyalty to an individual German state. Although there were sporadic acts of resistance in Tyrol and in North Germany in 1807, by and large anti-French resistance was not as widespread and intense in Germany as in Spain. However, out of the wars of Liberation a new all-German ideology emerged that had more of a cultural than a political slant. Its heralds, men like Fichte, E. M. Arndt, and Joseph Goerres, emphasized the moral and cultural superiority of the Germans over the vile and superficial French. At the same time they favored greater participation of the burghers in running the state.[27] Here were the beginnings of that union of liberal and nationalist attitudes that were to become so characteristic of German political thought in the nineteenth century.

Army reformers like Scharnhorst and Gneisenau were aware that a people's army was required to fight against the foreign usurper. They realized the handicaps of the aristocratic monopoly of the officer corps and demanded that citizen-soldiers and citizen-officers replace mercenaries and peasant conscripts who did not know what they were fighting for. They advocated universal conscription. These changes, which were bound to raise the status of the middle classes, were not popular with the members of the old establishment. While the Junkers and their allies could only protest against the reforms during the years of national emergency and liberation, they managed to water down many of them soon after the defeat of the Napoleonic armies in the Battles of Leipzig in October, 1813, and Waterloo in June, 1815. Though not all the reforms could be eliminated in 1814–15, the overriding purpose of the Congress of Vienna, that unique bartering place of large and small powers, was the restoration and, as far as possible, the preservation of the old order. Certainly the days of the First Empire had gone for ever, but the dawn of the Second seemed still far away.

[27] For the far-reaching reforms of Stein and Hardenberg in Prussia, see Chapter 5.

4

The Spirit of Weimar, 1775-1832

GOETHE, MADAME DE STAËL, AND WORLD LITERATURE

Germany? Where does it lie then? No map of mine seems to show it. Where that of culture begins, that of politics ends.
GOETHE AND SCHILLER

From their joint satirical poem, Xenien (1796).

A Glance at the City of Weimar

In the *Age of Louis XIV* Voltaire describes four islands of culture in the endless and often rough stream of history: Athens under Pericles, Rome under Augustus, Italy in the Renaissance, and France under Louis XIV. Had Voltaire lived fifty years later, he would probably have acknowledged a fifth illustrious period, the period of Weimar, the age of the classicism of Goethe and Schiller between 1780 and 1830. There are two aspects that make this age so fascinating to the later observer. First, the fact that the peak of literary creativity was not reached in one of the major states, such as Prussia or Austria, but in the capital of a small principality, Weimar, which had a population of some 6,000 inhabitants. An enlightened and progressive prince, Karl August, Grand Duke of Saxe–Weimar, set out to attract leading writers and to make his capital the center of an elite. It was owing to the lack of an overall national capital, as well as to the deliberate efforts of Karl August that "Weimar" became a byword for cosmopolitan universalism just as "Potsdam" was to signify the essence of Prussian militarism and nationalism. The pluralism of the German states encouraged some towns, in which a court resided, to develop into centers of art and scholarship, and allowed Weimar to achieve international cultural fame.

The second fascinating aspect is that German classicism coincided with other significant philosophical and literary developments in Germany. While some of the older romantics at least paid lip service to the Olympian achievements of Goethe, the spirit of German Romanticism was very different from that of Schiller and Goethe. The great contemporaneous stimulus of German philosophical speculation expressed itself in an outpouring of philosophical systems that began beginning with Kant and Fichte and ended with Schelling and Hegel. The flowering of literature, philosophy, and music in that period determined to a large extent the special German concept of "*Kultur.*" W. H. Bruford has pointed out that the important distinction Germans have since made between "culture" and "civilization" goes back to that time. Culture, in this sense, refers to the higher manifestations of the human mind—to its expressions in religion, philosophy, literature, art, and music.

Since 1800 Germans have been inclined to draw a distinction between culture and civilization on the one hand and between culture and "*Bildung*" on the other. While the term "civilization" in the German sense may include polished manners, it refers largely to technological and social "know-how," to the rules of the technical and the social game. *Bildung* is a more individual term that means personal cultivation and the degree of culture which the individual is able to obtain. In this period Wilhelm von Humboldt, thinker and diplomat became its supreme symbol. During the period roughly between 1750 and 1830, beginning with the dramatic critiques of G. E. Lessing and ending with the speculations of Hegel, the elite in Germany was little concerned with improving the technological and material standards of life. Instead, the period witnessed "a single sustained effort of the German mind to make sense of its own peculiar world." At a time when the Germans were politically divided and powerless, the German idea of *Kultur* gave them a focal point, an ideal for which to strive. "Many members of the intellectual elite began to see in the realisation and propagation of this ideal the specific mission of the Germans." To these people culture had become "a supreme good, and ideal to live for." [1]

[1] W. H. Bruford, *Culture and Society in Classical Weimar 1775 1806* (Cambridge, 1961), p. 3.

As W. H. Bruford has shown, the cultural elite of Weimar was based on the fusion of two cultural groups—that is, of people derived partly from the aristocracy and partly from the middle classes—all residing in a small country town. It was a fairly static society in which everyone knew and accepted his place, and its various social classes were dominated by a long-established routine. Unlike the imperial cities, Weimar lacked a complex class structure, for there was no proper middle class between the general mass and the handful of court nobles, more successful professional men, and higher officials. As in other residential seats of a monarch or prince, the main social division lay between those who were and those who were not "*hoffähig*"—that is, were or were not admitted to the court. To obtain this privilege, a person had to be titled. Even Goethe (1749–1832), coming as he did from a patrician family and enjoying the charismatic prestige of a recognized genius, reluctantly accepted the Duke's proposal in 1782 that he be raised to the nobility. In a similar way, his fellow poet Friedrich Schiller, the champion of freedom of thought, and Herder, theologian and interpreter of the poetry of the nation, were ennobled twenty years later.

The elaborate bureaucracy of Weimar was recruited partly from the nobility and partly from academics with a university training in law. Such a hierarchy, with its ranks and subdivisions, was found to some extent all over Germany, though it permeated the social system most deeply in Prussia. Whereas these social distinctions were taken for granted, everyone was free to participate in culture and to escape from the prosaic limitations of the existing order into a realm of thought and beauty. Any achievement in personal cultivation or "*Bildung*" could serve as a channel of liberation from the drudgery of what was then widely regarded as a preordained order.

Roughly three classes were discernible in the Weimar society of 1820. The upper class usually had an income range of 600 to 3,000 Thalers per annum and was comprised of a few leading civil servants, including State Minister von Goethe (whose annual income was 3,100 Thalers), other court personnel, and some prominent merchants and bankers.[2] Its lowest rank included officials, ladies-in-waiting, actors, clergymen, grammar-school masters, and shopkeepers, all with an average yearly income of 600–700 Thalers. Next came the class of mastercraftsmen, with an income of between 200 and 600 Thalers. Their lowest rank was made up of head clerks, lieu-

[2] See the table in the Appendix to W. H. Bruford, op. cit.

tenants, barber-surgeons, and teachers. Last was the journeyman class, with less than 200 Thalers per annum. Its highest rank included messengers, sergeants of the gendarmerie, other types of teachers, actors, shop and innkeepers, and even hawkers. Altogether, there was a close interrelation between the amount of income and social status. This small and not particularly impressive-looking town centered, as did so many other "residential towns," on the palace; it was a place of narrow streets and houses for the most part small and mean, and was perhaps more like a large village than a town; it was here that a distinguished foreign visitor discovered German culture.

Madame de Staël on Weimar and German Literature

Madame Germaine de Staël, who first visited Weimar in 1804, was well qualified to interpret German civilization to her fellow countrymen. A Parisian by birth and upbringing, and a daughter of Necker, the famous banker and minister, Madame de Staël was a refugee from Napoleon's dictatorship when she wrote her outstanding book on Germany, De l'Allemagne (1815). In it she attempted to convey the image of a new epoch in German culture and of Goethe as its greatest representative: German literature in all its originality, she explained to her French readers, dated back scarcely forty to fifty years. The French had been so absorbed in politics for the last twenty years that they were ignorant of literary trends abroad. Thus her book interpreted German literature from a fresh viewpoint; and in fact introduced it not only to France but also to England, Italy, Spain, and other countries. Madame de Staël had the temperament, though perhaps not the outlook, of a modern journalist. Although she impressed others with her cleverness and stimulating comments, her unending loquacity caused some embarrassment in the well-tempered milieu of Weimar classicism. After one of his meetings with her, Goethe observed: "It was an interesting hour. I could not get a word in; she speaks well, but a great, a very great deal." Obviously she wanted to show off and to make Goethe inclined to answer her many questions. Today this journalistic technique is a matter of course, but it was then unknown in Germany. As a result, Geheimrat (Privy Councillor) Goethe became cautious and somewhat reserved. Madame de Staël stayed too long in the small capital city, and in the end Goethe often avoided her. Yet he was genuinely pleased that she was writing on Germany and urged her on to publish a book. When it was published in 1813 and Goethe read it the following year, he felt that this was a work that would increase German self-confidence. The Germans would hardly recognize themselves in this portrait, but the work would help them to realize the great step forward they had taken. Later, in 1823, he called *De l'Allemagne* "a mighty battering ram that made a great breach in the antiquated prejudices which stood like a Wall of China separating us from France."

Madame de Staël realized that the differences between the two national literatures had deep roots in the diversity of national attitudes. She declared French literature to be the most classical of all modern literatures, and German literature the most romantic. There existed no fixed style in German literature; above all everything was "independent and individualistic," whereas French literature was primarily social. There was a great difference, she found, in the relationship of the author to his public. In France, the public conditioned the author; in Germany it was the reverse—the author moulded his public. In France, a country with many more intellectuals than Germany, the author had to constantly consider the critical reactions of the public. In Germany authors felt themselves to be above their critics and therefore were little inclined "to curtail the length of their works, and they rarely stop at the right time." The different degrees of sociability prevalent in the two countries influenced the character and impact of literary works. French writers felt that they were always in society, even when composing. The German author was basically solitary. "In France one scarcely reads a work except in order to talk about it; in Germany, where one lives almost alone, one wants the work itself to keep one company."

What struck Madame de Staël particularly was the contrast between the often painful obscurity of much German writing, and the clarity of style regarded as indispensable in French literature. German writers did not trouble themselves with their readers. Since their works were received and commented on as oracles, they were able "to surround themselves with as many clouds as they please." The different degree of dependence on the public also affected the author's style. In German prose the style was often too careless, while in France a much greater importance was attached to it, with a premium on such social merits as beauty, charm, grace, wit, taste, order, propriety, clarity, and a sense of proportion. The elites of the two countries should strive to learn from each other, said Madame de Staël. She wanted the French to become more religious and the

Germans "a little worldly." She saw both sides of the national balance sheets. The German poet was a born idealist, for it was the ideal as such that excited his enthusiasm. French writers had to realize that there were other standards than good taste. After all the laws of society were not everything, and genuine emotions were also valuable.

Goethe appeared to Madame de Staël as a representative of what she regarded as German romanticism rather than as a classicist. In her eyes he possessed all the main characteristics of the German genius to an eminent degree: "a great profundity of ideas, the charm of which gives rise to imagination—a charm more original than that arising from the German spirit; finally, a sensibility which is sometimes fanciful." *Faust* is seen not only as the peak of Goethe's creative work, but also as the epitome of the German mind. The French observer disliked its lack of form and taste, the absence of proportion and moderation. Madame de Staël was wrong to describe Goethe as romantic, but she was clear-sighted in regarding the Faustian qualities of insatiability and an endless search for a better future as characteristic of the German mind, if such a collective term is permissible.

The French writer noticed that admiration for Goethe took extraordinary forms in Germany. It led, she discovered, to "a kind of brotherhood whose rallying cries" served "to make the initiated known to each other." These unorganized but vocal communities of Goethe fans appeared to the foreign observer as a kind of literary freemasonry without a ritual. Foreigners expressing admiration for Goethe met with scorn if they also ventured some reservations and did not worship completely at the shrine.

The Individual, the Nation, and World Literature

Goethe was both a man of the world and a detached genius. Even as a minister in the small but progressive state of Saxe–Weimar social problems never occupied his mind very much. Like so many poets and philosophers, he was more concerned with Man than with men. In his autobiography, *Dichtung und Wahrheit*, he tells how he and a small group of cultivated people with whom he mixed in Frankfurt in his early twenties did not bother about reading newspapers, but concerned themselves rather with the study of Man: "It was our aim to get to know Man as such, we gladly let men do as they liked." In fragmented Germany, divided as she was into so many unequal parts, there was no incentive for a man of Goethe's exceptional imagination and insight to bother about current affairs and politics. Even in his later years, Goethe never shared the sense of social obligation and concern of Lessing or Schiller. Goethe was predestined to be an individualist: he was the offspring of a father who belonged to the city's patrician class and who was able to retire early from all professional duties, and of a mother who had been brought up in one of the few leading families of the town, yet had managed to follow her own happy temperament. His early freedom from social concerns and obligations remained with him, in a way, all his life.[3] In 1775, Goethe had exchanged his freelance life in Frankfurt, "responsible to nobody, responsible for nothing" for a position of highest authority in Weimar that gave him, along with the ruler and a handful of others, complete charge of the welfare and behavior of the population. It was a remarkable change. Yet in 1814 Wilhelm von Humboldt could observe that Goethe belonged "althogether to the types indifferent to everything that is political and German."

Even as a member of the rather enlightened establishment of Grand Duke Karl August—one of the first rulers in Germany to grant a constitution—Goethe always remained something of a *Privatmensch* ("a private person"). Yet while a law unto himself in many ways, Goethe sometimes seemed to have felt that his non-political attitude was typical of many Germans. In 1807 he remarked to Cotta with a good deal of satisfaction that the Germans had never been politically important and that their significance consisted in their disproportionate concern with the arts and sciences.

Like Madame de Staël, Goethe was aware of the trend toward isolationism in German intellectual life. In the course of a long and fame-filled life, Goethe made many statements and comments on Germany and the Germans, some of which seem to be contradictory. He was always more interested in the cultural life of his nation, and in the great contributions that Germans could make to literature and scholarship, than in the idea of a unified German nation-state. Too much has been made of his remark to Eckermann in 1828 that he was not worried that "German unity might not be achieved. Our good roads and future railways will play their parts in it." Germans, he then suggested, should above all be united in love for each other

[3] Barker Fairley, A *Study of Goethe* (Oxford, 1947), p. 242.

and should always unite against a foreign foe. Although Goethe favored a German Customs Union (the *Zollverein* came into existence in 1834, only two years after his death[4]) he was not a German nationalist. He was in favor of a uniform currency and passports that would be valid in all German states. "There should be no more talk of distinguishing between one's own land and foreign lands among German states," he observed.

Goethe's emphasis on greater conformity does not mean that he thought in terms of political unification. He was primarily concerned with culture, and this to him was only feasible through a multiplicity of cultural centers. "But if anyone imagines that the unity of Germany should consist," Goethe added, "in this very large empire having a single large capital, and that this one large capital would be beneficial to the development of single great talents and to the welfare of the great mass of the people, then he is mistaken." The idea of cultural uniformity was obviously abhorrent to him. National culture would never flourish if confined to one center. "Let us assume," he remarked "we had in Germany only the two court cities [*Residenzstädte*] of Vienna and Berlin, or even only one court city: I should like to see what the position of German culture would be, or even that of the widespread prosperity that would go with it."

Goethe pointed to the twenty German universities, the numerous theaters, and the big cities with their individual characteristics. All of them would lose their significance if they were subordinated as provincial cities in a German empire. He felt that the capitals of kingdoms and principalities such as Dresden, Munich, Stuttgart, Kassel, Brunswick, and Hanover exuded great and vital stimuli into the neighboring provinces. Independent city-states such as Frankfurt, Bremen, Hamburg, and Lübeck were great and magnificent, and their impact on the prosperity of Germany was incalculable. The question was, "would they still remain what they are if they lost their own sovereignty and became part of some large German empire [*Reich*] as mere provincial towns?" Goethe had reason to doubt this. When Goethe spoke of Germany, he nearly always had the cultural community of all German-speaking people in mind. Political diversity, to him, in no way impeded the common culture, which was equally at home in Vienna and Prague and to a lesser extent in Zurich. Goethe welcomed this cultural diversity, but any exclusive

[4] See Chapter 5, pp. 118-19.

nationalism was alien to this outlook. He disliked all narrow Germanophiles and the inclination of German romantics to become Teutonic chauvinists.

Goethe also regretted the excessive amount of theorizing and of philosophical speculation to which so may Germans were given. He contrasted this with the pragmatic mentality of the English: "Whilst the Germans vex themselves with solving philosophical problems, the English with their great common sense laugh at us and win the world." "If only," he remarked in 1828, "one could teach the Germans to acquire less philosophy and more activity after the model of the English." In contrast to the Germans, English visitors —many of them young Etonians—impressed him by their instinctive sureness of themselves, by their ability to act reasonably and in a practical manner, and by their self-confidence, which other nations did not always like but which was very different from the unstable arrogance—originating in a lack of self-assurance—that was sometimes to be found in Germans.

A trend toward greater extroversion can be discerned in Goethe's long and uniquely fruitful life. In his later years he was well aware of the limitations of the "cultural elite world" in which he lived, and toward the end of his life he showed a keen interest in the social experiments in the New World. He praised its freedom from decaying castles and outdated traditions. At the age of seventy-six he explained to Eckermann "that it was only in the decadent ages of society that poets and artists became inward-looking and self-preoccupied. In all the great progressive ages the creative mind concerned itself with the outer world." As we have seen, Goethe welcomed the incipient changes toward an era of industrial expansion, of better roads and easier communications, although he does not seem to have anticipated the questions and problems of a more egalitarian society that Alexis de Tocqueville, the French political scientist, was to perceive shortly afterwards during his celebrated visit to the United States.

To later German generations, Goethe's universalism and his emphasis on self-cultivation became a symbol that they thought highly of in theory but were unable to follow in practice. Goethe retained his belief in a total humanity to the end. In his novel *Wilhelm Meister*, Jarno remarks that "it takes all men to make humanity and all our strength jointly to make the world." As a minister of state Goethe took his attachment to a monarchic establishment for granted, but as a writer he insisted on being free and uncommitted. Shortly before his death he made his life-long position explicit. "If a writer wants his work to be politically effective," Eckermann reports Goethe as saying in March, 1832, "he must attach himself to a party, and as soon as this happens he is finished as a poet: he must part with his intellectual independence and unbiased outlook, and draw the cap of narrow-mindedness and blind hatred over his ears."

If German classicism had any missionary zeal, it was to further "the good, the noble, and the beautiful," and these values were not restricted to any particular territory or nation. Goethe had his own reply to the well-worn phrases of patriotism. "And what does it mean," he asked searchingly, "when we say 'to love one's country,' and what does it mean when we speak of 'patriotic endeavor'? If a poet has endeavored all his life to fight pernicious prejudices, to eliminate narrow-minded views, to enlighten the mind of his people, to purify their taste and ennoble their attitudes and ways of thinking, what better things could he do than that, and how could he act in a more patriotic manner?"

Goethe was a universalist at a time when German literary and political romanticism concentrated on the German folklore and national traditions. It was he who opened the window to a wider world by conceiving the idea of a "world literature." As he explained, this term did not simply mean that "different nations should inform themselves about one another and about each other's work, for in this sense it has long since been in existence and is still growing." Talking to Eckermann on July 15, 1827, Goethe called it "a very good thing" that "with the close intercourse between Frenchmen, Englishmen, and Germans we have a chance of correcting each other's errors. This is the great advantage that world literature affords, which will in time become more and more obvious. Carlyle has written the life of Schiller and has estimated him throughout as it would have been difficult for a German to do. On the other hand we can judge Shakespeare and Byron, and know how to evaluate their merits, perhaps better than the English themselves." "World literature" is thus conceived as a link not only between national literatures but between the nations themselves. Like his contemporary, the French utopian reformer St. Simon, Goethe in a way anticipated UNESCO and the efforts at intellectual cooperation between nations in our age. His non-romantic vision of world literature as a new and voluntary tie between nations suggested "an intellectual interest in each other, a mutual helping and supplementing of each other in the things of the mind"—an ideal which even today is more proclaimed than carried out.

WILHELM VON HUMBOLDT: THE CLASSICAL GERMAN LIBERAL

Wilhelm von Humboldt (1767–1835), the understanding friend and admirer of Goethe and Schiller, has been well described as "a latter-day Greek . . . to whom it was vouchsafed to withdraw from life, voluntarily devoting himself like a Greek to his own service and that of the community, and to the study of ancient Greece." [5] But this is not the full story. Humboldt was also a classic cultural liberal, the champion of aesthetic individualism. Though his ideas had little influence on his countrymen, they later impressed the great English pioneer of liberalism, John Stuart Mill, who drew attention to them in his famous essay On Liberty (1859). To Humboldt, the idea of Bildung meant the right and the duty of the individual to develop fully and freely. Yet the same man who wanted to see the sphere of the state restricted to a minimum later gave a strong impetus to reforming the state-controlled universities after the Prussian defeat by Napoleon's armies, and represented his country at the Congress of Vienna.

The brothers Wilhelm and Alexander von Humboldt were contrasting figures. Alexander (1769–1859), the outstanding explorer, geographer, anthropologist, and archaeologist, was an extrovert who made many important discoveries in Latin America and Central Asia, then under Tsarist control. Wilhelm, the pupil of the great classical scholar F. A. Wolf and a student of comparative linguistics, looked introvertedly to the realm of the human mind and developed a corresponding ethical attitude. To him "the first true law of ethics" ran: "Cultivate yourself!" (Bilde Dich selbst!); and the second law: "Influence others by what you are!" While Humboldt's views on the state changed to some extent after he had gained experience as a diplomat and administrator, his historical significance lies in his early ideas on the individual and the state, and in the conviction that "what matters alone is Bildung; although by itself it does not make one happy, it is the first precondition of all happiness."

With the philosophers Herder and Kant, Wilhelm von Humboldt shared a dislike for the absolutist state in the eighteenth century

[5] D. F. S. Scott, Wilhelm von Humboldt and the Idea of a University (Durham, 1960), p. 9.

because it looked at the individual as only a cog in a wheel. Like Goethe, Humboldt believed reason to be a creative faculty. "What makes man intrinsically a thinking and willing being," he wrote once, "is his intellectual nature. As a sensual being he is dependent on sensual forces, but as an intellectual being he is able to create for himself an ideal of perfection and independence according to which he can live."

Humboldt's major essay, "Ideas on an Attempt to Define the Limits of the Activity of the State," was published only in parts during his lifetime, but it caused a stir among Western liberals like J. S. Mill in England and Laboulaye in Belgium when it appeared in full in 1851. In it Humboldt discussed both the purpose of Man and the purpose of the state. In the spirit of Weimar, he defined the purpose of Man as "the highest and most truly harmonious formation of his capacities to an integrated whole." To achieve this two conditions were required: liberty and a wide variety of individual experience. Only with their help could the potentialities in man become a reality. Humboldt's image of man stressed the need for both "individual vigor and manifold diversity." To him a wealth of different individualities was the focal point and strength of a worthwhile civilization. From this position Humboldt insisted that the functions and tasks of the state be very restricted. Unlike Hegel and so many later German writers on politics, he allowed the state only a negative function. It should provide security but never attempt to promote happiness. This concept of the state has been criticized for limiting the state's role to that of a night watchman who protects the individual from attack and provides security, but is not concerned with human welfare.

Apart from ensuring this security through the police and armed forces, Humboldt rejected any steps "to increase the positive welfare of the nation—all its care for the country's population and the maintenance of the people," no matter whether expressed "directly by means of institutions for the poor" or "indirectly by promoting agriculture, industry, and trade." In other words, he disapproved of "every measure taken by the state which has for its purpose the preservation or furtherance of the physical welfare of the nation." Humboldt was afraid that the government's attitude in any of these measures, however wise and salutary, could "produce a uniformity and an alien mode of behavior in the nation." To him it made for conformity; it stifled the creative forces in the individual; it killed his spontaneity and willingness to act. For, maintained Humboldt,

"Man's mind, like all his other faculties, is shaped only by his own active efforts, his own inventiveness, or his own application of the inventions of others." Not only did state regulations involve some sort of compulsion—and any compulsion was anathema to Humboldt —but they also induced man "to rely more and more upon external tuition, external guidance, external assistance rather than to think of a way out for himself." As Humboldt saw it, what suffered most from the state's excessive care for its citizens was "the spirit of initiative and the moral backbone."

Again and again Humboldt comes back to his central theme that "the state should withhold itself from all care for the welfare of the citizens and should not go a step further than is required for safeguarding internal and external security. To no other purposes whatsoever should it limit their liberty."

The fields which the state must not touch included education. It therefore seems somewhat ironic that fifteen years later as a high state official, Wilhelm von Humboldt was concerned with the reorganization of schools and with the planning of a new university. After a short legal apprenticeship at a Berlin court, Humboldt, who was then financially independent, had for many years lived a private life, entirely devoted to his studies. Yet, as was fitting for a man whose family belonged to the educated aristocracy, he had seen a good deal of the world, had lived abroad in Paris and Spain as well as at the family castle of Tegel near Berlin. Even when he was appointed Prussian envoy to the Holy See in 1802, the post, a sinecure, left him ample time for his own studies. Only the collapse of Prussia forced him to return to Berlin. In 1808, he took over the section for religious denomination and education in the Prussian Ministry of the Interior, and became a member of the State Council.

Educated entirely by private tutors after the fashion of the ruling class, Humboldt himself had never visited a school, nor read a book on education. Yet well-prepared as he was by his own efforts at self-education and equipped with a constructive mind, "in the one solitary year of his tenure of office, German education was given a new aim and emphasis." [6] (D. F. S. Scott). Like J. G. Fichte, the philosopher,[7] Humboldt was greatly influenced by the ideas of the Swiss educator, Johann Pestalozzi, who suggested that the pupil himself must find out things and develop his aptitudes, and that the

[6] D. F. S. Scott, op. cit., p. 10.
[7] See below pp. 112–14.

teacher should act as a friendly guide rather than as a drill sergeant. Humboldt and his two able assistants in the ministry, Süvern and Nicolovius, agreed that the teaching in the primary schools should follow the Pestalozzi pattern. At the secondary schools or *Gymnasium,* the student's mind was to be trained and equipped, largely by way of the classics. At the university too, the emphasis would not be on vocational training, but on developing new perspectives on a wide search for truth and on encouraging the intellectual growth of the individual to its highest extent. Humboldt regarded learning, or *Wissenschaft,* as a creative activity. It was not the task of the university to pass on textbook knowledge, but to promote the infinite search for truth by students and professors jointly. A variety of views was necessary and stimulating, for complete academic freedom was essential.

Humboldt the philosopher was an idealist, Humboldt the diplomat and administrator a realist. It was one thing to choose men of differing views for the new University of Berlin, another to discover how awkward some of these professors could be. Humboldt called them "this most intractable and most difficult-to-satisfy class of individuals with their eternally conflicting interests, their envy, their jealousy, their lust for power, their one-sided view. . . . Managing scholars is no better than being in charge of a troupe of actors!"

After serious disagreements with his superior, Chancellor von Hardenberg, over the structure of a new state council, and frustrated in his expectation that in the reorganization of the ministries he would be made Minister of Education, Humboldt resigned in April, 1810, before the university opened. He was soon appointed Prussian envoy to Vienna, a post he held for the next five years. His interest in politics had grown meanwhile. It was largely his achievement as Prussian plenipotentiary at the Congress of Prague in 1813 that Austria gave up her neutrality and joined Prussia and Russia against Napoleon. In later years he regarded this success for which King Frederick William III awarded him the Iron Cross (at that time a rare distinction for a civilian), as the most important event in his political career. At the Congress of Vienna he was second to Chancellor Hardenberg, who led the Prussian Delegation; von Humboldt showed great professional skill in opposing Talleyrand, the wily French Minister for Foreign Affairs, whom no other delegate but he could match. At times they were like two wrestlers and all the other delegates were onlookers.

Ten years earlier, Humboldt had been a cosmopolitan individualist, and in his own words, "felt most patriotic beyond the Alps," in Italy; but now he identified himself with Prussia. "Believe me," he wrote to his wife, "there are only two good and beneficial powers in the world, God and the Nation [Volk]. What is in between is absolutely no good, and we ourselves are only good insofar as we put ourselves close to the nation." Humboldt, the aesthetic elitist, now believed in the force of the people. As he wrote to his wife in October, 1815, "All the strength, all the life . . . all the freshness of the nation can only lie in the people, nothing can be done without the people and they are constantly needed." A reformed Prussia, in which the citizens participate in the administration of their towns and districts, was now Humboldt's ideal. Prussia should be freed from all recognizable defects in her administration and constitution and should become a model. It could then act like a magnet to draw the rest of Germany to herself.

The people who had fought for the survival of their country in the wars of liberation, were now much more interested in the affairs of the state. "The new state institutions," he remarked in the autumn of 1814, "which are bound to result quite naturally from such a [political] crisis and which would spontaneously emerge from the minds of the citizens, even if the governments don't want them, will claim the individual for the state much more than in former times." Although not a democrat, Humboldt realized that no government could ignore the wishes of the people. The government should be both firm and fair.

In 1819 Humboldt, then a state minister in Berlin, clashed again with Hardenberg because the chancellor did not allow him sufficient scope and disapproved of his proposals for a reform of the outdated system of Estates still prevailing in the Prussian Provincial Assemblies, which Humboldt wished to replace by a modern national representation. In fact, both Humboldt, who resigned, and Hardenberg, who was soon forced to resign, ran counter to the waves of reaction instigated by the *Junkers* against the liberal reformers. Humboldt led a contemplative life for his remaining sixteen years, devoting himself as a private citizen to classical and linguistic studies.

When in January, 1818, he went through the letters he had received from Schiller some twenty years earlier, he reflected on the change of emphasis that had since occurred. It struck him that not a single reference to public events could be found in the poet's letters. Now hardly a letter could be written without them. "I will not assert," Humboldt wrote to his wife, "which attitude is better, the one of today or that of the past. Anything in that field was then regarded as quite separate from the scientific life and would only have disturbed it. Today one believes that man cannot reach his true fulfillment, his true value, if, in whatever position he may find himself, he does not take a lively interest in what goes on in the state. There is no doubt that science and literature and also the reflecting mind profited from the former attitude. However the present age might demand something different; the character of our nation may now have gained, and science may benefit from its fruits." At least one cannot stop the tide. "It is no good trying to turn back the wheel of the age. The past has gone and no one can have it back."

In German history Wilhelm von Humboldt remains a great, if solitary figure near the peak of Weimar. Recently a German analyst aptly summed up his specific liberal attitude: "To give freedom and to use freedom, not in order to force things, but to awaken and further [man's] potentialities, to adapt oneself to reality, this has been Humboldt's maxim for life, which at the same time contained his political program." [8]

AWAY FROM WEIMAR: GERMAN ROMANTICISM

The writers of the school of romanticism were a generation younger than Goethe, Schiller, and Wilhelm von Humboldt. They had not escaped Goethe's enormous impact, and they admired his earlier writings and his erstwhile enthusiasm for Shakespeare. Friedrich Schlegel (1772–1829) called Goethe's novel *Wilhelm Meister* one of the three outstanding monuments of the age, the other two being the French Revolution and Fichte's philosophy. There was a strange love-hatred in the romantics attitude toward the sage of Weimar. As Friedrich Schlegel expressed it at the age of twenty: "The overall concept of his [Goethe's] works is the imprint of a selfish soul, gone cold. *Werther, Goetz von Berlichingen, Faust, Iphigenie,* and some other lyrical pieces mark the beginnings of a great man, soon turned into a courtier." Goethe on his side detested romanticism, which he regarded as incompatible with his own preference for the classical. "The classical I call healthy and the romantic diseased," he told Eckermann in 1829. What he disliked in the protean and diffuse writings of the German romantics was their con-

[8] Eberhard Kessel, *Wilhelm von Humboldt: Idee und Wirklichkeit* (Stuttgart, 1967), p. 237.

tempt for measure and form and their disregard for clear demarcation lines between the disciplines.

The romantics were subjective where Goethe and Humboldt desired to be objective. They preferred synthesis to research, a play with words and ideas to clear concepts, and startling aphorisms to a harmonious balance between content and form. With the earlier generation, the angry young men of the *Sturm und Drang* movement of the 1770s, they emphasized feeling, intuition, and the cult of genius. They disliked the dry and often pedantic rationalism of the German Enlightenment. At first they were radicals who, after a short spell of enthusiasm for the French Revolution and the rights of man, sought refuge in a strong state and in the *fata morgana* of community life. Most of the romantics came from the middle classes, with the exception of the fine figure of Novalis (1772–1801), who died young and whose real name was Friedrich von Hardenberg. Owing to their social origin, these men had little chance for a major career in the petty German states, and they preferred to escape into the realms of fancy and imagination or write for reactionary and conservative governments. During their earlier period, however, they were deliberately nonconformist and hated the philistine. The brothers Friedrich and August Schlegel shocked a society not yet prepared to tolerate bohemians by marrying divorced women. Romantics often changed from an excessive individualism in their youth to an equally excessive authoritarianism and reverence for the establishment in later years. To some extent the reason for this fluctuation is to be found in the lack of a political tradition and in the helplessness of these sons of burghers before well-established authority.

Johann Gottlieb Herder (1744–1803), the godfather of the German romantics, was a stimulating theologian and philosopher of history; he was one of the discoverers of folk literature and had a profusion of ideas, but he lacked order and clarity. This admirer of Homer, Luther, Shakespeare, and Rousseau proved an ardent champion of divination, setting faith above intellect and the genetic approach to history above the rationalism of science. The romantics shared Herder's conviction that nature and history can best be understood intuitively and with the help of poetry. Although a good European and by no means a nationalist, Herder believed that the divine idea expressed itself in different ways in different nations. He drew attention to the role of common language deeply imbedded in subconscious and semiconscious layers as the root of all literature, and he collected folk songs and folk poetry of many peoples. Herder equally turned against the arbitrariness of the absolutist state and the dogmatic rules of the French classic drama. The romantics followed in Herder's steps, refuting the claims of analysis and reason in favor of intuition and poetical feeling. They rejected Kant's warnings on the limitations of the human mind, as well as the Western doctrines of natural rights and of the social contract as the foundations of society. For a poet like Novalis, philosophical thought and political action should be viewed in the light of religion and poetry. When the cataclysm of the French Revolution and the impact of the Napoleonic wars frightened many Germans, the romantics sought refuge in an idealized image of the distant past and the German middle ages, and hoped for a return to the feudal society that had definitely ended.

Perhaps the real contribution of German romanticism was its emphasis on the diversity of people, nations, and cultures. In his early days, Friedrich Schlegel shared the interest of the classicists in ancient culture and believed that the Greek city-state was the highest type of political organization. Later, he and his brother, August Wilhelm, became interested in the Orient and were among the first to draw attention to its literary and philosophical achievements. They longed for universality, for a synthesis of poetry, thought, art, and religion. The same longing found a major expression in Novalis's fragment of 1799, "Christendom or Europe." It is a eulogy for the Middle Ages and by stressing its "sense of unity, order, and purposiveness" he "opposes by implication his own age." [9] Both the supreme Pontiff and the hierarchy of the medieval Church were depicted as wise, benevolent, and helpful. If the internal corruption of the Church finally resulted in the rise of Protestantism, in Novalis's view, these reformers went too far themselves in making the spirit of rebellion permanent. There existed for Novalis a clear if distant connection between Protestantism and the French Revolution.

The antithesis to the French Revolution and the corresponding enthusiasm for Edmund Burke, its critic in England, is even more clearly reflected in the career of the political writer, Adam Müller (1779–1829). Some have considered Müller an ideological opportunist who changed his point of view when it suited him. Indeed, he turned from Protestantism to Catholicism in 1805; he served the re-

[9] H. S. Reiss, *The Political Thought of the German Romantics* (Oxford, 1955), pp. 24–25.

formist Prussian Chancellor Hardenberg for a time, but then turned to Austria and became a propagandist for Metternich and Austrian Consul-General in Saxony. Yet he remained firmly consistent with his basic political philosophy in rejecting liberal individualism. To him the individual was only a small, transitory part of social life and had no rights against the state, which must be seen as an organism, not as a machine. The state embraced everything and was "the totality of human affairs, their union into a living whole." Medieval society was an organic society, and modern society must again become one. Like the infinitely more penetrating and non-romantic Hegel, Adam Müller had his own system of dialectics. He believed in the principle of polar opposition. In social life, the fundamental clash of opposites is between space and time. Space produces the opposition of the sexes, the masculine and feminine poles. Besides the principle of coexistence in space (*Nebeneinander*), there is also the principle of continuance in time (*Nacheinander*), where the opposites of youth and age produce both change and stability, radicalism and traditionalism. The severity of law corresponds to the masculine element in society; the clemency of love, to the feminine element. In this play on principles, economics looks ahead to the future, law back to the past.

Adam Müller shared Burke's opposition to the economic liberalism of Adam Smith, but in his worship of the state and the community Müller went much further than Burke. A more genuine mind, though no less turgid a writer than Müller, was J. G. Fichte (1762–1814), whose eccentric idealism influenced many of the younger German intelligentsia. Although changing his ideas repeatedly, Fichte remained an honest and profound and often unrealistic philosopher. The son of a weaver, in his youth he nourished a resentment against the eighteenth-century establishment and pleaded for individual rights. At that time, Fichte had an unbounded belief in the power of reason, which he thought was fully able to explain both the cosmos and society. He looked upon the phenomenal world as the creation of the mind and an extension of consciousness. The world as non ego can only be patterned in the consciousness of mind. Consequently there can be no rights higher than those of the individual. Rational man must insist on freedom of thought, which is the main objective of politics. In this early stage Fichte took over both the idea of natural rights, and that of the social contract from Western thinkers. Gradually, however, he came to realize that social life as such was not made by the individual but formed an unavoidable part of human experience. His work, *The Closed Commercial State* (1800), has been called a "plan for a socialist utopia." No longer did Fichte see the state as merely the sum total of the individuals forming it, but a being with a structure and meaning of its own. He visualized a planned state that would satisfy the individual's right to work and ensure that everyone could live by his work. The individual was no longer the judge of the state; on the contrary, he had to submit himself to the wisdom of the statesman. In some ways Fichte anticipated the idea of economic self-sufficiency of the state, which is characteristic of fascist systems in the twentieth century. Fichte also made the curious suggestion that a state must extend to its natural frontiers. Once all states had done so, there would be no further need for war.

After the collapse of Prussia and her occupation by French troops, Fichte tried to evoke national pride in his listeners by glorifying Germany as the philosophical nation. Far from being an imperialist, he denounced all efforts to imitate England and her colonial empire. He saw Germany's work in science and philosophy as her contribution to civilization. His patriotism was German, not Prussian, when he urged that Prussia take the lead in the struggle for German unity, anticipating in a way the course of German history half a century later.

Fichte now stressed the insignificance of the individual and the importance of a reformed nation-state. The more the Germans suffered the shame of defeat and invasion by Napoleon's armies, the more passionately did Fichte point out their cultural mission. German culture, he proclaimed in his *Addresses to the German Nation* (1807), was more highly developed than any other. The Germans were a primeval nation with a deeply original language; it was not an artifact like French. The Germans must discard all foreign ideas as detrimental to their freedom. They should realize the unique quality of their language and combine to form a unified state which they could then identify themselves with completely. While each child is entitled to an education, only the state can direct it. Fichte, who warmly endorsed the work of the great contemporary Swiss educator Pestalozzi, demanded state-organized teacher training. By 1812, Fichte the authoritarian had long replaced Fichte the Jacobin and radical. With the older Fichte began the community idolatry that can be traced from the romantics to the Pan-Germans and the racialists, and on to the crude doctrines of the National Socialists in the twentieth century. The rationalism of state planning and the irrationalism of the cult of community coexisted uneasily in Fichte's speculative mind.

The antirationalist spirit of romanticism and its preference for the genetic approach can also be clearly traced in Friedrich Savigny (1779–1861), a leading German jurist and founder of the historical school of law. To him all law arises as customary law. It is created by custom and by what people believe, and is systematized only later by jurisprudence. Law results from the impact of national forces and not from the arbitrary decision of a single legislator. Legislation is an organic part of a nation's life; first it is the unconscious product, later it is made conscious through jurisprudence. Law can never be autonomous or static; it must be considered in the context of national history. Thus it is the spirit of the nation (*Volksgeist*) working through every individual that creates positive law. The nation whose will is expressed by the "national spirit" has a natural unity, based on a common language and a common legal tradition, which forms a bond between the past and the future. To Savigny this tradition is the judge of all new developments. It was obviously an extremely conservative view that did not allow for the impact of new political and social forces and prevented reform; even outdated or evil institutions had to be viewed as part of the historical process.

Such an ideology could easily play into the hands of the powers of restoration and reaction. The emphasis on the subconscious forces of the community could serve to conceal the German middle classes' deep sense of political inferiority. Fichte's later ideas, those of Adam Müller, and Savigny became tools of the Prussian conservatives and the nationalists in the Second Empire. Yet it would be a mistake to overlook the far-reaching impetus romantic thought as a whole has given to the study of history and of many languages and literatures. The emphasis on the individual and the unique, the stress on the historical role of images and symbols rather than ideas, has proved just as fruitful as the vague romantic belief in the *Volksgeist* and the subconscious community ties have proved abortive and even dangerous.

The trouble with German romanticism was not its wealth of aphorisms, its antiphilistinism, its longing for the infinite and for intuitions, but its aversion to clear concepts and its over indulgence of synthesis at the expense of sober insight into reality. It is also paradoxical that while the romantics inspired the development of an historical sense and a lively interest in the variety of history, they also produced a highly idealized picture of feudalism in the middle ages. They saw feudalism as a society "in which there was no strife between the Crown and the Estates, in which the noblemen honoured the arts and the merchants followed the example of the Hanse." The romantics were unable to realize that the collapse of Germany under Napoleon's armies "was to a large extent due to the fact that the feudal system in Germany was not superseded in time, as had happened in France and England." [10]

[10] Reinhold Aris, *History of Political Thought in Germany from 1789 to 1815* (London, 1936), p. 315.

5

Towards an Industrialized Society, 1815-1850

Some Major Social and Economic Developments in the Nineteenth Century

There are three social and economic landmarks that transformed the predominantly agricultural Germany of the early nineteenth century into the modern industrial and commercial power of the Second Empire. First, the Stein–Hardenberg Reforms in Prussia to a large extent removed the feudal restrictions of the Estates, which in some German states lasted until the Revolution of 1848. Second, the formation of the German Customs Union in 1833 helped greatly in establishing Germany as an economic unit. Third, the rapid expansion of industry and banking between 1850 and 1870 accelerated the economic pace of the country, though it still concentrated largely on the home market.

In a memorandum to King Frederick William III in September, 1807, K. A. von Hardenberg, later a minister of state, shrewdly considered the lesson from the French Revolution and recommended for Prussia "timely reforms from above." "Democratic rules of conduct in a monarchical administration—such is the formula, it appears to me, which will conform most perfectly to the spirit of the age." The Stein–Hardenberg Reforms ended the occupational barriers of the old system. Commoners could now acquire country estates and noblemen were no longer debarred from working in commerce and industry. The power of the guilds was abolished, and free competition was

116

allowed full play. Agriculture became part of a liberal economy. All serfdom was officially abolished by an edict of 1807. Peasants became "free," yet at the same time they lost the protection of the lord of the manor, who had often taken a patriarchal interest in them. For their part, the peasants had not only worked for him but had also shown him a deference hallowed by the tradition of centuries. The old feudal system characteristic of large areas of Prussia such as Brandenburg, Pomerania, East Prussia, and Lower Saxony was never the same again. However, through the ordinances of 1811 and 1816, the reforms were soon watered down by Stein's successor, Hardenberg, who, vacillating and careless, yielded to pressure from the dissatisfied landed aristocracy. Consequently, the reform did not extend to all the peasants, and certain categories of them were not emancipated until 1850. Of those who gained their freedom earlier, the majority had to give half the land they occupied to the landlord in order to obtain freehold tenure of the other half. This made many of the smaller holdings unviable, particularly when additional expenditure for necessary equipment became necessary. In addition to the loss of land the peasants had to compensate the landlord in cash or in kind for the loss of compulsory services that they had so far rendered to him. Under the old position the government had protected the peasant, and land owned or leased by him could not be taken away from him.[1] Now, this was no longer so, "with the result that large numbers of peasants were after 1816 simply evicted from their lands and became farm laborers." [2] In fact until 1850 the lords found themselves "deprived of only a fraction of the forced labor at their disposal." They profited from the service of landless agricultural workers, and the use of modern methods in agriculture enabled them to meet the increased demand for their produce from the quickly growing population in the towns. After 1850 this growth was further increased by farm workers who migrated to the city where rapid industrialization demanded many hands.

In most other parts of Germany only the revolution of 1848 brought about the peasants' liberation. In Austria, where the power of the high nobility had prevented agrarian reform for over half a century, the efforts of a young idealistic politician, Hans Kudlich, were

---

[1] The new freedom for the peasant also meant the disappearance of some fringe benefits in the form of money payments, natural produce, food, even sometimes a share in the harvest.

[2] Walter M. Simon, *The Failure of the Prussian Reform Movement: 1807–1819* (Ithaca, 1955), p. 99.

crowned with success in 1848, and the emancipation of the peasants became state law.[3] Although the Austrian landowners also received money compensation for the loss of land and jurisdiction, it was kept within reasonable limits. In both Prussia and Austria the disappearance of the last traces of the feudal system and the "liberation" of the peasants did little harm to the old ruling class. In fact, the peasants proved to be the most loyal and conservative supporters of the establishment during the remainder of the century.

The Customs Union

The *Zollverein*, or Customs Union, was the result of a strong desire for greater economic unity and cooperation, which made itself felt after the Napoleonic Continental System had ended. The Continent was then flooded with cheap British goods, and the sale of Continental products suffered accordingly. As Friedrich List (1789–1846), an economist of vision and prophet of protectionism, pointed out, Germany was in the position of a youth who had to wrestle with a mature man. In such an unequal situation there could be only two objectives: economic unification and a stronger promotion of industry, which would enable German products to compete with those from abroad.

Prussia set the trend toward economic unification after 1815. Prussia had suffered from the separation of some of her newly acquired territories in Central and West Germany from the bulk of her territory. The Prussian Tariff Law of 1818 was intended to create internal uniformity of tariffs and to extend them to the petty and medium-sized states in North Germany that formed enclaves between the disconnected Prussian territories. The bad financial position of these states played into the hands of the Prussian statesmen. The policy of uniform tariffs was pursued soon afterwards in other areas of Germany. By 1828 three different systems had been formed—The Prussian–Hessian Customs Union; the South German Customs Union, uniting Bavaria and Württemberg; and the Central German Customs Union, which was largely directed against Prussia. The amalgamation of the Prussian and the South German organizations in 1829 opened the way for the much wider German Customs Union, which went into effect at the beginning of 1834.

The formation of the *Zollverein*, which covered an area of 8,253

---

[3] See below, p. 130.

square miles and a population of 25 million, changed both the economic map of the country and some of the economic habits of its member states. In spite of repeated and protracted efforts by her statesmen in the 1850s and 1860s, Austria remained outside the Customs Union. In fact the continuous, though not necessarily overt, competition between Prussia and Austria for hegemony in Germany was largely decided by economics. Austria had declined greatly after the worldwide economic crisis of 1857. In 1862 the Austrian Foreign Minister Rechberg could claim that the German question was "concentrated on the questions of tariffs and trade." In the end the success of the Prussian armies in 1866 "only confirmed the economic outcome." [4] In the struggle between the different Prussian and Austrian currencies, the former prevailed. Prussian trade and tariff policy was the lever; and renegotiating the Zollverein in 1865 was the starting point that Bismarck used to secure a Prussian solution to the German question.

Parallel with the development of the Customs Union, the network of railways that had spread all over Germany in the 1830s and 1840s gradually extended. Friedrich List, who had studied the role of the railways in the U.S.A., proved right in his prediction that in Germany the railways would bring people from different areas and states into contact with each other, develop a feeling of common growth, create a wider market for many goods, and ease and accelerate their exchange. The first German railway lines were built to connect the adjacent Bavarian towns of Nuremberg and Fürth in 1838. By the end of the 1840s, each of four German areas had its own railway system: North and Central Germany, with Berlin at the center, the lower Rhine region centering on Cologne, Southwest Germany with Frankfurt-on-Main, and Bavaria with Munich and Nuremberg as her railway centers. Until the 1860s most of the railway companies were privately owned, but under Bismarck they were gradually put under state control. The Constitution of the Second Empire expressly laid down the right of the Reich to insist on common lines of policy, tariffs, and a coordinated timetable. The result was the uniformity of the state-owned railway system, the Reichsbahn—with one exception. It remained Bavaria's privilege to run and control her own railways.

As in other countries, the development of the railway system led

[4] Helmut Boehme, Deutschlands Weg zur Grossmacht (Cologne, 1966), p. 182.

to an increased demand for coal and iron and also facilitated mass sales and therefore mass production of many goods. Considerable capital was required for investment to finance the expensive building of railway lines and the improvement of trains. For some years railway shares were regarded as the most important stocks on the German exchanges.

Before considering the late but dynamic expansion of German industry and banking in the 1850s, a word should be said about the decline in the position of the artisan, who became the victim of the changeover to an industrialized society. The abolition of the guilds and the unfettered freedom of trade operated against the artisan and facilitated the growth of factories. Soon there were too many small-scale masters; many artisans ended up as factory hands as a result of overcompetition. And the fact that their wages were inadequate resulted in increased factory work by women and children. An awareness of the social question—of the plight of the proletariat —came later in Germany than in England and France. It was only in the 1840s, when the embittered weavers of Silesia destroyed textile machines in despair, that some enlightened members in the Prussian establishment began to take the problem seriously. By and large, however, the middle classes were much more concerned with constitutional problems and with the desire for German unification.

Yet there can be little doubt that the serious depression of the 1840s paved the way for the uprising of 1848. By 1848 the earlier prosperity, based on the expansion of railway lines and factories, had come to an abrupt end, and Germany was plagued with an economic crisis. It coincided with the serious famine of 1846 that troubled Europe from Ireland to Prussia. The failure of both the grain and the potato crops deprived the lower classes of their staple food. With an average increase in the cost of food in Germany of about 50 percent between 1844 and 1847, it is not surprising that famine, disease, and unemployment created opposition amongst the masses to the established order. After 1845 many journeymen and apprentices found themselves out of work, or had to earn a living as unskilled day laborers. With the proletarization of the handicraftsman in the 1840s, the artisan masses became "the shock troops of revolution, whereas the employees of iron foundries and locomotive works were as a rule only interested by-standers in the great events of 1848."[5] Thousands of Germans emigrated, many of them to the

[5] Theodore S. Hamerow, *Restoration, Revolution, Reaction: Economics and Politics in Germany 1815–1871* (Princeton, 1958), p. 80.

United States, less for reasons of liberal conviction or political persecution than in order to secure a safe livelihood. Yet the loss of 2.5 million Germans to overseas countries between 1830 and 1870 did not seriously affect the constant growth in population inside Germany. By 1850 her total population (excluding the Hapsburg Empire) totaled over 35 million, second on the Continent only to Russia's 61 million. By 1870 Germany's population, at 41 million, considerably exceeded that of France (35.7 million) and Great Britain (26.2 million).

The 1850s were different from the 1840s. Though politically stagnant with the restitution of the old powers, the period made great steps forward in the new economy through dynamic developments in industry, investment, and banking. While there was a worldwide wave of economic expansion stimulated by the discovery of gold in California and Australia, Germany perhaps profited more from it than some other European countries. By then she had banks with capital of over 150 million dollars and railway companies with capital of more than 105 million dollars, while companies with shareholders in mining, iron-ore production, machine production, shipping, and other branches of industry reached a total capital of 97.5 million dollars. Corresponding to her complex political structure was Germany's multitude of banks that were entitled to issue their own banknotes. In 1870 they numbered 33. Between 1850 and 1870 no fewer than 114 different kinds of paper money were in circulation. However, in the Second Empire the new government owned the *Reichsbank* (built upon the Prussian Bank of 1847), and gradually acquired a practical monopoly on issuing notes. Following the example of France in the 1850s, a new type of German bank developed, the *Industriebank*. Its main function was to obtain funds for the founding, maintenance, and expansion of industrial enterprises.[6] Among them were the four "big-D" banks: the Darmstädter Bank founded in 1853; the Disconto Gesellschaft, founded in 1856, and later spurred on by the successful war against France and the indemnity extracted from it; the Deutsche Bank (1870); and the Dresdner

---

[6] Three influential Prussian bankers, Adolf Hansemann, Gerson von Bleichröder, and Georg von Siemens took the view in 1866 that an expansion of Prussia was required in an age in which the country changed increasingly from an agricultural-mercantilist into an industrialized-capitalist society. They took a great risk in providing the necessary funds for it. Hansemann and Siemens were pioneers in the development of the new type of industrial bank.
See H. Boehme, *Deutschlands Weg zur Grossmacht* (Cologne, 1966), pp. 202–).

Bank (1872). As a director of the Dresdner Bank commented in 1908: "In Germany our banks are largely responsible for the development of the empire, having fostered and built up its industries. It is from 1871 that our real development dates, and it is since that year that our great banks have been organized." The banks helped to float companies and granted long-term credits to industrial firms. Bankers took a big hand in controlling the policy of industrial concerns, while a number of industrialists were on the boards of banks.

Between 1871 and 1914, Germany became a highly developed industrial society, although politicians often preferred the term "agricultural-industrial state," since it was official policy to protect agriculture and the farmer's interests without impairing industrial development. The Wilhelminian Empire witnessed a striking expansion in coal, steel, and iron production. The coal output increased from 34 million tons in 1870 to 149 million in 1900, and then nearly doubled to 277 million. The production of iron grew from 1.3 million tons to 7.5 million in 1900, and to 14.7 million in 1914. No less impressive was the rise in steel production from 300,000 tons in 1870 to 6.7 million in 1900, and to 14 million in 1914. In fact German steel production surpassed that of England after 1900. At the outbreak of World War I, Germany was the largest producer of iron and steel in Europe and the second largest producer of coal. Much of the coal, iron, and steel industry was now concentrated in the Ruhr area, which had taken the lead in production from Upper Silesia in the 1870s and was soon clustered with ever-growing and interlinked towns.

J. M. Keynes has argued that the Second German Empire was "built more truly on coal and iron than on blood and iron." The Krupp firm is a symbol of the strength of Germany's iron and steel industry. Founded in Essen in 1811 by Friedrich Krupp, its beginnings were inconspicuous. When its founder died prematurely in 1826, work at the foundry had almost ceased and the firm was near bankruptcy. However, his stoical and resolute son Alfred had only one ambition and obsession: making and selling crucible steel. In twenty years of hard work he introduced many improvements: the melting shop was fitted out with a new forging press, and a wooden power hammer was installed. The *Zollverein* enabled the ambitious Alfred Krupp to get orders from all over Germany, and by 1834 the output of Krupp's factory trebled. "Krupp steel must be above suspicion," was Alfred Krupp's motto; he was the type *par excellence* of the self-made entrepreneur—ruthless, single-minded, domineering. "We have no time for reading, politics, and all that sort of thing," he said proudly.

Alfred Krupp never filled any public office, but he proved to be both a stern boss and remarkably shrewd at advertising his goods. They were represented at the fashionable industrial exhibitions in Prussia, England, and France. By the early 1860s Krupp had become the biggest producer of cast steel on the Continent and had secured the German license for the new Bessemer process, which revolutionized steel-making in the second half of the century. It was not by chance that the rise of the Prussian-German Empire and that of Krupp coincided. Only after Prince (later King) William took control of Prussia did Alfred Krupp obtain a large order from the Prussian army. In 1861 the king made him Privy Councillor. In October, 1864, Bismarck visited the firm in Essen. It was the beginning of what Krupp biographer Peter Batty has called "the 'special relationship' between the Essen firm and the authorities in Berlin." [7] At the same time, Krupp's products reached many countries: "to own a Krupp cannon was for monarchs and megalomaniacs the status symbol of the age." [8] When Alfred Krupp died in 1887, he was the richest man in Europe. His son Friedrich established excellent relations with Wilhelm II and followed the Kaiser's advice to engage in shipbuilding at Kiel. In the fifteen years before World War I, Krupp helped the expansion of the German navy by building nine battleships, five light cruisers, thirty three destroyers, and ten submarines for it. In 1914 Krupp's "Big Bertha" pierced the steel fortresses of Liège in Belgium; and their "Long Max" shelled Paris from a distance of seventy-five miles in 1918, thus opening a new phase in modern warfare.

There was an equally marked expansion in other branches of German industry after 1870. The textile industry intensified its production between 1875 and 1905 by no less than 1,400 percent, expanding in Saxony, Northern Bavaria, Württemberg, and the Rhineland. German exports of textiles increased fourfold between 1883 and 1913 as compared with a mere twofold expansion in the British textile export trade. More significant still was the dynamic rise of the German chemical, optical, and electric industries that had developed from scratch in Germany and were enhanced by the fact that most important inventions in these fields were made by Germans.

[7] Peter Batty, *The House of Krupp* (London, 1966), p. 75.
[8] *Ibid.*, p. 83.

In all sectors of industry the trend towards concentration and rationalization was unmistakable, particularly in the twentieth century. This was the age of the cartels, of vertical and horizontal combinations of formerly independent firms, and of joint syndicates for selling. There had been only four cartels in 1865, but by 1900 their number had risen to 300 and by 1911 to 600. The fact that by 1900 the firms in the coal industry, and in the heavy metallurgic and chemical industries were in relatively few hands facilitated an understanding between the owners. A favored type of industrial cartel was the syndicate which, in addition to determining the selling prices and the amount of production among member firms, had its own sales offices for them. Cartelization took place in the chemical industry in 1904. For some years there had been a sharp rivalry between the two major firms in South Germany, each of which combined at first with other firms until in the end, during World War I, they amalgamated to form a single organization—I. G. Farben. The effect of this trend did not always work to the advantage of the German consumer. Owing to Bismarck's protective tariffs and the impact of the cartels, the home consumer paid a price above that on the international market for a large number of manufactured goods. On the other hand, the cartel organization, which did away with competition at home, at the same time made competition abroad easier.

Freedom or National Unity: The Problems of 1848

The map of Germany was greatly simplified after the Napoleonic invasion in 1806: instead of 234 principalities, there were now only 39. The medium-sized states—Bavaria, Württemberg, Baden, and Hesse—remained. As we have seen, the Napoleonic wars made an impact on educated Germans, stimulating an upsurge of nationalism and a longing for German unity.[9] Baron vom Stein, the Prussian reformer, declared in 1812: "To Germany alone and not to any part of it am I devoted with all my soul." He wanted to see Germany great, united, and strong in order "to maintain her independence and nationality between Russia and France." Prince Metternich, Austrian Chancellor and a leading figure at the Congress of Vienna in 1814–15, regarded such ideas as subversive. He still thought in terms of the pre–1789 establishment and rule of the aristocracy. The thirty-nine principalities now formed the loose German Confederation

[9] See Chapter 3, pp. 92–93.

seated at Frankfurt, where Austria's will prevailed. Austria and Prussia both rejected the idea of granting a constitution and persecuted students and professors who dreamt vaguely of a synthesis of liberalism and nationalism.

At this time a new student movement, the so-called *Burschenschaft*, spread from Jena to all the German universities. Its ideology was a confused mixture of Christian-Germanic and liberal ideas. The students favored a united and free empire under the leadership of a medieval emperor. Their colors were black, red, and gold—later to be adopted by the revolutionaries in 1848 and again by the founders of the Weimar Republic. In 1817 at the Wartburg Festival in Central Germany, the students celebrated both the 300th anniversary of Luther's revolt against the Catholic Church and the anniversary of the Battle of Leipzig in 1814, when Napoleon was defeated. They burnt the writings of some conservative reactionary authors and also a copy of the Napoleonic code of laws. The rebels were both liberal and nationalist, and Metternich and like-minded reactionaries saw in them a new type of German Jacobin. The assassination in 1819 of the Russian agent Kotzebue by a fanatical student of theology, Karl Ludwig Sand, alarmed Metternich, and he pressured the German Confederation into accepting the "Karlsbad Decrees." They put all universities under severe state control, dissolved the *Burschenschaften*, and forbade their colors.

In Prussia, King Frederick William III had promised earlier some form of political representation; but when this idea was implemented after the war, it was restricted to provincial diets only, where most of the population was not represented. Only in some South German states (Bavaria, Baden, Württemberg) and in Saxe–Weimar were constitutions granted in the years immediately after the Napoleonic wars. The public discussions at the Diet of Baden in Karlsruhe caused a sensation, and diplomats from other German states watched them from the gallery. This was a novelty, for Austria and Prussia knew no parliament until 1848. When King Frederick William IV of Prussia felt obliged to arrange a combined meeting of representatives of the provincial diets in 1847, he did so because he needed their consent for a new tax to construct a planned railway from Berlin to East Prussia. But the deputies, mainly moderate liberals, were only prepared to grant the means if the king was willing to hold sessions of the combined diet periodically. This the king refused to do—though belatedly, in March, 1848, he was forced to give in after the outbreak of the revolution in Paris.

The great political question for the liberals in the 1840s was whether preference should be given to national unity or political liberty. One school of thought that favored constitutional liberalism had its stronghold in South West Germany, particularly in Baden. Champions of constitutional freedom and authors of an influential political dictionary such as Professors Karl von Rotteck and K. T. Welcker of the University of Freiburg were deeply concerned about this question of priorities. As Rotteck once put it: "I want no other unity than one together with liberty, and I prefer liberty without unity to unity without liberty. I do not want any liberty under the wings of the Prussian and Austrian eagles." Another school represented by F. D. Bassermann, who came from Baden and was the leader of the moderate liberals in the Frankfurt Parliament declared in 1849, "If I knew that the unity and future greatness of Germany were to be secured through a temporary renunciation of the entire rights of freedom I should be the first to submit to such a dictatorship."

As a result of the impact of the French Revolution of 1830, constitutions were granted in some of the German states, among them Saxony and Hanover, although, King Ernest Augustus revoked the constitution in Hanover in 1837.

1848

There are diverse interpretations of the causes of the Revolution of 1848–49 in Germany. Theodore Hamerow has undoubtedly made a good point in stressing that "the great depression of the forties enabled the various groups in opposition to the Restoration, groups disparate in social composition and economic objective, to overcome their difference and form a single political force." This view maintains that the severe economic crisis in the 1840s "prepared the way for the spring uprising of 1848 by endowing the political opposition with popular support and forcing it to adopt more radical tactics." [10] It is a fact that the prosperity of the early 1840s was based on railway construction and the expansion of factories, which suddenly came to a halt after 1844. According to Hamerow, the depression of 1845–47 drove the urban artisans and manual workers into a partnership with bourgeois liberals and made possible the overthrow of the old order.

[10] Theodore S. Hamerow, op. cit., p. 75.

However the economic interpretation can be overdone; for although there was unrest among the weavers in Silesia and food riots occurred in Berlin in the 1840s, these had little direct political impact. It is significant that the two important political programs for reform drawn up shortly before 1848 were formulated not in Prussia but in the more liberal atmosphere of Baden, in South West Germany. In September, 1847, a group of southern radicals led by two lawyers, Gustav von Struve and Friedrich Hecker, drew up the Offenburg Program, a list of demands that included the abolition of standing armies and their replacement by a people's militia, or national guard; a German parliament elected by the people on the basis of universal suffrage; freedom of the press; freedom of religion and of teaching; trial by jury; the accountability of all ministers and officials; and the abolition of all privileges. The new radical tone of the program was expressed in demands for the education of all children, the protection of labor and the right to work, the adjustment of relations between capital and labor, and an administration both popular and economical. More moderate were the liberal opposition deputies from Baden, Württemberg, and Hesse, who assembled a month later in Heppenheim, near Darmstadt. These people pleaded in a restrained tone for the establishment of freedom of speech and assembly and the reform of justice and administration. They demanded a constitutional monarchy for Germany as a whole, and constitutional governments for all states. Both factions joined in the so-called "Preparliament" in Frankfurt at the end of March, 1848, after the outbreak of revolution, first in Vienna and then in Berlin. The preparliament was revolutionary and entirely ignored the Confederate Diet and the state governments. Differences soon arose between the moderates and the radicals. The moderate majority insisted on a national assembly to be elected by the whole nation that would devise a national constitution.

The celebrated National Assembly which met in May at the Church of St. Paul in Frankfurt-on-Main was composed of 799 members, out of whom at least 653 or 81.6 percent had a university education.[11] The lower classes were little represented as there were no peasants, only a few small shopkeepers, and no deputy who belonged to the "industrial proletariat." On the other hand, in the Austrian parliament or Reichstag, convened in Vienna at the same time, no

[11] At least 764 or 93.5 percent of the deputies had attended a secondary school (Gymnasium). See Frank Eyck, The Frankfurt Parliament: 1848–1849 (London and New York, 1968), Chapter 3.

less than 92 deputies were peasants. In Frankfurt property and education prevailed.

The regulations provided for one deputy for every 50,000 inhabitants. However, as recent research has shown, the elections were conducted in various ways. They followed the existing franchise in states that already possessed constitutions. In other states the prerequisite of being an independent citizen precluded many workers and domestic servants from voting. The result was an assembly of notables confined to the upper middle class. Only men known to the public could attract votes, and only the wealthy and educated—the scholars, lawyers, and civil servants—were known. The men elected to the Frankfurt assembly had been largely prominent in the liberal gatherings of the March revolution, while others had sat in the various chambers and legislatures of individual states. Broadly speaking, three main groups evolved in the Frankfurt Parliament, a right, a center, and a left. But these groups took time to form and were never rigid: men moved from one group to another on particular issues. The middle-class liberals of the center were the most numerous, but they also varied a good deal in their opinions. There was a right wing as well as a left wing. The center was a broad and optimistic party that contained future Reich ministers and lesser-known followers. The unchallenged head of the left was the popular Robert Blum of Leipzig, often acknowledged in Frankfurt as a leader of the working class. Later, the left split into the smaller extreme left, which called itself the Democratic Party and was led by Arnold Ruge, a champion of the Democratic Republic, the People's Sovereignty, and the Congress of All Nations; and the moderate left, which included Robert Blum and the scientist Karl Vogt. Similarly, the right was made up of an extreme and mainly pro-Austrian wing and a moderate wing, composed of Prussian officials and led by Joseph Maria von Radowitz and Georg Ernst von Vincke.

The National Assembly had to face three major problems. There was first the national problem: should the new German Empire include or exclude Austria? The "Lesser Germans" (*Kleindeutsche*) favored a nation-state without the Hapsburg Empire, which was largely composed of non-Germans. On the other hand, the "Greater Germans" (*Grossdeutsche*) wanted the Germans of Austria included, but they differed as to how this "Greater Germany" might be formed.

The second main problem involved the choice between unitarianism and federalism. The Lesser Germans were unitarians. They favored a strong empire represented by the Reichstag and a Reich ministry that would be largely independent from individual states and would have far-reaching powers to enable them to decide on major issues from a national point of view. In their opinion the federal member-states should only have limited rights; and, in particular, Prussia should not become too strong or independent. Apart from the Republicans who aimed at a unitary republic, the Greater Germans were federalists who favored the greatest possible independence of the individual states.

Finally there was the constitutional problem: should the new state be a parliamentary or merely a constitutional state? The Lesser Germans saw their model in the English parliament and accordingly pleaded for two houses of parliament—a lower house to be elected by the people, and an upper house with half its members appointed by the state governments and half from the diets of member-states. The Republicans among the Greater Germans wanted a strictly parliamentary democracy with one chamber only.

It has been said that the Frankfurt Parliament was "too much of a university and too little of a political stock exchange." [12] There was indeed something very academic and impractical about the endless discussion of human rights during the winter of 1848–49. One of the first steps of the assembly was the creation of a central authority. In a speech on June 2, 1848, Heinrich von Gagern, the president of the Frankfurt Parliament, insisted "that the future central authority must be placed in the hands of a regent with responsible ministers." The regent elected was the Austrian Archduke John, who then formed a parliamentary Reich ministry. However, it soon became evident that the regent was without real power, because he commanded no army of his own, and received the homage due to him from the troops only in the petty states, but not in Prussia or Austria. The news of the June battles at the barricades in Paris frightened the German bourgeoisie, and the revolutionary tide gradually ebbed away. One important feature of the revolutions of 1848 in Germany and Austria is the fact that the army remained with the old order and was not affected by the revolt, far different from France in 1789 and Germany in 1918.

Limitation of space does not allow for a discussion of the simultaneous revolutions in the Hapsburg Empire, of the events following the fall of Chancellor Metternich in March, 1848, and the formation

[12] Veit Valentin, 1848: Chapters of German History (London, 1940), p. 272.

of more liberal governments. Revolutionary élan had gradually weakened, and the revolutionaries were defeated in Vienna by the imperial troops at the end of October.[13]

After the imperial troops had conquered the capital, the police took drastic steps against the students and other radical elements. Most Viennese had long tired of "anarchy," as they saw it, and preferred order, even if it was heartless and ruthless. The peasants, who had been granted the abolition of all feudal ties and burdens by a bill championed by Hans Kudlich and accepted by the Constitutional Assembly in Vienna in August, 1848, showed little further interest in the revolution and remained indifferent to the return of the old powers.

By crushing the revolution in Vienna, the imperial army under Windischgrätz indirectly brought about a compromise between the Lesser and Greater Germans in the Frankfurt Parliament. The new prime minister of Austria, the resolute and ruthless Prince Felix zu Schwarzenberg, on whose express order Robert Blum had been executed, insisted that the entire Hapsburg Empire be included in the new German Reich. This was impossible in the eyes of all the parties at Frankfurt. Austria was to remain outside the new empire. The disappointed Greater Germans now accepted an hereditary emperor; and the Lesser Germans agreed on universal, direct, and secret suffrage. The result was a constitution both unitary and parliamentary, with an hereditary emperor, an imperial ministry, and a parliament, or Reichstag, consisting of a lower house elected by the people and an upper house composed of representatives from the member-states. Uhland, the South German poet, had declared himself in vain against the hereditary emperor in an impressive speech that he delivered to the assembly on January 22, 1849. "The Revolution and an hereditary emperor: this is a youth with grey hairs," he said. "No head will shine over Germany which is not anointed with a full drop of democratic oil." He was in the minority. Most deputies sided with the Lesser German Dahlmann, a liberal historian, who maintained that there was "absolutely no future possible for Germany without Prussia. . . . At last Germany, as such, must enter the group of great political powers of the Continent: that can only come to pass by means of Prussia, and neither Prussia without Germany, nor Germany without Prussia, can find salvation. . . ."

After the acceptance of the constitution, a deputation from the

[13] On this theme see R. J. Rath, *The Viennese Revolution of 1848* (Austin: University of Texas Press, 1957).

National Assembly went to Berlin and offered the hereditary crown of emperor to Frederick William IV of Prussia, but the king refused. At first the real reasons for his rejection of the German crown were concealed, but his hatred of the revolution became known. He disliked the "crown from the gutter," permeated, as he put it, with "the hateful odor of the revolution." Second, had he accepted the crown it would probably have meant war with both Austria and Russia. Tsar Nicholas I had earlier resented Frederick William's overtures to the German revolutionary movement in March 1848. At that time the unstable king had made some large concessions and had even proclaimed that in the future "Prussia would be absorbed by Germany." There followed a succession of Prussian cabinets during 1848, extending from the liberal ministry of Camphausen to the reactionary ministry of Count Brandenburg. Each cabinet leaned more to the right than its predecessor. By November the military, who had left Berlin in March by order of the king, had returned; and the popular General Wrangel forced the dissolution of the Prussian National Assembly at the end of the year.

However, if reaction was as successful in Prussia as elsewhere, it did not mean that things after the revolution were exactly the same as before. For the first time the king had been obliged to grant a constitution with two houses of parliament; and although its final form was imposed upon the country, parliament could not be ignored. The events of the revolution forced the land-owning nobility to form a party of their own, the Conservative Party, which tried to win as much support as possible from the masses against the liberal tide using the slogan "with God for King and Country." Frederick William IV, an artistically inclined man but by no means a strong character, became more and more dependent on a conservative camarilla that was determined to win back the exclusive control which they had lost for some months during the tempestuous days of 1848.

The revolution in Prussia and Austria followed a pattern similar to that in France: first, it gathered momentum, then it reached a climax, and finally it ebbed away with the old powers gradually reasserting themselves. There is no doubt that the traditional German thirst for order and for obedience to the "powers that be" remained deeply rooted. The events of June, 1848, in Paris seemed to have frightened the German middle classes even more than their French counterparts. As Hans Rothfels has emphasized, many Germans feared then that a radical development in France would mean an attack on the Rhine area or a revolutionary offensive to the east. A strong fear of the "red spectre" made members of the middle class more inclined to accept the reaction. The desire for tranquillity, a return to normal, and business as usual was not only a bourgeois preserve but "was also very much felt by the lower middle classes whose small margin of existence was threatened by economic paralysis." [14]

Thirty years after the Revolution of 1848, one of its leading figures in the Prussian National Assembly, the democrat Hans Viktor Unruh, observed retrospectively: "In spite of the many great mistakes then made on all sides . . . the events of 1848 form the basis of our present political development and of our present political condition, which no Liberal and no Conservative who is not a reactionary would wish to exchange for that before 1847." To some extent this was a rationalization, but Unruh's further remark is undoubtedly valid: "All of us were political dilettantes in 1848. We clung to the constitutional blueprints of Rotteck and Dahlmann and thought that we could achieve everything we desired by drafting paragraphs of a constitution. We have had to learn through bitter experience that the only things that matter are the actual changes made in the state."

Many Germans continued to suffer from what may be called a "national inferiority complex." Prince Chlodwig zu Hohenlohe–Schillingsfürst, who was later to become the second chancellor after Bismarck, wrote in 1847: "One reason for dissatisfaction being universal in Germany—and every thinking German feels it deeply and painfully—is the nullity of Germany vis-à-vis other states. . . . It is sad and humiliating not to be able to say proudly abroad, 'I am a German!'—not to see a German flag flying on ships nor find a consul, but to have to say: 'I am a Kurhesse, a Darmstädter, a Bückeburger, my fatherland was once a great and powerful country but is now split into thirty-eight fragments.'" [15] The impotence of the National Assembly in Frankfurt and the return of the old powers made many Germans feel that what really mattered was not freedom but power. The reaction against the theorizing of the Frankfurt professors was perhaps best expressed ten years later by Julius Froebel when he wrote: "The German nation is sick of principles and doc-

[14] See the article by Hans Rothfels, "1848—One Hundred Years After," in 1848: A Turning Point?, ed. Melvin Kranzberg, Problems in European Civilization (Boston, 1959), pp. 71–79.
[15] Quoted in Sir Lewis Namier, Vanished Supremacies (London, 1958), p. 63.

trines of literary greatness and theoretical existence. What it wants is POWER! POWER! POWER! and whoever gives it power, to him it will give honor, more honor than he can imagine." [16] A liberal constitution in a united national state remained the ideal of many men of the older generation, but they gradually realized that this would remain a mere daydream until German unity could be brought about through power and strength. The man to personify that power and to create a united Germany, not from below but from above, was Otto von Bismarck.

GERMANY AS HEINRICH HEINE SAW HER

When he spoke of Germany, Heinrich Heine (1797–1856) lacked Goethe's dispassionate, Olympian detachment. Through temperament and personal fate Heine did not belong, like Goethe, to the establishment, but was a member of the mobile intelligentsia of a later generation. He spent only the first half of his life in the country of his birth; the second half he spent in France, part political refugee and part political playboy. He became the first great *Feuilletonist* (feature writer) of the German press by making politics, literature, and social life palatable and interesting for a wider reading public. He also functioned as a go-between and interpreter who undertook to explain German philosophy and literature to the French and French politics and social doctrines to the Germans. Irreverent and witty, shrewd and often amusing, a liberal without any party attachment, sometimes aggressive, sometimes restrained, sometimes romantic, usually cynical, Heine was a novel personality in German literature. His jibes at the philistines and narrow nationalists at home, his antipathy to restrictive conservatives, his mockery of Metternich's police organs and the multitude of censors in Germany made him both disliked at home and attractive abroad. Out of place in pre-1848 Germany, in the era of *Biedermeier* and official quietude, he threw more light on its weaknesses and perhaps its charm than any other German author.[17]

Born in Düsseldorf, in the Rhineland, in 1797 of Jewish parents,

---

[16] Quoted in Heinrich von Srbik, *Deutsche Einheit* (Munich, 1942), III, 5.

[17] *Biedermeier* is a term used to indicate the idyllic and contented German family life between 1815 and 1848, "the retreat from a larger social scene into the private sphere." This attitude has been depicted in the paintings of M. von Schwind, Ludwig Richter, and Karl Spitzweg. See the essay "Biedermeier," by M. J. Norst, *Periods in German Literature*, ed. J. M. Ritchie (London, 1966), pp. 147–168.

Heine retained a natural sympathy for Napoleonic France; for it had been the French dictator who put an end to the old order and emancipated the Jews in the Rhineland. Heine studied law and the arts at the universities of Bonn, Göttingen, and Berlin. In Göttingen he found that "the ordinary professors knew nothing extraordinary and the extraordinary professors nothing ordinary." In Bonn he heard A. W. Schlegel, the romantic interpreter of Shakespeare and Oriental poetry; in Berlin he listened to Hegel, then the acknowledged star among the German philosophers. Heine felt disappointed when in October, 1824, he visited Goethe; the two men had little in common. Although he became a convert to the Protestant church, his enemies continued to attack him as a Jew. The publication of the *Book of Songs* and of the second volume of *Reisebilder* made him famous, but the appearance of the third volume of *Reisebilder* evoked official disgrace; the authorities declared the work subversive and banned it in the whole of Austria and in the Rhine province. When Heine visited Württemberg, a plainclothes policeman promptly took the poet to the frontier and expelled him as an undesirable person.

In April, 1831, the German and Austrian governments took drastic steps against Heine and other independent writers of the "Young Germany" school; and Prince Metternich, the Austrian chancellor, issued a warrant for Heine's arrest.[18] Soon afterwards Heine left Germany for Paris; and he spent nearly all the rest of his life abroad. In Paris he became a political writer and an interpreter of Germany to the French and of France to the Germans. There he developed into a figure of world literature, into a "world citizen in exile" (Hermann Kesten).

Heine was not an educator or a moral reformer, but a shrewd observer and a perceptive and forceful satirist. He was also a romantic poet. To Heine, the romantic poet, Germany was both the *Biedermeier* country of small towns and petty states, and of nightingales, the Lorelei, and folk sagas. It was the land of Luther, of Lessing, and of Kant. Heine, the social critic, disliked smug philistines and petty-minded bureaucrats—the petty rulers and the subservient masses so jealous of title and rank. He was not a political doctrinaire or even a politician with a constant "line": for all his criticism of German society he was never a fully fledged radical like the less-talented but more consistent Ludwig Börne, for some years a fellow writer

---

[18] The "Young Germany" school is discussed in E. K. Bramsted, *Aristocracy and the Middle Classes in Germany* (Chicago, 1964), Chapter 9.

in the pleasant exile of Paris. A witty phrase or a startling *bon mot* were often more important to Heine than a definite political approach. As William Rose has said so well, "Heine was driven by the idea of human liberty, but for all the venom with which he tipped his sword he fought as a poet, not as a political thinker." [19] Even Karl Marx, with whom he was on friendly terms in Paris during the 1840s and who admired his poetry, was inclined to make allowances for inconsistencies in Heine's political views. "I am a constitutionalist. I am for freedom," Heine once wrote. "Perhaps the best solution would be a monarchy governed by republicans, or a republic governed by monarchists."

Yet Heine had no illusions about the strengths and weaknesses of the German national character. The man who could sigh in exile:

Deutschland, denk ich Dein in der Nacht,
bin ich um den Schlaf gebracht.

[When I think of you, Germany, in the night,
I cannot regain my sleep.]

perceived clearly the servility and longing for conformity of so many of his countrymen. In 1836 Heine wrote to Varnhagen von Ense: "the German is obsequious by nature and the cause of the people is never popular in Germany." Earlier, in his *English Fragment* (1830), he had drawn his famous comparison of the different attitudes to liberty of the Englishman, the Frenchman, and the German. "The Englishman," Heine suggested, in his inimitable way, "loves liberty like his wedded wife. He possesses her; and if he does not treat her with tenderness he still knows how to defend her like a man if need be. . . . The Frenchman loves liberty like his chosen bride. He is aglow for her, he is aflame, he throws himself at her feet with the craziest protestations, he fights to the death for her, he commits a thousand follies for her sake." The German loves liberty as he does his old grandmother, as part of a fairytale. It is true that "the German will never turn his old grandmother out completely; he will always let her have a place by the fire where she can tell fairytales to the children. Should freedom ever vanish from the earth—which God forbid—a German dreamer would find it again in his dreams."

It was the pre-Bismarckian, pre-Darwinian, pre-Marxist Ger-

[19] William Rose, *Heinrich Heine* (Oxford, 1956), p. 93.

many, the land of petty states, profound philosophers, and romantic poets that Heine thus characterized—and amiably ridiculed. But he took the German contribution to philosophy and literature seriously and tried to explain its trends to the French public in two brilliant works, *On the History of Religion and Philosophy* (1834) and *The Romantic School* (1835). Although not an abstract thinker himself, Heine nevertheless managed to give a simplified but masterly account of the religious and philosophical trends in Germany since the Reformation. He rejects as superficial French attempts à la Madame de Staël to understand Germany through her novelists and poets alone. German thought will remain "a cumbersome puzzle" as long as the importance of religion and philosophy in Germany is not realized. Heine's own clarity and distinctness contrasts with the style of German philosophers, which he describes as "thorough, immeasurably thorough, very profound, but also equally incomprehensible." His long essay "On the History of Religion and Philosophy in Germany" clearly reveals the impact of the Utopian movement of St. Simon in France, which attracted Heine greatly. In this book, "three main themes are developed; firstly the conflict between spiritualism and sensualism in German culture; secondly, the defeat, in the course of a religious and philosophic revolution, of spiritualism and the restoration of the pantheism native to Germany; thirdly the transformation into action of the revolution already achieved in the field of thought." [20]

How did Heine see the overall significance of German philosophy? He assures us that it is a matter which concerns all mankind, and emphasizes that "a methodical nation like the Germans had to begin with the Reformation; only after that could it concern itself with philosophy; and only then could it proceed to political revolution after its completion." As though foreseeing the worldwide impact that Hegel's greatest pupil and opponent, Karl Marx, was shortly to make, Heine saw revolutionary forces at work behind German philosophical doctrines "which only wait for the day when they will break through and fill the world with dismay and admiration."

At the same time, Heine realized with rare insight the interconnection between the new German philosophy of nature and the "demonic forces of old German Pantheism." Anticipating in a way the brutal aggressiveness of twentieth-century German nationalism, Heine conceded that "Christianity—and this is one of its finest

[20] C. P. Magill in his introduction to *Zur Geschichte der Religion und Philosophie in Deutschland* (London, 1947).

merits—somewhat softened down that brutal German lust for fighting. If one day the taming talisman, the Cross, breaks up, then the wildness of the old fighters, the nonsensical fury of the Berserkers of which the Nordic poets say and sing so much, will rise once more." Then the day of the Germans will come, and the French will be well advised to let the Germans alone and not meddle with their affairs; for the German fury (*furor Teutonicus*) will be dangerous. In any case, Heine advised the French to be on their guard. No matter whether Germans were to be ruled by the Crown Prince of Prussia, later King Frederick William IV ("a romantic on the throne of the Caesars," as his contemporary David Strauss called him), or by the radical democrat Doctor Wirth, the French had always to be prepared; they should remain quietly at their post, rifles under their arms. "I mean well by you," said Heine, "and it almost gave me a shock the other day when I heard that your minister intended to disarm France."

Heine was the last man to wish for a war between the two nations, to each of which he felt a strong affinity. As he was to express it in his last will and testament: "It has been the great task of my life to work for a cordial harmony between Germany and France and to frustrate the intrigues of the enemies of democracy who exploit international prejudices and animosities to their own advantage." For years he had been in favor of a *rapprochement* between the two countries. In June, 1832, he wrote from Paris in the leading German newspaper *Augsburger Allgemeine Zeitung*: ". . . in recent times both of us, Frenchmen and Germans, have learned much from each other. The former have accepted much German philosophy and poetry, and we on our part have done the same with the political experiences and the practical sense of the French. Both nations resemble those Homeric heroes who exchange their weapons and armor on the battlefield as a token of friendship."

Heine managed to give the Germans a lively impression of the character and the fascination of Paris, of Paris's relationship to France compared with that of any major German town to Germany. Goethe had said to Eckermann in March, 1830, that "Paris is France, all the important interests of her great fatherland are concentrated in the capital, and they have their proper life and real echo there. . . . With us in Germany such a thing is not possible. We have no city, we have not even a country, of which we can say definitely: here is Germany."

Although Heine himself for a time favored the French monarchy, he realized that it was doomed. A republic was inevitable in France because of the incompatibility of the national character with royalty. The Germans, however, were in a different position. Their belief in authority had not yet evaporated, and nothing significant was pushing them towards a republican form of government. They had not outgrown their belief in monarchy; their reverence for princes had not been violently disturbed; they had not experienced a revolt against a monarch, or as Heine put it, "the disaster of a January 21st" (1793), when Louis XVI was beheaded. The Germans still believed in authorities, in great power, and in the police.

During the last few years of his life, in the mid-1850s, Heine thought that the future might belong to the communists, a prospect that both frightened and fascinated him. As he saw it, there were two arguments in favor of a communist regime. The first resulted from a premise Heine accepted—i.e. that "all human beings have the right to eat." The second argument was that communism would form the chief opposition to the new nationalism in Germany, to "those false patriots, whose love of their fatherland only consists in a stupid resentment of foreign countries and neighboring peoples and which spits its venom against France every day."

At the end of his life, lying helpless and tormented with pain on a mattress in Paris, Heine was frightened by the thought of the Teutonic nationalists on the other side of the Rhine. They had first sounded their anti-French fanfares in 1840, but the revolution of 1848 had silenced them somewhat. Now, he lamented, "these saviors of the fatherland are setting the tone again in Germany, and continue to shout by permission of the highest authorities." Ending on a sardonic and confident note, Heine predicted the day would come when a fatal blow would destroy that foe—and the great poet could go to his last rest freed from all worry.

6

Bismarck and the Second Empire, 1850-1890

The time for ideals has passed. German unity has descended from the world of dreams to the prosaic world of reality. Today politicians must ask less what is desirable than what is obtainable.
JOHANN MIQUEL, A LEADING LIBERAL POLITICIAN (1866)

THE ROAD TO POWER POLITICS

Two men changed the political map and the balance of power of Europe profoundly in the nineteenth century: Napoleon I and Bismarck. For fifteen years Napoleon imposed the will of post revolutionary France on Europe and forced most of it into an empire. By 1815 the empire was broken, never to return. Bismarck, on the other hand, founded a United Germany through three wars, established her as the central power in Europe, and tried to obtain security for her by an elaborate system of alliances and pacts.

Otto von Bismarck (1815–1898) was a Prussian country aristocrat, a *Junker* by origin, but a *Junker* with a difference. For though his father came from the old Prussian nobility, his mother was the daughter of a high civil servant burgher ennobled by the king. In his complex inheritance Bismarck combined proud self-reliance, an aversion to obeying others, and roots in the Pomeranian soil with a rare versatility of mind, a resolute will to power, and an ability to readjust and to grow. After studying law at Göttingen and Berlin, he joined the Prussian Civil Service for a while, but soon resigned and devoted himself to running his father's country estate. As a deputy

139

to the provincial diet, he was deeply opposed to the revolution in Prussia in 1848 and to the liberal and democratic tide. At that time he still favored the traditional antirevolutionary alliance of the three conservative monarchies, Russia, Austria, and Prussia.

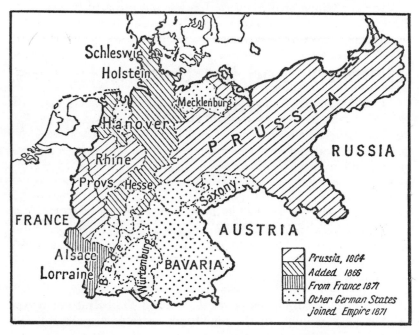

THE GROWTH OF THE GERMAN EMPIRE, 1864–1871

Bismarck's first diplomatic appointment came in May, 1851, when the king sent him as Prussian envoy to the Confederal Diet at Frankfurt, which had survived the turmoil of 1848–49. There he gradually became convinced that the peaceful coexistence of Prussia and Austria could not last and that there was not sufficient elbow room for both powers within the Germanies.

In December, 1862, soon after his appointment as Prime Minister of Prussia, Bismarck told the Austrian minister in Berlin that the relations between Austria and Prussia were bound in the end to lead to war if they were not improved soon. To avoid an armed conflict Bismarck suggested that the Hapsburg monarchy should "move the center of its gravity eastwards, to Hungary." In other words,

Austria should give up her claim to control Germany, particularly North Germany, which Prussia regarded as her natural sphere of influence. If Austria accepted this advice, Prussia would become her faithful ally. Otherwise catastrophe would follow.

It was a telling prediction. Austria was not prepared to give way. Bismarck lured the heedless Austrian statesmen into an adventure which could only end in surrender or war by involving Austria as an ally in a war against Denmark in 1864 and afterwards in the control of Holstein, a territory next door to Prussia but hundreds of miles away from the Hapsburg monarchy.

In 1862, Bismarck's key appointment had been widely regarded as a desperate attempt by King William to find a way out of the conflict with the liberal majority in Prussia's lower house over his pet project, army reform. The bitter feud over the proposed extension of military service from two years to three and of the reorganization of the reserve forces, the *Landwehr*, was in fact a power struggle between king and parliament; for the state was to be run either by the nobility or by middle-class commoners.

Bismarck treated the liberal majority in parliament with undisguised contempt. He lectured them on the soundness of realism in politics (*Realpolitik*), remarking acidly that "the great questions of our time are not decided by majority decisions but by blood and iron." Soon afterwards the king, having become fainthearted, told Bismarck in the course of an interview that he could foresee how things would end: "In front of the [Berlin] Opera House under my windows, you will be beheaded and a bit later I shall be myself." In reply, Bismarck contended that they all had to die sooner or later, and could they lose their lives more decently?: "I myself in the fight for the cause of my king, and Your Majesty by sealing your royal rights of divine grace with your own blood." To many leading liberals Bismarck was nothing but "a shallow *Junker*," the champion of arrogant and ruthless reaction. Although the government dissolved the diet again and again, the liberals were always returned with substantial majorities. Seen in retrospect, this opposition during 1862–66 proved "indeed, the only one in the whole history of constitutional Germany which could effectively depend upon their voters." [1]

[1] Erich Eyck, *Bismarck and the German Empire* (London, 1950), p. 61. This opinion is not shared by Otto Pflanze in his work *Bismarck and the Development of Germany: The Period of Unification 1815–1850* (Princeton, 1963), Chapter 10.

The lightning victory of the Prussian armies at Königgrätz (or Sadowa) on July 3, 1866, meant both a military defeat for the Austrian troops, due to the superior quality of Prussian guns and military organization, and a severe setback for the Prussian liberals, although many of them personally welcomed the victory with the same national pride as did their conservative adversaries. Bismarck did not allow himself to be carried away by this success but, against the desire of the king and his generals, displayed a conciliatory attitude towards the Austrians as well as the Prussian liberals. In both cases he was clearly motivated by pragmatic long-term aims and considerations. He wanted to treat Austria leniently to prevent her from later becoming an irreconcilable foe to his secret plans for German unification. Similar tactics can be discerned in Bismarck's handling of the liberals, who were largely the party of the propertied and educated urban middle classes. Bismarck's Indemnity Bill of 1866, by which he asked the diet to belatedly legalize the expenses that the state had contracted and the taxes it had collected during the parliamentary crisis, was a master stroke; for it split the liberals permanently and reduced their strength through the secession of the "National Liberals." Unlike the remaining Progressives, the National Liberals were prepared to make their peace with the dexterous prime minister, trusting that he in his turn would accept some of their ideas on legal and economic reforms.

Bismarck treated the Austrians with great consideration, but he was savage towards some of their North German allies. Hanover and other territories in North Germany, including the former Free Imperial City of Frankfurt-on-Main, were annexed. Even the private property of the blind king of Hanover was confiscated and a heavy fine imposed on the city of Frankfurt. The remaining North German states were ready to join Prussia in the North German Confederation, of which the King of Prussia became President and Bismarck Chancellor. The Constitution provided for two chambers; the Reichstag was based on universal suffrage; and the upper house, or Federal Council, was comprised of representatives of the member-states; these formed the model for the Constitution of the Second Empire of 1871. Among the National Liberals in the new Prussian Diet were many men from the territories newly annexed by Prussia, who regarded Bismarck as a liberator rather than as a reactionary, and strongly favored a policy of accommodation. Not a few prominent liberals underwent a change of heart. Tired of the fruitless support of a doctrinaire line, they readjusted themselves to the strong and demanding personality of Bismarck and made their peace with him, hoping to satisfy both their insistence on constitutional freedom and their desire for national power.

Bismarck's own views also changed to some extent between 1864 and 1871. In a speech to the diet in January, 1864, he had accused the liberals with their wider German sympathies of "opposing the national spirit of Prussia." Only slowly did he change his emphasis from a conservative Prussia to a federal Germany under Prussian leadership.

After the formation of the North German Confederation and its Reichstag, he cautiously considered a kind of *Anschluss* of the South German states. By 1869, Bismarck had found in German nationalism "the moral force with which to expand and buttress the power of the Hohenzollern monarchy against the hazards of European politics and the pressure of social change." [2] Bismarck proceeded slowly, aware of both the strength of German particularism and the danger of French intervention. He knew that wide circles in South Germany had an aversion to being ruled by Berlin. Although he officially acknowledged the river Main as the line separating the North of Germany from the South, he secretly managed to conclude offensive and defensive military alliances between the North German Confederation and the South German states.

The question of whether or not Bismarck—the consummate tactician—deliberately worked towards a war with France has occupied historians for a century. Bismarck was very conscious that a war would provide a focal point for national animosity and self-assertion and would obliterate the separatist trends in South Germany. Looking back, neither the French nor Bismarck was guiltless. There is enough evidence to prove that Bismarck was determined to put the France of the fading romantic adventurer Napoleon III in her place and to humiliate her. The French emperor insisted on concessions and compensations for the services he felt he had rendered Bismarck before the Prusso-Austrian war by bringing Italy and Prussia together in a common front against Austria. An explosive situation developed between the two countries, and only a spark was needed to set it aflame. This was provided by the candidacy of a Hohenzollern prince for the vacant Spanish throne. With a German as King of Spain, France would have to reckon with two potential enemies at her frontiers. Although Bismarck denied it, it is fairly certain that he

[2] See Otto Pflanze, "Bismarck and German Nationalism," in *American Historical Review*, LX (October 1954–July 1955), 548–66.

had a hand in engineering the candidacy of Prince Leopold of the South German Catholic branch of the Hohenzollerns. In July the French foreign minister asked the French ambassador in Berlin, Benedetti, to see the Prussian king, then at the spa of Bad Ems in the Rhineland, and to demand from him "if not to order at least to advise" Prince Leopold to withdraw his candidacy. In fact, King William himself disliked the Spanish proposal. On July 12, Leopold's father, Charles Anthony, bowed to pressure and withdrew his son's candidacy.

However, Napoleon III and Gramont foolishly went further and instructed Benedetti to demand from King William that he would never authorize a renewal of Leopold's candidacy, a demand which the irritated king firmly but politely rejected. When Bismarck received a telegram on July 13 in Berlin from the king's secretary on Benedetti's interview with William in Bad Ems, he reedited it for publication, giving it a sinister and provocative ring. If the king had behaved more like a dove, Bismarck behaved like a hawk, and was applauded by his friends, the Minister for War, von Roon, and the Chief of the General Staff, Hellmuth von Moltke. The French cabinet promptly took up the gauntlet and answered with a declaration of war. By doing so, it played right into the hands of Bismarck, who felt a war was necessary to unite Germany under Prussian leadership. Perhaps Bismarck was a warmonger, but the French lacked the foresight and leadership to call his bluff and avoid the trap that he had prepared for them.

The quick successes of the German armies soon appeared to justify Bismarck's tricks. His demand for the annexation of Alsace-Lorraine helped to make the war, in the words of Otto Pflanze, "a popular national crusade in Germany." The war also helped to win over the south and to obtain its agreement to a constitution modeled on that of the North German Confederation. Even in Bavaria the war fever had run high, and the anti-Prussian Patriots' Party was unable to stem the patriotic tide.

Although Bismarck knew how to exploit German national sentiment to the full when it suited him, he can be regarded as a nationalist only in the sense that the power and welfare of the new empire was his highest concern in international affairs. He carried the old ideas of *raison d'état* and balance of power into the new framework of much stronger and more competitive powers. Bismarck was a nationalist in the sense that he worked incessantly to maintain the military strength and the international prestige of the Prussianized

Second Empire. His "internationalism" was only an arrangement to secure a balance of power with one or two other big European states. He had no inclination to destroy and incorporate the Austrian monarchy for the sake of a "Greater Germany." Bismarck regarded the Austro-Hungarian Empire as a bulwark against the Slavic flood into Eastern Europe. He was never a Pan-German. However, Bismarck would use the rhetoric when it suited him of nationalist aggressiveness or intense national self-assertion as, for instance, in the famous sentence in his Reichstag speech on February 6, 1888: "We Germans fear God, but nothing else in the world."

Before 1866, "the Prussian nation" commanded Bismarck's primary emotional allegiance. Only in 1866 and 1867 did he declare repeatedly, "my highest ambition is to make the Germans into a nation." Later he used the phrase "establishment of the German nationality" to describe his life's work. Dynastic loyalty and national sentiment were inseparable in his mind.[3] Elsewhere, the modern nation-state meant rather a state based on popular sovereignty, a conception thoroughly disapproved of by this Machiavellian *Junker*. After 1871, Bismarck, the "Iron Chancellor," was averse to the idea of preventive wars on the whole although he often used bullying tactics. He was obsessed by what he called "the nightmare of coalitions" and worried by what he saw as the sinister conspiracy and threat from international forces such as the Catholic Church and Marxist socialism. To sum up, Bismarck was neither a cultural nationalist nor a racialist, but an admirer and exponent of the strong nation-state on a dynastic basis.

A SEMICONSTITUTIONAL MONARCHY

The Second German Empire, the product of three wars of aggression, was created in 1871 from above and not from below. In the words of the Preamble of the Constitution of 1871, it was to be "an Eternal Covenant for the protection of the federal territory and for the promotion of the welfare of the Reich, concluded by the King of Prussia in the name of the North German Confederation with the South German princes." Bismarck used underhanded methods to obtain signatures to the Covenant, including bribery to win over the reluctant King of Bavaria, Louis II, and his emissary at Versailles, Count Holnstein. He also had to cajole his own king, William, into agreeing to become the German *Kaiser* (emperor), a "promo-

[3] Cf. Otto Pflanze, "Bismarck and German Nationalism," op. cit., p. 561.

tion" little to the taste of the monarch. Even when talked into accepting the position King William would have preferred the title "Kaiser of Germany."

Bismarck proved as shrewd and tactful in handling the other German princes as he was in his approach to William. Avoiding emphasis on unitarian features, he made considerable concessions to the particularist currents in some of the South German states. In Bavaria and Württemberg, the kings retained command of their troops in time of peace, control of their own railways, and considerable postal and currency concessions. There were also some special commercial rights enjoyed by the three Hanseatic cities of Hamburg, Bremen, and Lübeck. The *Länder* were represented in the Federal Council, or *Bundesrat*, where Prussia commanded the largest number of votes (seventeen out of a total of fifty-eight), although it was not a majority. However, since any proposal to change the Constitution could be blocked by only fourteen votes, Prussia or the combined three South German states were given the chance to veto all changes of which they disapproved. The Federal Council was intended as a counterweight to the Reichstag, based on universal male suffrage, a concession to democracy at the time that was not found in many other countries. There were thus three unifying forces in the Constitution: the emperor, who remained King of Prussia as chief executive; the chancellor, who was responsible only to the king; and last and least, the National Parliament, or *Reichstag*. It was a skillful but somewhat artificial equilibrium of forces.

Bismarck liked to point out the difference between this semiconstitutional German monarchy and the parliamentary monarchy of England. In Germany the chancellor and the ministers (who were only his assistants) were not responsible to parliament; there was neither an imperial cabinet nor a recognized opposition in the English sense, and Bismarck could use the parties as tools however and whenever it suited him. No German party ever obtained an absolute majority. Although Bismarck had some respect for the English parliamentary tradition, he genuinely doubted that such a system would work elsewhere. There were, he felt, circumstances in English history favorable to such an institution that were completely lacking in other countries.

Bismarck half felt and half posed as "a loyal servant of his royal master." Because the world in which he lived was complex, the attitudes he adopted were somewhat ambiguous. On the other hand, he belonged by birth and education to the old world of traditional

European diplomacy, which had seen its heyday in the seventeenth and eighteenth centuries. Yet with the advance of industry and technology in the nineteenth century, he had to reckon with and to utilize modern mass movements. It was no longer sufficient to play on the European chessboard of traditional diplomacy; he also had to cajole and threaten leaders and members of parliamentary parties at home. But there was a personal rub to it: "Bismarck's world in which he felt at home and moved with complete security was the grand world of the courts and aristocratic society. . . . Even when he desired to he was unable to negotiate with deputies and party leaders as skillfully as with ambassadors and foreign ministers of other powers." [4]

For some years Bismarck regarded the two parties represented in the Reichstag and in most German state parliaments, the Social Democrats and the Catholic Center Party, as conspiratorial elements, as *Reichsfeinde*, enemies of the empire. It would be wrong to see Bismarck as the exclusive author of the *Kulturkampf* (cultural struggle), the clash between the Second Empire and the Roman Catholic Church; for the opposition from the liberals to the declaration of the infallibility of the Pope at the Vatican Council of 1870 was strong in many countries, and anticlerical hostility to the claims of Pius IX was not confined to Germany. In England a liberal Catholic of the stature of Lord Acton was no less critical of the Pope's claims than was a German scientist, the professor of anatomy Rudolf Virchow, who actually coined the term *Kulturkampf* in a speech in parliament. However, in the last analysis it was Bismarck who turned the existing antagonism between science and clerical orthodoxy, between liberal freethinkers and ardent supporters of Rome, into a full-fledged political clash between church and state, between the German Empire and the Holy See.

Both at home and in foreign affairs, Bismarck aimed at a balance of power—a traditional concept, it is true, but one to which he gave his own interpretation. His skillful balancing of the forces underlying the various institutions of the Second Empire has already been mentioned. The authoritarian government dependent upon the consent of the states in the Federal Council was to some extent counterbalanced by the lower house, which was based on universal male suffrage; this made Germany equally remote from Tsarist absolutism and

[4] Franz Schnabel, "The Bismarck Problem," in *German History: Some New German Views*, ed. Hans Kohn (London, 1954), pp. 76–77.

Western parliamentary systems. The balancing in foreign affairs act was more difficult and required constant readjustment. Bismarck was not only a virtuoso in keeping five balls in the air simultaneously, he also insisted that Germany have only one potential enemy at a time—a policy that led to his system of alliances and supplementary pacts. The chancellor put security before adventure; and although he could make threatening speeches and defiant gestures during European crises (like those of 1875 and 1887, which both involved a resurgence of nationalism in France), his policy was directed towards securing the status quo and taking only limited risks. The Balkans, he declared emphatically during the Balkan crisis of 1877, were "not worth the bones of one Pomeranian grenadier," adding that "in Egypt I am English, in Bulgaria I am Russian." His attitude towards the acquisition of colonial territories for Germany was similarly cautious. Bismarck was Europe-centered; he was not oriented toward the world overseas. Although he used the tension between France and Britain during the mid-1880s as a welcome opportunity for the acquisition of German colonies in Africa and in the South Pacific, he never allowed himself to be distracted by colonial issues. As he once remarked: "My map of Africa lies in Europe. Here lies Russia and here lies France, and we are in the middle. That is my map of Africa."

It can be argued that Bismarck, the "Honest Broker" of the Congress of Berlin in 1878, pursued a negative rather than a positive policy, since his main aim was to isolate France and to avoid a conflict over the Balkans between the two conservative Eastern powers, Russia and Austria–Hungary. Through his calculated system of alliances and additional treaties, of which the Reinsurance Treaty of 1887 is the most famous example, Bismarck aimed to avoid full-scale conflicts rather than to create them. "We are sated," he declared early in the new empire, and perhaps the fact that his foreign policies can be described paradoxically as those of a "bullying pacifist" bears this out. But what about the less-satisfied powers? Their urge for expansion had to be restrained, as in the cases of Austrian–Hungary and Russia, or directed into different channels, as with France, whose expansion in North Africa and Indochina under Jules Ferry was looked upon with favor by the German chancellor.

It seems doubtful whether Bismarck was fully aware of the economic and social impact of the belated but intense Industrial Revolution in Germany. He left economic matters largely in the experienced hands of Rudolf Delbrück, president since 1871 of the imperial chancery. Delbrück, whose outlook on economic matters was akin to that of the National Liberals, welded together a "free trade" front of agrarian interests, commerce, liquid capital, and the export industry.[5] He drafted the new laws on trade and factory law, common weights and measures, and a common currency, which were required first for the North German Confederation, and four years later, for the Second Empire. After 1870, a uniform currency was created and a central state bank, the *Reichsbank*, was set up to discharge functions similar to those of the Bank of England in Britain. Delbrück became the classical exponent of the liberal trade policy of the Reich. When he suddenly submitted his resignation in April, 1876, it meant the beginning of the end of the liberal era. The change was the outcome of the world depression of 1873, which had a negative effect on the expansion of the German economy. At a time when the home market was shrinking and both agrarian and industrial interests were seriously threatened by superior foreign competition, the slogan of "laissez-faire" had lost its attraction. The demand for protection was first raised by steel manufacturers but spread quickly to other branches of industry. The farmers, including the influential *Junkers* east of the Elbe, also clamored for protection. They had to face competition now not only from Russia but from North America which, helped by improved transport conditions, could undercut German agricultural products on the world market.

Having become aware of this situation in 1878, Bismarck came out with a program of economic and tariff reforms. His new general tariff extended to all industrial and agricultural imports. This reversal of the former liberal trade policy was welcomed by the alliance of sectional agricultural and industrial interests. In the end the protectionist tariff was accepted in the Reichstag by the two conservative parties and the Center Party, the great majority of whom had long favored protectionism, and was opposed by the Progressives and the Socialists. The issue caused a split among the National Liberals. The left wing seceded from the party in 1879 and joined the Progressives five years later. Bismarck had successfully weakened his former allies and had formed a new ruling class consisting of heavy industrialists and *Junkers* that was to outlast his own regime. Free trade was now taboo, and governmental liberalism was discarded in favor of "Prussian hegemony and a German conservative state." [6]

⁵ See Helmut Böhme, op. cit., second chapter.
[6] Helmut Böhme, op. cit., pp. xii, xiv.

Bismarck's fierce hatred of the Social Democrats and his resolve to crush them expressed itself in the Antisocialist Laws he submitted first to the Reichstag in the spring of 1876. When he found the National Liberal Party with few exceptions disinclined to vote for it, he used the pretext of a second attempt on the life of Kaiser William in June, 1878, for dissolving the Reichstag. A fresh "law against the dangerous activities of the Social Democrats" put before the new Reichstag was again opposed by the Social Democrats, the Center Party, and the Progressives, but was fully supported by the two conservative parties. Having lost thirty seats in the election, the majority of the National Liberals now gave it their reluctant blessing. The Antisocialist Laws aimed at stamping out the movement altogether. Though it did not prevent the election of Social Democrats to the Reichstag and did not interfere with their parliamentary activities there, it banned all Social-Democratic organizations and their press. Socialist politicians and organizers were ruthlessly expelled from towns, and many of them went abroad to Switzerland and England. Yet the votes polled for the Social Democrats rose constantly and had nearly trebled by 1890. So in the long run Bismarck's Antisocialist Laws proved as much a failure as had his anti-Catholic legislation earlier.

One could perhaps dismiss the "Iron Chancellor" as a complete reactionary in domestic affairs were it not for his own brand of "state socialism." In the year in which he issued the draconic Antisocialist Laws, Bismarck told one of his officials, "If the worker had no more cause for complaint, the Social Democrats would lose their grass roots." To him, concentrated legislation that introduced an elaborate state insurance system for sickness, accident, and old age in 1880 was a means to safeguard political stability. As he put it to his assistant, Moritz Busch, in June, 1881: "The state must take the matter in hand. Not as alms but as a right to be provided when the will to work is no longer able to operate. Why should only persons incapacitated by war, or if a public servant, by old age, have a pension, and not a soldier of labor? This thing will succeed. It has a future. It is possible that our policies will perish when I am dead. But state socialism will make the running. Everyone who takes up this idea will govern." To this limited extent, Bismarck can be called one of the fathers of the modern welfare state.

The idea and practice of Bismarck's "state socialism" fits in well with that strange medley of political and social forces that the Second Empire presents to the historian. In the midst of rapid industrialization German society remained quasi-feudal. The sociologist Max Weber, perhaps the shrewdest contemporary critic of Wilhelminian Germany, emphasized the "feudal prestige" then symbolized in Germany "by way of giving satisfaction through the duel and by acquiring the rank of officer of the reserve; by way of a traditional student's life that stresses badges of rank, fencing scars, and thus diverts from real intensive work." [7] Most of these students later occupied leading positions in the governmental and industrial establishment. It was largely left to the less-privileged strata to perform the "real intensive work" that still remained characteristic of so much of German life. The society of the German Second Empire was indeed full of paradoxes and contradictions. For in this "industrial feudal society" and "often authoritarian welfare state," [8] a much stronger trend towards antimodernism, a more vigorous questioning of the new industrialized city atmosphere prevailed than in contemporary France or England.

A new ideological dichotomy developed in the Second Empire: between *Gemeinschaft* (community) and *Gesellschaft* (society)—culture and civilization—with a positive evaluation of the former and a negative evaluation of the latter. This dichotomy goes back to the musings of early romanticism,[9] but it gained momentum from the widespread distaste for the discomforts of a rapidly industrialized society.

One important aspect of this semifeudal society was the lack of groups who strongly felt the need for religious freedom and variety. In contrast to Britain and the United States, there were no Methodists, Unitarians, and Quakers in Germany; and the role of religious nonconformity was altogether negligible. There was in the Second Empire (and also later in the Third Reich) a strong preference instead for a potted synthesis, for an all-embracing *Weltanschauung*. This largely explains the influence of nationalist writers of the genre, ranging from Paul Lagarde (an eccentric professor of oriental studies) and the anonymous "Rembrandt Deutsche" (Julius Langbehn) to the English renegade H. S. Chamberlain with his readable racialist concoction, *The Foundations of the Nineteenth Century* (1899), and, later, to the National Socialist doctrines of Hitler's *Mein Kampf*

[7] Max Weber, *Gesammelte Politische Schriften*, 2nd ed. (Tübingen, 1958), p. 40.
[8] Ralf Dahrendorf, *Society and Democracy in Germany* (London, 1965), pp. 61–62.
[9] See Chapter 4, pp. 111–15.

and Alfred Rosenberg's *The Myth of the Twentieth Century*. Germans were inclined to believe in the "expert," especially the expert in synthesis and oversimplified formulae who could explain all the complex aspects of society and the universe from a common denominator.

The belief in the expert also lay at the root of the Bismarck cult that was so widespread among the educated and the uneducated alike after 1870. There were only a few clear-sighted critics of that cult. One of these was Theodor Fontane (1819–1898), the eminent novelist and sage. Although admiring Bismarck's Machiavellian statecraft with which he had managed to unite the Germans, Fontane did not overlook the flaws in Bismarck's character, even if he confined his criticism to the private correspondence. "One must forever recall the giant achievements of his genius, if one does not wish to be repelled by his dishonesty, which rests on the crassest contradictions," he wrote in a letter.[10] He felt "truly disgusted by this unending tendency to cheat, by this total foxiness." As a writer, Fontane admired "the genius which speaks from every one of his sentences," and felt, as he put it in a letter in 1894, that the critical remarks made by Bismarck in retirement "always hit the nail on the head";[11] but Bismarck's ruthless egoism was repellent to him. "Always I, I, and when things go wrong, complaints about ingratitude and a sentimental North German tear," the author wrote to his daughter, "Wherever I see Bismarck as a tool of Divine Providence, I bow before him. Wherever he is simply himself—country squire and captain of the dike and man out for his own advantage—I dislike him profoundly." [12] Few Germans were able to see so clearly the contradiction in the man who was largely responsible for the semifeudal structure of the new industrialized German society—a society where many a head of family felt and behaved like a pocket-sized Bismarck, at least at home. Had not Heinrich von Treitschke, the ardent contemporary nationalist historian, proclaimed that subordination began in the family?

[10] Quoted in Joachim Remak, *The Gentle Critic: Theodor Fontane and German Politics 1848–1898* (Syracuse, 1964), pp. 50–51.
[11] *Ibid.*, pp. 51–52.
[12] *Ibid.*

7

The Germany of William II, 1890-1918

> For I cannot allow my government to take a line like this without being on the spot to supervise the consequences carefully and take a hand. In any case it would be unforgivable and make me look as if I were a mere constitutional monarch. Le roi s'amuse! And all the time we are heading for mobilization. That must not happen with me away.
>
> KAISER WILLIAM II
>
> Comment made on a Norwegian cruise during the Moroccan crisis in July, 1911.

THE KAISER: A DILETTANTE IN POLITICS

William II was certainly a more complex personality on the imperial throne than either his grandfather William I or his father, amiable Frederick III whom fate allowed only ninety-nine days as emperor. His mother was a daughter of Queen Victoria, a capable but emotional woman, aptly described by Lord Granville as "very clever but not very wise." Handicapped to some extent by his physical disability, a withered left arm, William was "the product of two cultures, not of one," that of the Prussian *Junker* and of the liberal English gentleman; and he often gave the impression of a hearty toughness for which he had no natural aptitude.[1] Holstein has rightly portrayed him as a man "with more dramatic than political instincts" and a great artist in conversation. By tempera-

[1] Michael Balfour, *The Kaiser and His Times* (London, 1964), p. 83.

ment impulsive, impatient, and often tactless, his lack of a sense of proportion caused Bismarck much regret. The many marginal comments on diplomatic dispatches reveal his vanity, his bouts of absolutist conceit, and his inclination to theatrical pose. There was a lack of sober pragmatism in this monarch who always wanted to have his own way, yet was in constant need of praise from others and liked every day to be Sunday. His love of shining armor and oratorical gestures frequently misled him as well as others. Like Frederick William IV, he disapproved of any trend towards democracy. As he once observed when crown prince: "Democratic principles can only create weak and often corrupt pillars of society. A society is only strong if it recognizes the fact of natural superiorities, in particular that of birth." Later as emperor, he insisted that "the will of the King is the supreme law." [2]

William liked to pose in a constitutional state as an absolutist ruler by divine grace, as Frederick William IV had done fifty years earlier. He allowed himself to be influenced by people outside the government and listened to the advice of courtiers and officers on important decisions and appointments. The influence of certain courtiers was considerable, and some critical parliamentarians and journalists proved right in their suspicions. That a ruler who liked to emphasize that he was his own master could allow himself to be influenced by a court clique is one of the paradoxical aspects of the period. When the Kaiser rattled his sabre, it seemed a parody of Bismarck's earlier defiance, which was at least based on a genuine and not on a mere institutional prestige. Yet William II could appeal to a strong militarist tradition when boasting that "the soldier and the army, not parliamentarian majorities and decisions, have welded the German Empire together. I put my trust in the army." In his retirement Friedrich von Holstein deplored the Kaiser's lack of "all sense of what is fitting," calling it "a misfortune both for him and the German Reich."

When he came to the throne, William was convinced that he had a mission to fulfill. As he told the Brandenburg Assembly in February, 1892, "We are destined for great things. I am leading you to marvelous times." William wanted to appear supramodern, and his interest in new achievements in industry and technology was genuine; yet he remained wrapped up in antiquated concepts of absolutist rule. There was a discrepancy between appearance and

[2] Entry in the Visitors' Book of the City of Munich.

reality, pose and truth, which throws a pecular light on the last of the Hohenzollern monarchs. If there was a good deal of the actor in him, his stage was unfortunately not the theater but the world, and *Weltpolitik* was the field for which he possessed more inclination than aptitude. As a boy William was subjected to a strong dose of Calvinist austerity and hard work by a tutor.[3] Yet Queen Victoria once complained to Empress Augusta that Willy was getting spoiled by too much kindness. Spoiled, often naughty, and sovereign only in his public attitudes, the boy could hardly be expected to gain balance and wisdom. If some blame later lay with the emperor for not making a greater effort to overcome his weaknesses, more lay perhaps with his official and unofficial advisers for playing up to his weaknesses and exploiting them for the benefit of personal or political interests. "The sad fact remains that the two tendencies [his own instincts and inclinations to showmanship and self-aggrandisement and those of his entourage to influence him in the wrong directions] encouraged one another, and that taken in combination they resulted in untold damage to William, to Germany, and to the world."[4]

THE POLITICAL PARTIES

Different from England and the United States, the opposition was not a recognized element in the German political system. Ministers were not chosen from the members of parliament; and while it was necessary to make sure of a majority in the Reichstag or the diets for its support, the government could afford to ignore and even despise any opposition groups. Another distinct feature of the German political scene was the existence of two big parties, each of which represented a complete outlook on life. The Social Democratic Party was largely, though not entirely, based on Marxism,[5] and the Center Party was based on the doctrines of the Catholic Church. The German Social Democrats, under the firm leadership of Wilhelm Liebknecht and August Bebel, rejected any compromise with the powerful authoritarian regime, the *Obrigkeitsstaat*. The Center

[3] M. Balfour, op. cit., p. 77.
[4] *Ibid.*, p. 166.
[5] The two earlier socialist rival groups, the German General Workers' Association, founded by the brilliant orator and philosopher Ferdinand Lassalle shortly before his death in 1865 and the rather Marxist Social Democratic Workers' Party, had amalgamated at a congress at Gotha in 1875.

Party, however, comprising all strata of Catholics from the West-phalian aristocratic landowners to shopkeepers and Christian trade unionists, was fundamentally a rather conservative party led by notables and priests. Adamant in the defense of the Church and its faith, the Center Party was not basically antagonistic to the ruling system so long as Catholic interests were safeguarded. After the failure of the *Kulturkampf*, neither Bismarck nor his successors were averse, if necessary, to coming to terms with the Center Party. Both the Center and the Social Democrats combined the functions of a doctrinal organization and a pressure group. Their many affilia-tions through women's auxiliaries, youth associations, and trade-union groups gave them a special comprehensiveness. Whereas the Center formed part of the establishment in some of the South German states, particularly in Bavaria, the Social Democratic masses remained isolated. They were denounced for their internationalism as "fellows without a fatherland."

In their Erfurt party program of 1891, the Social Democrats demanded a general, equal, and secret system of voting in all elections and direct participation of the people in legislation through plebiscites. Twenty years later, in their manifesto before the elec-tions of 1912, which made them the strongest party in the Reichstag, the Social Democrats pressed for the introduction of a parliamentary government. The German workers were by no means conscious revolutionaries. In their modest dwellings, a portrait of the Kaiser was often found hanging side by side with a certificate of their time in the army and a picture of "the Counter-Emperor, August Bebel." Bebel, the son of a Prussian sergeant-major, as leader kept the reins of the party (known as the SPD) tightly in his hands and made it a model of cohesiveness and organization.

Through its efficient mass organization, its numbers, and its emphasis on doctrine in the party press, the SPD became the leading socialist party within the Second International between 1889 and 1914. "The German working class," wrote the French socialist leader Jean Jaurès after the Congress of the International in Copenhagen in 1910, "has an increasingly positive and strong will. It is marching by the light of an idea towards a new social order: but it knows it can only go there by stages. Through its cooperatives and unions it wants to become an immediate force. And it wants to transform political institutions, infuse them with democracy in order to make the guarantees of peace more sure and bring about social evolution more freely." [6] The strongest conviction Jaurès brought back from the congress at Copenhagen and a brief visit to Germany was "that neither Europe nor Germany itself forms an impenetrable block of conservatism and militarism." It was a fair, but all too optimistic verdict.

Compared with the SPD, the Center Party had less strength in the big industrial areas. Its strongholds were in regions with a predominantly Catholic population, such as Silesia, the Rhineland, and Bavaria. In the absence of a party congress, Catholic men of property and education played an influential role in it.

There were two conservative parties—the orthodox *Deutsch Konservative*, who had approved of anti-Semitism in their Tivoli Program of 1892, and the more liberal Free Conservatives, who dated from 1866, the year in which the pro-Bismarckian National Liberals had seceded from the intransigent Progressives. Both conservative parties relied for support on the pillars of the establishment, the landowning aristocracy, the civil servants, and the parsons of the Protestant Church.

The National Liberals had much support from heavy industry and the financiers. Like the Center they were largely a party of dignitaries (*Honorationen*), but remained more loosely organized than the parties on the left. [7] The left liberals represented perhaps the most individualistic and for many years the most fragmented party, though all of them were in favor of free trade. In 1910 the three existing left liberal groups amalgamated into the *Fortschrittliche Volkspartei* (Progressive People's Party) with a program that included a democratic franchise in the states and a ministry composed of parliamentarians.

Friedrich Naumann is perhaps the most interesting figure among the left-wing liberals. A Protestant parson in Berlin with an unusual understanding of the problems of modern mass society, he fully realized that the old establishment was out of date and that a new synthesis was needed between the modernized monarchy, the middle classes, and the workers. He failed in his efforts to bring about this synthesis. The German middle classes were disinclined to put pressure on their government and administration. Three German sayings often quoted before 1914 reflect their attitude: "Public servants are

[6] Quoted in James Joll, *The Second International* (London, 1955), p. 143.
[7] See Theodor Nipperdey, *Die Organisation der deutschen Parteien vor 1918* (Düsseldorf, 1961).

the State"; "Politics corrupts the character"; and "The best constitution is a good administration."

Max Weber, a judicious critic of the German political scene, deplored the power of the Wilhelminian bureaucracy and demanded the right of members of parliament to make and influence decisions. "A nation," he wrote in 1917, "that would *only* produce good officials, estimable clerks, honest merchants, capable scholars and technicians, and loyal servants, but would otherwise put up with the rule of *a bureaucracy free from control* behind pseudomonarchical phrases, would not be a nation of masters [*kein Herrenvolk*] and would do better to devote itself to its day-to-day affairs instead of being vain enough to bother about world destinies."

WELTPOLITIK AND WAR AIMS, 1890-1918

A. The "New Course" Under Four Chancellors

The dismissal of Bismarck by the young Emperor William II in March, 1890, caused a sensation both inside and outside Germany. For twenty years the "Iron Chancellor" had been the ultimate authority, the man who made the final decision in everything. Now the young Kaiser had forced the aging giant to submit his resignation. There had been disagreement between Bismarck and the new self-confident monarch over a variety of issues for some time. Obviously the Second Empire had been founded on a special relationship, that between an exceptional chancellor and a monarch who admired him and was quite willing to play second fiddle to his political genius. But the young William II thought differently. He wanted "to play first violin and be the conductor at the same time and the chancellor would at most have to play second violin beside him." [8]

The fact that members of parliament were excluded from the combined post of chancellor and Prussian prime minister narrowed the choices to the spheres of the court, the army and the diplomats. The choice fell on General Leo von Caprivi—an honest, straightforward character with a good deal of common sense, but lacking experience in the many fields that came under the competency of the chancellor's office. At home he was in favor of cooperation between all elements of the right, center, and left and

[8] Erich Eyck, *Das Persönliche Regiment Wilhelms II* (Zurich, 1948), p. 16.

opposed to a social revolution. In foreign affairs, he followed the personal whims of the Kaiser and the advice of Friedrich von Holstein, the most influential official in the foreign ministry. Shunning all public responsibility, Holstein was a suspicious and devious character who worked at the ministry seven days a week. He possessed a sharp intelligence and an unrivalled knowledge of foreign affairs, gained through his extraordinary industry; but he often functioned like a spider busy weaving his web of secret machinations and intrigue. Although earlier historians have been inclined to overrate his influence, Holstein's distrust of people and his sinister, deep pessimism were an undoubted handicap.

Caprivi had the courage to resign in October, 1894, having become tired of the caprices and impositions of the Kaiser. His immediate successor, Prince Chlodwig zu Hohenlohe-Schillingsfürst, former Prime Minister of Bavaria and German Ambassador to Paris, was unable to say no to the Kaiser's often erratic and unreasonable moves and decisions. Bernhard von Bülow who succeeded him as chancellor from 1900 to 1909, managed to handle his imperial master more skillfully and keep a better balance between him, his ministers, and the Reichstag. Like Metternich, Bülow was a master of tactics and expediency, although he lacked the ability to pursue the same aim consistently. In spite of undeniable brilliance, Bülow lacked moral strength, and his superficial amiability was not balanced by real conviction. Admiral Tirpitz, a stronger and more candid character, said of Bülow that an oiled eel was a leech compared with him.

What was the Kaiser's "New Course" after Bismarck's dismissal? With the decision not to renew the German Reinsurance Treaty with Russia, which, they argued, would undermine Austria's confidence in Germany, Holstein and the Kaiser were in favor of an independent stance that would allow Germany to choose between the British lion and the Russian bear as it suited her. In 1890, a German rapprochement with England, favored by Holstein, seemed to materialize through an agreement on the exchange of Heligoland and Zanzibar. The men in the German foreign ministry did not want to commit Germany to any particular foreign policy; they preferred to keep a "free hand," erroneously convinced as they were that Tsarist Russia and the Third Republic of France would never join hands. Yet the apparently impossible happened. The secret military convention concluded between the French and Russian chiefs of staff in 1893 was far-reaching. If either of the two powers was attacked by Germany or by another power with her support, both partners would turn on Germany. Their cooperation would last as long as the Triple Alliance existed on the other side.

In Germany, ex-Chancellor Bismarck expressed resentment and concern about the dilettantism of the "New Course," yet its champions put their confidence in the shifting focus of the international power struggle from Europe to Asia and Africa. With the imperialist interests of France and England clashing in Africa, and those of England and Russia in the Middle and Far East, it seemed safe to base German foreign policy on the dogma of the inevitable permanence of such antagonism. Indeed, Holstein and others in the Wilhelmstrasse hoped to compensate Germany for the loss of her close ties with Russia by a rapprochement with Britain. The trouble lay in the wobbly position of German foreign policy.

When in the spring of 1898 Joseph Chamberlain, Secretary of State for Colonies in Salisbury's cabinet, proposed to the German Ambassador in London, Count Hatzfeldt, an agreement between the two nations that would amount to a defensive alliance, he added significantly that if they should not reach such an understanding, England would have to come to terms with France or Russia. At that time German public opinion was sharply anti-British owing to England's action in the Boer War. For this and other reasons the German leadership neither accepted nor rejected Chamberlain's feeler, but encouraged Hatzfeldt in his attitude of "leaving the issue open."

Early in November, 1899, the Kaiser and Bülow, then Secretary of State for Foreign Affairs, visited London. A few days after their departure, Chamberlain, in a speech at Leicester, made a far-reaching plea for cooperation with "the Great German Empire," and stressed the similarity of the Anglo-Saxon and Teutonic races and the value of an alignment between England, the United States, and Germany. Bülow's reply in the Reichstag displayed little enthusiasm for the idea, and the disappointed Chamberlain felt he had been cold-shouldered.

Holstein's influence continued undiminished when Bülow became chancellor in October, 1900. He was opposed to German concessions to Britain on individual issues, but he demanded as a matter of principle that Britain join the Triple Alliance. This proved unacceptable to Salisbury and his cabinet. Some form of defensive Anglo-German alliance was then quite feasible, but the German demand for "all or nothing" turned out to be a fateful blunder.

While an Anglo-French rapprochement was regarded as un-
likely in Berlin, Chamberlain and the Foreign Secretary Lansdowne
turned to France. When the Entente Cordiale was signed in April,
1904, it had exactly the limited and specific character that the Germans had rejected in their plan for an Anglo-German pact. Anglo-
German relations remained ambiguous afterwards, due to a large extent to their naval rivalry during the decade before World War I.
At the end of the nineteenth century Germany was the leading
military power on the Continent, but only the sixth or seventh naval
power. Then Admiral von Tirpitz, the energetic, skillful, and purposeful State Secretary for the Navy for nearly twenty years (1897–
1916), proclaimed the need for a German navy "for the protection
of the country, against which even a first-rate naval power would
be unable to take the offensive." Tirpitz's ambitions were assisted
by the navy complex of the Kaiser, who coined the slogan that
"Germany's future lies on the water." In 1896, Germany possessed
only 6 battleships and 4 cruisers, compared with 33 and 130 respectively on the British side. By 1904 however, her navy stood in a relationship of 1:2 to Britain, and she was planning to change this ratio
to 2:3. When Britain tried to make her lead competition-proof by
building the new, superior type of dreadnought, she was displeased
to see the German navy soon follow suit. The Kaiser was not prepared to comply with the suggestion made by Edward VII during
a visit to Germany that the Germans either stop or slow down their
naval program. William II would rather fight, for to him, as he explained to his guests, it was "a question of national honor and dignity." And yet the Kaiser told the British public in his famous interview with the London *Daily Telegraph* in October, 1908, that they
were "mad, mad, mad as March hares" if they feared the German
fleet. He declared himself to be a true friend of England, but insisted
that Germany have a powerful fleet to protect her worldwide commerce and be able to champion her manifold interests in any quarter
of the globe.

The undiplomatic and tactless interview not only evoked a storm
of indignation in the Reichstag and the German press against the
Kaiser, but also led ultimately to the termination of Bülow's chancellorship. Bülow declared in the Reichstag that in the future nobody could take responsibility, and the authority of the crown would
not remain unimpaired if the sovereign did not show the necessary
restraint. The Kaiser never forgave him this public censure. When
Bülow's majority block of parties in the Reichstag broke down the

following spring over an increase in taxation, the chancellor was allowed to resign (July, 1909).

His successor, Theobald von Bethmann Hollweg, was not a diplomat but an administrator by training; he was a man of great integrity and industry, with many of the virtues of the Prussian official. Yet his position as chancellor was fraught with difficulties. He had to face much criticism for the actions of others in the Reichstag, where the opposing Social Democrats became the largest party in 1912. Bethmann's strength was his comparative sincerity, which created a foreign confidence that Bülow had never enjoyed. There was, however, a streak of Hamlet in him that made it hard for him to decide at the right moment. It must be said in fairness that probably only a man of the caliber of a Bismarck could have found a way out of the many waves of crisis in which the European powers found themselves embroiled, prodded as they were by strong army and naval interests and by an ever-growing emphasis on national prestige. Bülow had been unable to prevent the Anglo-Russian rapprochement that was highlighted by the agreement of the two powers in 1907 on Persia, Tibet, and the Far East. However, this was still an agreement of limited scope, and no obligations of military and diplomatic support ensued from it. In 1907 the two pacts—the Triple Alliance and the Triple Entente—still "stood side by side." Seven years later, however, they faced each other.

Between 1908 and 1913, the Moroccan and Balkan crises intensified the general feeling of insecurity and were responsible for stepping up the international armaments race. At the beginning of 1913, an army bill was submitted to the Reichstag increasing the strength of the German army by 130,000 men. In retaliation France extended the service of her recruits from two years to three. At the end of the year Russia augmented her army to 1,420,000 men compared with Germany's 761,000 (soon to grow to 820,000) and France's 750,000. Everywhere the prestige of the military—officers and general staffs—had grown dangerously while that of civilians, diplomats, and politicians had correspondingly decreased, particularly in Germany. Though few people wanted a war and even fewer had a clear concept of what a modern war would mean, the general belief in peace was in decline. Many felt that Europe was sitting on a powder keg and that any spark might explode it.

It is outside the scope of this book to examine the fateful developments leading from the assassination of Archduke Francis Ferdinand, the heir to the throne of Austria–Hungary, and his wife at the end of June to the outbreak of the European war early in August, 1914. Within ten days what first seemed a localized conflict between Austria–Hungary and Serbia developed into a world conflagration that was to determine the fate of millions of people. The Austrians, who, not without reason, regarded the Serbians responsible for the Sarajevo murders, sent a severe ultimate to Serbia. When all its stipulations, except one, were accepted by the Balkan power, Vienna was still not satisfied and declared war on Serbia. By this act the system of alliances, forged over forty years, came into operation. Backing Serbia, the Tsar ordered a general mobilization of the Russian army on July 31, and Germany promptly responded the next day by declaring war first on Russia and then on her ally France. These powers looked on Germany and Austria as aggressors. However, the fact that Germany was involved in war with the reactionary Tsarist system made it easier for the German Social Democrats to toe the line and fight in the defense of their "superior" country. After the German invasion of Belgium, an event that the harassed German Chancellor Bethmann Hollweg admitted represented a breach of international law, England declared war on Germany on August 4, a step few Germans expected.

In all the countries involved, the masses were enthusiastic about a war the duration and impact of which they did not foresee. It was as if an immense tension, fed everywhere by propaganda, had been released.[9] With many of their leaders the masses slid into the war as if it were nothing but a ferocious football match. All expected their side to win and the conflict to be decided by Christmas, 1914. It was a tragic illusion, and it made the opponents all the more inclined to pin the responsibility for the war on their enemies.

B. German Imperialism Before and After 1914

If imperialism was rife on all sides, the German brand of it had its specific character: there were imperialists both on the right and on the left. Those on the right gathered in a number of pressure groups such as the Pan-German League, the Naval League, and the Colonial Association. Although before 1914 the Pan-German League never had more than about 22,000 members, these belonged mainly to the economic and intellectual elite—professors, teachers, industrialists, merchants, and shipbuilders. Under its chairman, Heinrich

[9] See the interesting reflections by James Joll in his Inaugural Lecture, 1914: The Unspoken Assumptions (London, 1968).

Class, the League worked for the integration of all German elements throughout the world, adding a nebulous racism to a fierce nationalistic plea for the extension of the German state. The aim was an economic combination of all peoples of Teutonic origin in Europe and overseas, with a large colonial empire for German settlement and economic exploitation.

A liberal imperialist like Friedrich Naumann could ask the question in a popular pamphlet in 1897, "What is nationalism?" and define it as "the urge of the German people to spread their influence all over the globe." In addition to the emphasis on building a powerful navy, he demanded "the achieving of equality both in prestige and in actual fact, with the other world powers in the coming world system of states." Looking back, we can see that "the liberal imperialists and with them wide circles of the upper classes were prepared to accept the risk of a European war rather than renounce the ultimate offensive aim which they had set themselves at the turn of the century." [10]

Professor Fritz Fischer's massive work *Griff nach der Weltmacht* has caused a recent controversy about German war aims in World War I.[11] Basing his conclusions on an impressive amount of documentation, Fischer maintains that although the German government perhaps did not actually desire war in 1914, it was under the spell of the "risk of war" ideology and encouraged its only reliable ally, Austria–Hungary, to bring about a war with Serbia when it seemed doubtful that it could be localized.[12] This mentality was further reflected in the far-reaching, aggressive German war aims put forward during the first year of the war not only by various vested interests but, as Professor Fischer has shown, by the German government itself. Fischer reveals the consistency of Bethmann's outlook before and during the war. For some time before 1914, he had been in contact with men who favored the idea of a German-controlled Central Europe. He had also believed that if Germany avoided any suspicion of provocation in a war against Russia and France, Britain might content herself with "an intervention, at first diplomatic, in

---

[10] Ludwig Dehio, *Germany and World Politics in the Twentieth Century* (London, 1959), p. 76.

[11] *Grasping for World Power*, a more significant title than that of the English translation, *Germany's Aims in the First World War* (London, 1967).

[12] This view is also shared by the distinguished Italian historian Luigi Albertini. While not finding any of the nations participating in the world war guiltless (including his own), he underlines Germany's heavy responsibility for the Austrian declaration of war on Serbia.

favor of France after her defeat." Fischer has perhaps read too much into Bethmann's report of December, 1912, for it was intended to influence the Kaiser against the proposed heavy increases in the German navy, which the British regarded as German provocation. Was the German chancellor really as Fischer presents him, a full-fledged, incorrigible annexationist? One is more inclined to agree with Golo Mann's verdict that Bethmann was "conciliatory and weak, too weak to be entirely genuine, good-natured and eager for applause. He wanted to remain on top and please everyone. . . . And of course Bethmann thought in strictly monarchic and Prussian terms, and like most politicians of his day in most countries he was not always opposed to changes of frontier by war-like means. But an *Eroberungsbestie*, a 'beast of conquest,' he was not." [13]

On the other hand, in the flush of the startling initial successes of the German armies, Bethmann's blueprint for German war aims of September, 1914, became comprehensive. It demanded "security for the German Reich in the west and the east for all imaginable time." France had to be "so weakened as to make her revival as a great power impossible for all time." Russia was to "be thrown back as far as possible from Germany's eastern frontier and her domination over the non-Russian vassal peoples broken." [14] These demands were similar to, although not necessarily identical with, the ambitious schemes of conquest put forward in memoranda by the large industrial and agricultural vested interests during the next twelve months.

At first the Germans succeeded both in the west and the east. Following the Schlieffen Plan, they overran Belgium quickly and occupied Northern France; while in East Prussia General von Hindenburg and his subordinate, General Ludendorff, inflicted a heavy defeat on the Russian invaders at Tannenberg. However, the Battle of the Marne in September, 1914, put an end to the German advance on Paris and to German hopes of knocking France out of the war quickly. The movement of the war stopped. Between November, 1914, and March, 1918, the bitter trench fighting with its barbed wire, mines, and flame-throwers was practically static and never moved forward more than eight or ten miles. Both sides tried vainly

[13] Golo Mann, "1914: The Beast in the Jungle. Dr. Fritz Fischer's Thesis," *Encounter* (November, 1968).

[14] Later this demand was largely fulfilled by the harsh Treaty of Brest–Litovsk, imposed on Bolshevik Russia by the German high command in February, 1918.

to effect a breakthrough. In 1916, the Germans attempted to take Verdun and failed in spite of the heavy losses they inflicted on the French. Similarly, the French and English failed in Flanders and in the murderous Battle of the Somme. In the east the Germans did better, despite some Russian advances into Austrian territory in 1915 and 1916. Their major chance in the east came with the Russian Revolution of 1917, which shortly allowed the German armies to concentrate on the fight in the west.

The aura of the Kaiser, who was unable to provide effective leadership, gradually receded. The masses put their trust instead in Field Marshal Paul von Hindenburg and his ruthless right-hand man, General Erich Ludendorff, who had jointly taken over the Supreme Command of the war in August, 1916. Economics played an increasingly important role in the war. England effectively used the weapon of economic blockade, but suffered serious losses herself in shipping and imports through German U-boat warfare. While the German Battle Fleet, so highly publicized before the war, proved of little significance, the U-boat became the German "miracle weapon," or *Wunderwaffe*. The question of restrictions on the use of U-boats became a vital issue. As long as she felt she could not ignore the attitude of the neutral powers, particularly the United States, Germany had to exercise some moderation. In January, 1917, the Kaiser decided in favor of unrestricted U-boat warfare, which caused President Wilson to break diplomatic relations with Germany and to declare war on her three months later. The long-postponed German decision proved a major blunder, as her admirals' hope that the U-boat would force Britain to her knees within six months was not fulfilled.

At home food and textile rationing brought hardship. The townspeople resented the war profiteers and the peasants who seemed to be in a privileged position; and the bureaucratic centralism of the rationing departments in Berlin fostered a dislike in the provinces, particularly in South Germany. If in August, 1914, the nation had been united and the emperor could say that he no longer knew any parties but only Germans, by 1917 the political mood had changed considerably. The emperor's importance dwindled. The revolution in Russia encouraged left-wing elements in Germany who disapproved of the continuous support of the war effort by the Social Democrats. The radical deputies from the traditional party had already seceded in April, 1916, and had formed the Independent

Socialist Party. The group around the determined Marxist Karl Liebknecht even favored a Bolshevik revolution in Germany.

In July, 1917, three major parties in the Reichstag, the Social
Democrats, the Center Party, and the Progressive Liberals, passed a
joint resolution in favor of moderate war aims. They declared themselves against "forcible annexations of territory" and for a "peace
of understanding and lasting reconciliation." They were sharply re-
buked by right-wing forces that had quickly organized a new mass
movement, the "Fatherland Party," led by the retired Admiral von
Tirpitz. Mostly representing the ruling establishment, these people
opposed the efforts of the majority parties to progressively democra-
tize the political system. The first step towards a parliamentary monarchy came in November with the appointment of a prominent
figure in the Reichstag, the aged Bavarian leader of the Center
Party, Count Hertling, as chancellor and prime minister of Prussia.
He was the second successor to Bethmann Hollweg, whose resignation had been enforced in July by General Ludendorff and Mathias Erzberger, a radical member of the Center Party. With Hertling as chancellor, another South German, the Progressive Liberal
von Payer, was made vice-chancellor. However, the two men of the
Supreme Command of the war, Hindenburg and Ludendorff, were
still the real rulers, and they disapproved of the left's demand for
the reform of the flagrantly unequal Prussian franchise. Although
the Kaiser promised such a reform at Easter, 1918, the conservative
powers prevented its implementation. It was very short-sighted to
withhold an equal vote from millions of workers who did their duty
in the trenches and in the munitions factories. When massive strikes
occurred in Berlin and Leipzig early in 1918, some Social Democratic leaders like Fritz Ebert joined in. While their aim was still
a modernized democratic monarchy, the more radical socialists now
thought revolution inevitable.

In the spring of 1918, the German armies in the west made two
desperate large-scale attempts at a breakthrough on a broad front.
Although they gained territory and prisoners and inflicted considerable losses on the enemy, the German goals were not reached either
in March or in May, and both times the grim battle exhausted
itself.

After the shattering defeats suffered by the German armies in
France in August and September, 1918, and after a separate bid
for peace by the disintegrating Austro–Hungarian monarchy and

the defection of Bulgaria, it was again Ludendorff who, at the end of September, shortly before he resigned, demanded that a German offer of armistice be issued without delay. It is ironical that in order to make it more effective, this autocrat suggested the formation of a parliamentary German government and even recommended universal suffrage for Prussia. The liberal Prince Max von Baden, who a few days later followed Hertling as chancellor, formed a cabinet with representatives of the majority parties. He was convinced that what Germany needed was a parliamentary monarchy. Yet it proved too late to rescue the old order. On November 9, Prince Max announced the abdication of the hesitant Kaiser without obtaining his consent. On the same day the Kaiser reluctantly left his headquarters and traveled to Holland, where he was granted asylum for the rest of his mismanaged life. Two days earlier, Friedrich Ebert, the leader of the Social Democrats, had told Prince Max that if the Kaiser would not abdicate, a social revolution would be unavoidable. "But I don't want it," he had added, "I hate it like sin."

Traditionally accustomed to revere authority, to worship the association of *General Dr. von Staat* (to use Thomas Mann's term), the Germans had little talent for revolution. Few politicians wanted more than reform, and even fewer thought in terms of revolution. Undoubtedly the masses, often hungry and disillusioned from the impact of the blockade and the bad news from the front, desired an end to military rule and a greater say in politics. The unforeseen collapse of all the German dynasties created a psychological and institutional void, the importance of which can only now be seen in retrospect. The sudden end of the monarchy soon led to the rise of political *ersatz* religions and evoked a longing for integration that the republic was unable to satisfy but was later successfully exploited by Hitler and the National Socialist movement.

8

The Unlucky Republic, 1918-1933

"An Improvised Democracy"

At noon on November 9, 1918, Phillip Scheidemann, the Majority Socialist leader, proclaimed "the German Republic" outside the Reichstag building in Berlin. Two hours later, Karl Liebknecht, the leader of the Communists, hailed "a free socialist republic" outside the Royal Castle in the same city. These symbolic acts indicated two possible alternatives for the new regime after the old powers had collapsed: a democratic republic after the Western model, or a Soviet Republic of Workers and Peasants after the Bolshevik pattern. It was by no means ruled out that Germany might turn into a Soviet system, as Lenin and Trotsky then confidently expected. At the end of October, the sailors of the Battle Fleet went on strike, frustrating the plans of the admirals for a decisive engagement with the English. A spontaneous signal for a revolt quickly spread from Kiel to many other German cities. When a band of left-wing socialists and writers in Munich led by Kurt Eisner proclaimed a free state, Soviets of Workers, Soldiers, and Peasants were formed. Councils of disgruntled workers and home-based soldiers soon sprang up all over Germany. On November 10, the Central Council of these new institutions in Berlin confirmed that the supreme authority was for the time being with the Six People's Commissaries of whom three belonged to the Majority Socialists (Ebert, Scheidemann, and Landsberg) and three

169

to the more radical Independent Socialists (Haase, Dittmann, and Barth).

On the extreme left was the Spartacist group, led by Karl Liebknecht and the brilliant theorist Rosa Luxemburg. Toward the end of the year it transformed itself into the Communist Party of Germany. Regarding themselves as the vanguard of the armed workers' revolution, the Communists did not contest the elections to the National Assembly which, they declared, would "become an organ of the counterrevolution." Lenin was convinced that Ebert would turn out to be Germany's Kerensky and Liebknecht her Lenin. The prediction proved wrong, and not only because Liebknecht and Rosa Luxemburg were murdered by Free Corps officers in Berlin in January, 1919. Already in December, a Reich Congress of all German Workers' and Soldiers' Councils in Berlin had decided by a considerable majority in favor of democratic elections to a National Assembly. Much earlier, during the night of November 9, Ebert had concluded a pact with the High Command of the army, now headed by General Groener. The army was prepared to acknowledge the new regime and to support it against the Bolshevist threat. Thus the authoritarian army of the day before backed the democratic regime of the new order. Ebert asked everyone to remain at his post so that the country would "not become a prey to anarchy and terrible misery."

While the pact between the new republic and the old army was to prove a heavy burden to the regime, it maintained law and order for the time being. What with the trying circumstances of the continued Allied blockade, and famine, economic crises, strikes, and revolutionary division, at least the unity of Germany as a nation-state was saved. In November, 1918, militarism, the arrogant rule of officers, many of whom were young and inexperienced, was greatly resented by the masses, and their pacifist feelings were probably stronger than their desire for socialism. In a vague way the masses who had served with considerable discipline in the trenches and munitions factories pressed for their share in the political process. There was also much talk of workers' participation in managing farms and factories by way of advisory councils (*Betriebsräte*). In Bavaria even advisory councils of pupils in secondary schools were established, but such advanced ideas and efforts soon petered out.

Although neither of the socialist groups that formed the new government were in favor of Bolshevik experiments, their aims differed. The Independent Socialists announced that they had joined the Council of People's Commissaries "in order to strengthen the revolutionary socialist achievements." The attitude of the Majority Socialists (SPD) was much more pragmatic from the beginning. Disposed toward reforming rather than revolutionary aims, they insisted on parliamentary democracy, social reforms, equal suffrage for men and women, and reform of the civil service and local government. They also proposed a moderate program of nationalization. In the harsh circumstances of the winter of 1918–19, some form of compromise between the new powers and the representatives of the old order was perhaps inevitable with the demobilization of millions of soldiers, the changeover from a wartime to a hazardous postwar economy, and the need for supplies and transport. The great majority of the civil servants accepted, as they put it, "the facts of the situation," but they did so without enthusiasm.

The old powers tried to crawl back slowly and cautiously. "They accepted the new master—the SPD, though not the Independent Socialists—for the sake of maintaining order while doing every thing in their power to prevent a revolutionary transformation of society." [1] Many Social Democrats were formalists with little vision or political instinct. In spite of some recent criticism of the term, it is safe to say that the outcome of the November Revolution was "an improvised democracy." [2] German democracy had not arrived as the result of an intense political mass movement, but as the product of an emergency situation after the failure of a gigantic war effort. The lightning speed of this sudden event revealed that the old regime had lost all power of resistance.

There was a good deal of political window-dressing among the parties before the elections to the National Assembly. The Old Progressives now called themselves the "German Democratic Party," the National Liberals turned themselves into the "German People's Party," and even the authoritarian Conservatives appeared in the new garb of the "German National People's Party," while the now-independent Bavarian branch of the Center Party styled itself as the "Bavarian People's Party." In the reelections in January, 1919, in which women could vote for the first time, the two socialist parties did not reach the expected majority. Out of a total of 421 delegates, the Social Democrats obtained 163 and the Independent Socialists only 22. Among the nonsocialist parties, the Center with 91 mandates and the Democrats with 75 scored over the two parties of the right,

[1] Reinhard Rürup, "Problems of the German Revolution, 1918–19," *Journal of Contemporary History*, III (1960), 126.
[2] See Theodor Eschenburg, *Die improvisierte Demokratie* (Munich, 1963).

the German Nationalists (44) and Stresemann's German People's Party (22). The government, formed as the "Weimar Coalition" by the Majority Socialists, the Democrats and the Center, had a three-quarters majority. The assembly gathered in the small town of Weimar in Thuringia as a matter of expediency in order to avoid the political strife and unrest in Berlin. It also seemed to be a symbol of the cosmopolitan spirit of the city of Goethe and Schiller in contrast to the discarded autocracy of Potsdam.

The transition from the old semiautocratic rule to the new democracy had come too suddenly. Authoritarian habits were deeply rooted; and the sympathies of many judges, civil servants, and teachers were not extended to the new regime. The unmistakable bias of judges showed itself in the strikingly disparate sentences imposed on right-wing and left-wing extremists. "Between 1918 and 1922, assassinations traced to left-wing elements numbered twenty-two; of these, seventeen were rigorously punished, ten with the death penalty. Right-wing extremists on the other hand, found the courts sympathetic: of the 354 murders committed by them, only one was vigorously punished and not even that by the death penalty. The average prison sentence handed out to these political murderers reflects the same bias: fifteen years for the left, four months for the right." [3]

The severe conditions of the Treaty of Versailles were very reluctantly accepted by the new government, which was blamed for them by many in the upper and middle classes. As Winston Churchill observed, "The Weimar Republic with all its liberal trappings and blessings was regarded as an imposition of the enemy. It could not hold the loyalties and the imagination of the German people." As so often with complex events and attitudes in history, this was perhaps not clearly seen in the early years of the republic by most contemporaries; but the course of events has since confirmed the astuteness of Churchill's comment.

The republican constitution-makers in Weimar had to face a number of major problems. Among them were the election and role of the president, and his relationship with parliament; the problem of the second chamber; the question of a unitary or federal structure of the new Reich; the relations between it and the individual states, now more modestly called *Länder*. The position of the Reich president was clearly, though perhaps not altogether judiciously, designed. It was felt that only a president who was not dependent on parliamentary majorities could form a true counterweight to the new

[3] Peter Gay, *Weimar Culture* (New York and London, 1968), p. 20.

Reichstag. Elected by the people for seven years, the president was to represent the Reich in international law, appoint and dismiss its civil servants, and be its supreme commander of the armed forces. All the president's decrees had to be countersigned by the Reich chancellor. Yet in case of a serious threat to public security—and such emergency situations happened in 1919—the president was entitled under Article Forty-eight to take measures on his own to restore public order. The faults of this two-edged constitution were revealed in the short history of the republic, which was unable to develop either the strong leadership of a presidential democracy of the American type or the ability to compromise of a responsible parliamentary system of the parties.[4]

But these weaknesses were not discerned in 1919, as the first president Friedrich Ebert was elected by the National Assembly and enjoyed the full confidence of its majority. The cabinet ministers, led by the chancellor, were responsible to the Reichstag. The suffrage was extended to women. Although the second chamber, or Reichsrat, had considerably less power than its predecessor in the Second Empire, it was again entirely composed of representatives of the Länder. As no Land could have more than two-fifths of the seats in the Reichsrat and as the offices of Reich chancellor and premier of Prussia were no longer held by the same person, the hegemony of Prussia had ceased to exist. Unfortunately the Weimar Constitution, described by President Ebert as "the freest in the world," came into operation six weeks after the German government accepted and signed the unpopular Peace Treaty of Versailles in June, 1919, a heavy burden which its opponents exploited to the full.

During the republic, no party ever obtained an absolute majority, not even in the elections of March, 1933, after Hitler had become chancellor. It was ominous, however, that the clear majority of the three parties of the Weimar Coalition of January, 1919, disappeared in the next election in June, 1920; instead of 77.7 percent of the total vote, the three parties this time polled only 44.9 percent. On the other hand, their opponents on the right increased their votes from 5.6 to 9.1 million and those on the left, including the Communists, from 2.1 to 5.3 million. The echo of Versailles, the deteriorating economic situation, and the state crisis evoked by the unsuccessful militarist Kapp *Putsch* (coup) in March, 1920, had all helped to

---

[4] In fact, during the Weimar period "the country was governed either by unpopular minority governments, by internally weak Grand Coalitions or finally by extraparliamentary authoritarian Presidential Cabinets." Karl Dietrich Bracher, *The German Dictatorship* (New York, 1970), p. 75.

undermine confidence in the Weimar regime. From 1920 until 1930, only minority cabinets or cabinets based on a "great coalition" were possible, the latter ranging from Stresemann's German People's Party to the Social Democrats, or from the Center to the German Nationalists, with the cracks of the internal tensions papered over.[5] The practice of "party barter" (*Kuhhandel*) developed, and the frequent turnover of cabinets gradually discredited the parliamentary system in the eyes of many voters. (The average life of the twenty cabinets of the republic was eight and one-half months.)

The socialists were represented in only eight of the twenty cabinets of the republic, and furnished a chancellor in three of them. The key position of the Center Party, on the other hand, is evident through its participation in all cabinets until the end of the Brüning government in May, 1932. In nine of them the Center provided the chancellor. By 1923, the scourge of inflation had reached its peak and had financially ruined sections of the middle classes, pensioners, and others living on a fixed income. The year began with the French occupation of the Ruhr and with President Poincaré playing Shylock and insisting on his pound of flesh—or better—coal, which was short in Germany's reparation deliveries. It ended in November with the Munich rebellion of Bavarian Premier Kahr and the Reichswehr General von Lossow pitted against the Reich government, which Adolf Hitler, leader of the small party of National Socialists, unsuccessfully tried to turn into a march on Berlin. In any case, the subsequent election of May, 1924, reflected the general shock and lack of confidence in the republican parties. The election reduced the Social Democrats to 100 seats, 6 less than the German Nationalists had achieved. The Communist Party rose from 17 to 62 seats; and the block of racialists, including Nazis, obtained 32 seats, which was more than the Democrats, who with only 28 deputies were on the downgrade. Yet in the following elections, held only seven months later in December, 1924, the stabilization of the mark through the stratagems of Dr. Luther, Minister of Finance, and of Dr. Schacht, President of the Reichsbank, and Stresemann's rapprochement with England and France, bore fruit. The spectre of extremism disappeared, the communists lost one-third of their seats, and the racialists more than one-half. On the other hand the socialists rose to 131 seats; all the parties in the middle improved their vote, but so did the German Nationalists, who reached 103 seats. By 1928, however,

[5] Cabinets of the Weimar coalition parties were, however, frequent in Prussia until 1932.

the Nationalists lost 30 seats while the Majority Socialists nearly doubled their number. Apart from the Center, there were too many weak, splinter parties in the middle. The outcome of the 1928 elections was the last "great coalition," led by the Social Democrat Hermann Müller as chancellor with Dr. Stresemann still as foreign minister. However, the steep rise in unemployment led soon afterwards to a sharp controversy between the deputies of the German People's Party and their Social Democratic colleagues in the cabinet.

With the dangerously growing number of unemployed, the cabinet had to either decrease its payments to the unemployed or force the employers and employees to make greater contributions to the Reich Insurance for the Unemployed. A reasonable compromise proposal was rejected by the socialist minister of labor, and in March, 1930, the "great coalition" came to an inglorious end. This was a fateful decision which played into the hands of the enemies of the republic. The sectional interests of the trade unionists had won out over any need to continue with an unspectacular government that enjoyed a clear majority in parliament. The next cabinet was headed by the Centrist, Dr. Heinrich Brüning. With him began a number of minority cabinets based on the authority of the president. Although the Social Democrats did not join Dr. Brüning's government, they tolerated it, along with the unpopular cuts the chancellor had to make in the budget and the salaries of public servants and workers. As the outcome of the growing avalanche of unemployment and dissatisfaction with the government's drastic attempts to contain the economic crisis, in the dramatic elections of September 1930 the moderate parties, including the Social Democrats, suffered heavy losses to the communists and the National Socialists, who became overnight the second strongest party in the Reichstag (the SPD still held first place).

Gustav Stresemann: Man of Compromise

Stresemann (1878–1929) was both the leading figure in his own party, the German People's Party (DVP), and an outstanding minister of foreign affairs from 1923 until his death in 1929.[6] He

---

[6] For recent interpretations of Stresemann's career and policies, see particularly Hans W. Gatzke, *Stresemann and the Rearmament of Germany* (Baltimore, 1954); Henry Ashby Turner, Jr., *Stresemann and the Politics of the Weimar Republic* (Princeton, 1963); and Anneliese Thimme, *Gustav Stresemann* (Hanover and Frankfurt, 1957).

came from the petty bourgeoisie in Berlin. After studying economics, he made his way as a manager in industrial organizations. In 1902 he founded the "Association of Saxonian Industrialists." In 1907 he was elected as a National Liberal to the Reichstag.

Ten years later he took over the leadership of his party. In the controversy over Germany's war aims, Stresemann was a committed annexationist. He was not opposed to a certain amount of democratization of the regime in internal matters; yet the November Revolution took him by surprise and embittered him. However, in the end he accepted the new situation.

At the end of 1918, some members of the left wing of the National Liberals joined with former Progressives in forming the new German Democratic Party, while most of the National Liberals followed Stresemann into the new German People's Party (DVP), which took its place to the right of the Democrats and to the left of the German Nationalist Party (DNVP). In the 1920 elections to the Reichstag, the German People's Party, which had received considerable support from the Ruhr industrialists, rose from twenty-two to sixty-five seats and became a political factor under Stresemann's flexible but firm leadership. The DNVP now entered the cabinet. Strangely enough, it was the assassination of the Center politician Erzberger in 1921 and of Rathenau, the foreign minister, in 1922 that led to Stresemann's greater commitment to the republic. During the chaotic year 1923 he at first fully supported the policy of the government of Chancellor Cuno of passive national resistance to the French occupation of the Ruhr. By August, however, the German economic situation had become desperate. One American dollar was equal to one million Marks, and long queues gathered outside the food shops. When the Social Democrats demanded that the policy of passive resistance be given up, the Cuno government fell and Stresemann became chancellor. By the end of September, he revoked the passive resistance. The national situation was turbulent. National unity was threatened by the left in Saxony, where a coalition government of socialists and communists had been formed, and from the right-wing government in Bavaria, which under Gustav von Kahr obstructed the execution of orders from Berlin. On November 8, Hitler proclaimed the national revolution in Munich in a sudden attempt to bully the conservative nationalists around Kahr and the rebellious Reichswehr General von Lossow into submission. In this emergency the cabinet in Berlin entrusted General von Seeckt with the Supreme Command of the army. Seeckt was not prepared to put up with the Munich revolt. After the Munich police had quashed the Hitler coup on November 9, there was no further talk of a march on Berlin.

Although Stresemann's chancellorship only lasted 100 days, he continued to hold the post of foreign minister successfully for the rest of his life. Stresemann pursued a policy of cautious revisionism in foreign affairs, which was backed by his own party and the parties of the former Weimar coalition. It aimed at the elimination of Allied military control of Germany, an early evacuation of French troops from the Rhineland, and a gradual diminution of German reparation payments. Though never mentioned by him in public, Stresemann also favored an annexation of Austria and a peaceful revision of Germany's eastern frontiers. To strengthen this policy, he felt that Germany should become a member of the League of Nations. The German Nationalists were emphatically against his insistence on the need for some accommodation with the new and more moderate governments in England and France. Stresemann was a pragmatist of genius. He recognized the realities of the postwar situation and wished to take advantage for his country of the gradual changes on the international scene. At the London Conference in August, 1923, Stresemann achieved what he had postulated during the previous year: support for the stabilization of the Mark, for which Dr. Schacht's Rentenmark had paved the way, through a loan of 800 million gold Marks from American bankers, the concession from Herriot for the evacuation of the Ruhr within a year, and a new regulation of the complex reparation issue. This was done by the Dawes Commission, which based its proposal expressly "on the assumption that the fiscal and economic unity of Germany will be restored." Although there was some fierce resistance from German Nationalists, in the end the necessary two-thirds majority for acceptance of the Dawes Plan was obtained in the Reichstag.

Stresemann went further in his efforts to bring Germany back into the comity of nations and achieve a revision of the Peace Treaty. Stresemann agreed with the idea of a mutual four-power security pact in Western Europe, first put forward at the end of 1923 by Lord D'Abernon, the enterprising British ambassador in Berlin. He felt that such an arrangement would free Britain to side with Germany in case of a new French march into the Ruhr. After lengthy negotiations between the four major powers, the final version of the security pact, signed in Locarno, Switzerland, on October 16, 1925, corresponded largely to Stresemann's blueprint. Belgium, France, and Germany agreed to refrain from any revision of their mutual boundaries, with Britain and Italy acting as guarantors. Yet there was an ominous omission. When France required a similar territorial guarantee for Germany's eastern frontier, Britain vetoed the idea. Stresemann refused any permanent settlement of Germany's eastern frontier. Instead, France and her eastern allies had to be satisfied with noncompulsory arbitration treaties between Germany and Poland and Germany and Czechoslovakia. Stresemann scored a further success at Locarno. Britain, France, and Italy agreed to sponsor Germany's nomination for membership in the League of Nations and for a permanent seat on its Council. After some unfortunate delays, Germany at last took her seat at Geneva during the autumn session of 1926.

On the other hand, the signing of the Locarno Pact made Soviet Russia suspicious of Germany's cooperation with the West. Stresemann had known for some time of the secret arrangements between Germany and the Soviet Union to facilitate German rearmament, but he placed a smaller value on their importance than did his antagonist General von Seeckt, the head of the Reichswehr. Stresemann had no high opinion of the military potential of the Soviet Army. In September, 1922, Seeckt in a secret memorandum to Chancellor Wirth had already stressed the need for close German cooperation with Russia at the expense of Poland. What Seeckt desired in the early 1920s, Hitler was to achieve later in 1939. Stresemann, however, was averse to such a drastic course. All he conceded was the need for a balanced position in Germany. With a view to placating both the Soviet Union and the German Nationalists, he agreed to the Treaty of Berlin of April, 1926, which reaffirmed the pledge of friendship between Germany and the Soviet Union of the Rapallo Treaty of 1922, and committed both parties to remain neutral in the event of an attack upon the other by a third power.

The bitter attacks on the foreign minister by the German Nationalists reached a new peak of fury in 1929 on account of his acceptance of the Young Plan, which put Germany's reparation payments on a different basis. Though the stipulations were hardly a masterpiece of constructive policy, they provided for a considerable reduction of the annual reparation sums in the near future and prepared the ground for an early evacuation of French troops from the Rhineland. When agreement on the Young Plan was reached in the summer of 1929, French Premier Briand agreed at last to the final withdrawal of the French occupation forces in the Rhineland by June 30, 1930, five years before the date stipulated in the Versailles

Treaty. It was a great achievement by Stresemann, but it came too late. He died on October 3, 1929. Three years later, at the Conference of Lausanne in June, 1932, Germany's reparations were reduced to a final payment of 3 billion gold Marks, which in fact was never made. Stresemann's policy had been justified, yet his name was maligned viciously by German Nationalists of all shades.

To sum up, Stresemann was neither a "good European" nor a crafty Machiavellian, as he has been depicted by different observers. He was a realist who thought primarily in nationalist terms as did most other statesmen of the age. He did not differ profoundly in this from Bismarck. His remark in 1927 was characteristic of his basic attitude in politics: "Nothing great created in this world has ever proved lasting without compromise."

It is to Stresemann's enduring credit that in his last ten years he preferred sober insight to indulgence in illusions. "There exists a great powerful party of Germans," he said in 1926. "They are the ones who are praying: 'Give us this day our daily illusion.' He who fights this party must have the courage to be unpopular."

Two Presidents: From Ebert to Hindenburg

Friedrich Ebert, the first president of the republic, (1919–1925), was a man without much education but who possessed a good deal of common sense and courage. As chairman of the Social Democratic Party from 1913 to 1919, he had acquired considerable political experience. Essentially a moderate, he possessed a singular strength of purpose and a wider vision than other leading members of his party. Stresemann was impressed by Ebert's tact and his insistence that the presidency must be a nonpartisan symbol of unity. Yet Stresemann told Lord D'Abernon that in Germany the man in the street, different from the intellectual, had "no affection for Ebert. . . . The truth is that the Germans do not want a president in a top hat. . . . He has to wear a uniform and a chest full of medals. When they see a man who wears a top hat as leader and who looks as though he might be a neighbor, then each says to himself, 'I could do that, too.' " [7] During his last years of office, Ebert felt obliged to bring a number of court actions for slander and libel. The constant abuse and the calumnies directed against him undermined Ebert's health and hastened his death at the age of fifty-four, in February, 1925.

[7] Quoted in Erich Eyck, A History of the Weimar Republic (Cambridge, Mass., 1962), I, 333.

There were seven candidates in the March election for president, ranging from the Communist Ernst Thaelmann on the extreme left to General Ludendorff, the candidate of the extreme right. The largest vote of 10 million went to the candidate of the moderate right, Dr. Jarres. The Social Democrats obtained 7.8 million votes for Otto Braun, prime minister of Prussia, and the Center Party nearly 4 million for Wilhelm Marx, a former chancellor. As none of the candidates achieved the required absolute majority, a second election in April was arranged, for which a simple majority would suffice. By a masterstroke Admiral Tirpitz suggested the military father-figure of the old regime, Field Marshal Paul von Hindenburg, as a new candidate of the right, and persuaded that retired warrior to accept the nomination in the national interest. The man whose portrait hung in countless German houses, it was felt, would appeal to many more than the usual voters on the right. The calculation proved right. Hindenburg was elected by 14.6 million votes compared with his two rivals, the Centrist Wilhelm Marx (13.7 million), also supported by the Social Democrats and the Democrats, and the Communist Thaelmann (1.9 million). There was an ominous ring in Stresemann's comment after his first meeting with the new president: "The main thing is not to let irresponsible people gain influence over him." (This was exactly what happened later after 1930.)

During his first years of office, Hindenburg rather disappointed his traditional friends, the German Nationalists. When in 1930 the bill that accepted the Young Plan for the settlement of German reparations (which was more favorable than the Dawes Plan) was passed by a majority in the Reichstag and signed by Hindenburg, the nationalist right, including General Ludendorff, abused the president. Hindenburg's relations with Chancellor Brüning, who was appointed in March, 1930, were odd. An outstanding member of the Center Party, Heinrich Brüning was a man of considerable intelligence and undoubted integrity. He had once worked in the Catholic trade union movement and was sympathetic to the worker. He had proved himself as an officer in the First World War. From that time he had retained a veneration for Field Marshal von Hindenburg that he was unable to discard when, as chancellor, he had to work with him as Reich president. With all his qualities Brüning "was not a skillful negotiator, he lacked the agility, the cunning, but also the absence of scruples and the demonic features of a Stresemann." [8]

[8] Theodor Eschenburg, op. cit., p. 248.

Yet the sinister tide of mass unemployment and political radical-ism on the right and left made the problems facing any chancellor of a dangerous magnitude. With the increasing political instability after the Reichstag elections of 1930 and the spectacular gains of the Nazis, it seemed imperative to Brüning that Hindenburg remain president for a second term; he persuaded the reluctant president to run again in the elections of 1932 and worked incessantly for his election. Yet the political constellation was now very different from that in 1925, when Hindenburg had been elected partly as a symbol of the faded glory of the old imperial colors, and partly as a stabiliz-ing factor. Seven years later, the ship of state was in much greater danger from the totalitarian mass movement of the extreme right.

Again, two ballots proved necessary in the presidential election. The two major candidates in both were Hitler and Hindenburg. The latter, Protestant Prussian and an old monarchist, was now supported by the Catholic Center Party, the Social Democrats, the trade unions, and the Jews. There was also an independent candidate sponsored by Hugenberg's Nationalist Party, Colonel Duesterberg, a leader of the ex-soldiers' organization, *Stahlhelm*, while the Communists ran Thael-mann once more. This time Hindenburg missed an absolute majority in the first vote by only 0.4 percent. Duesterberg, withdrew before the second vote, and the Field Marshal won a clear majority of 53 per-cent with 19,359,000 votes, as compared to Hitler's 13,417,000 and a mere 3,706,000 for Thaelmann.

Although Hindenburg's reelection was undoubtedly a success for Brüning too, Hindenburg brought about his resignation and that of his cabinet less than two months later. Brüning's dismissal was caused by backstairs intrigues in which General Kurt von Schleicher, head of the Minister's Office of the Reichswehr Ministry and close friend of Hindenburg's son, Oskar, played a leading part. Schleicher had earlier caused the downfall of his former patron, the Minister of the Interior, General Groener. Hindenburg, now eighty-two and becoming more and more inept, told Brüning soon after his reelection, with tears in his eyes: "I must turn right. The newspapers and the whole nation demand it. But you have always refused to do so."

After his resignation, Brüning recommended Goerdeler, later to become a leading figure in the anti-Hitler resistance, as his successor; but instead, Hindenburg chose Franz von Papen on Schleicher's advice. Before his fall, Brüning had been about to gain considerable concessions from the victors of 1918 on the issues of German repara-tions and rearmament. Schleicher, the grey eminence of German politics, had selected Papen for his conservative authoritarian attitude and his social poise; but in fact, in the words of K.D. Bracher, "no chancellor was ever chosen more frivolously." Papen had the confidence of Hindenburg and of Hugenberg's German Nationalists, but no other party supported him, not even the Center Party of which he had been a member. Papen, who aimed at a presidential dictatorship and vainly tried to bring Hitler into the government in August, 1932, achieved little during the six months of his rule. His most daring action was the forceful removal of the coalition government in Prussia under the socialist premier Otto Braun, in July, 1932. No resistance was offered.

Two elections to the Reichstag were held during the Papen regime. In the first, in July, 1932, the Nazis managed to increase their deputies from 107 to 230, but in the second, in November, they lost 34 seats and 2 million votes. Yet Papen now had hardly any support in the Reichstag, and a Communist motion of no-confidence was accepted with 513 against 32 votes. Schleicher, a cunning soldier and man of the world, had made Papen chancellor and now unmade him; he became his successor on December 2. Yet Schleicher's attempts to stem the brown tide proved an utter failure. He tried in vain to split the National Socialists by including the moderate National Socialist Gregor Strasser as vice-chancellor in his cabinet. The Socialists refused Schleicher's plan to build up a provisional authoritarian government in conjunction with the trade unions after they had created a general strike that was supported by the army. Papen took his revenge by entering into secret negotiations with Hitler in Cologne early in January, 1933, for an alliance between the Nazis, whose fortunes were at a low ebb at the end of 1932, and Hugenberg's Nationalists. Hitler insisted that he become chancellor and that the non-Nazi members of his cabinet agree to the elimination of Communists, Social Democrats, and Jews from public life. Hindenburg, who had previously not concealed his dislike of the "Austrian corporal's" entry into the government, now permitted Papen to pursue negotiations behind Schleicher's back. On January 30, the new cabinet took office with Hitler as chancellor and Papen as vice-chancellor. There were only two other National Socialists in it: Hermann Göring, prime minister of Prussia, and Frick, who was in charge of the Ministry of the Interior, which controlled the police. The sanguine Papen saw himself as a lion-tamer. "What more do you want?" he said to a conservative critic, "I have the confidence of Hindenburg. In two months, we shall have pushed

Hitler squealing into the corner." [9] It was an astonishing miscalculation by a man who had not even bothered to discuss with Hitler what policies the new government intended to pursue.

NATIONALISM DURING THE WEIMAR REPUBLIC

The Conservative Revolution

Nationalism in Germany between 1919 and 1933 displayed both traditional and new features. After defeat in the war and the sudden collapse of the old order in 1918, nationalism drew on injured pride, on a feeling of great loss in national prestige and wealth. This feeling was strongest among the former officers and other notable public servants, many of whom resented the change and the need for readjustment. Perhaps their resentment of the dictates of the Treaty of Versailles was natural, but their urge to find scapegoats and to make them responsible for the national disaster became pathological. The "stab in the back" legend that was spread by Nationalists like General Ludendorff and Professor P. N. Cossmann, a publicist in Munich, alleged that the German armies had not been defeated in battle, but had been forced to surrender owing to the treacherous subversive elements at home—the socialists and Jews who had engineered Germany's downfall. It is true that Jews had become more prominent in the political life of the republic than in the old empire; but their political views differed as widely as, for instance, those of Kurt Eisner, the radical socialist in Bavaria, and of Walter Rathenau, the far-sighted industrialist and foreign minister—both of whom fell to the bullets of nationalist fanatics.

If many people of the older generation were frustrated, resentful, or at least apathetic to the unglamorous new order the younger people were often bewildered and indifferent to politics, but they had an urge for a deeper orientation in their lives. The new nationalism was also less class-bound than the old and was more directed to the masses. Another characteristic of it was the cult of the life-force as opposed to mere intellect and reason, a belief in the irrational rather than in the rational. This worship of life and its corollary, the rejection of the critical function of the mind, permeated much of the antidemocratic and neonationalist thought. There was a great longing for a return to national community (*Gemeinschaft*) as opposed

[9] K. D. Bracher in *The Road to Dictatorship: Germany 1918–1933* (London, 1964), p. 118.

to the soulless contours of urbanized civilization. The drab, impersonal dealings of republican politicians was to be replaced by an organic, hierarchical system that was conceived by some as authoritarian, by others as a *Ständestaat*, a state based on a corporative system as in fascist Italy. Nationalism of the pre-Nazi kind meant a restoration, a "conservative revolution"—a term first coined by the Austrian poet and essayist Hugo von Hoffmannsthal. This paradoxical slogan envisaged a return to the values but not to the institutions of the Second Empire.

During the 1920s the grim experiences of World War I found literary expression in a number of novels that caused a stir. Their authors clearly belonged to two different schools. Novelists of the left wished to expose the shallowness and murderous futility of modern warfare—the raw deal experienced by the simple soldier. Novels like *Der Streit um den Sergeanten Grischa* by Arnold Zweig and *All Quiet on the Western Front*, a best-seller by Erich Maria Remarque, described the grim conditions on and behind the frontlines and illustrated with bitter irony the petty power of the commissioned and noncommissioned officers who were often, though not always, hated by their men.

The second type of war novel was more positive, although it did not tend to glorify life in the trenches. Using a precise and economic narrative, these novels undertook to recapture something of the hell of massive battle with the roar of big guns and the dramatic sordidness of clashing tanks. Ernst Jünger is the outstanding representative of this school. In his novels the war appears as a supreme test of endurance. As he puts it in the preface to *The Copse 125* (1925), a vivid account of a small but savage encounter between German and English troops near Arras in Northern France: "There is no good in asking 'What was the use of it all?' for we stood on the threshold of a realm that surpassed the limits within which a practical purpose can exist. Immortal deeds are absolute and from their outset stand in a realm apart. For the people, they are an eternal fount of strength. We survivors will always be proud to have belonged to the youth of such a time." If Jünger idealized the modern hard-bitten type of soldier, he set him side by side with the modern worker, the representative of the new age of technological progress and precision. The workers and soldiers of Jünger's visions formed the elite of their country, and they would respect the same elite in other nations.

Though profound and elegantly presented, Jünger's ideas were not those of a political philosopher. The case was different with Oswald Spengler, whose massive and fatalistic philosophy of history *The Decline of the West* caused a sensation at the end of the First World War.

Like the earlier and much more influential thinker Friedrich Nietzsche (1844–1900), Spengler scorned the belief in progress and universal humanitarianism. Instead he propagated a new synthesis in *Prussianism and Socialism* (1919). In this short book he castigated liberalism as an English invention that had befogged German professors and literati. Liberalism and Marxism were both declared obsolete. There was "for the workers only Prussian socialism or nothing" and "for the State only democratization or nothing." Similarly, there existed for the conservatives "only the choice between deliberate [Prussian] socialism or annihilation." Yet if Spengler recognized Germany's need for democratization, he also insisted that it needed "to get rid of the forms of Anglo-French democracy." Germany, he claimed had its own.

His intense dislike of liberalism was fully shared by Moeller van den Bruck. He too believed in a conservative regeneration that would produce a truly German type of socialism. To him Woodrow Wilson, the architect of the Treaty of Versailles, was the incarnation of liberal hypocrisy. In his book *Das Dritte Reich* (1925) Moeller demanded a party above all parties that would be all-embracing and both conservative and revolutionary.[10] The Germans should reject the parliamentary system of the Weimar Republic and put their faith into a mystical, neoconservative Third Empire that was to renew Europe. Moeller van den Bruck ended his life in despair in 1925. The Nazis took over his term of the "Third Reich" without acknowledging their debt to his ideas.

Hitler's Program

In this context we must briefly consider the main features of the program of the National Socialist German Workers' Party, formulated in Munich by Adolf Hitler in February, 1920. Founded by Anton Drexler, it was then only one of many extreme racialist and nationalist organizations that had developed in Bavaria after the dubious experiment with a soviet republic in the spring of 1919. Compared to the often vague ideas of Jünger and Moeller, the

[10] There is a condensed English translation by E. O. Lorimer, *Germany's Third Empire* (London, 1934).

Twenty-five Points Program of the NSDAP is clear, definite, and direct. Where the nationalist authors suggest, Hitler's small party *demands*—a phrase that appears again and again in the program. Mainly appealing to the *Mittelstand*, the various sections of the middle classes, including the farmers, it is clearer in its nationalist than in its "socialist" demands. The party was aggressively revisionist and propounded the idea of a "Greater Germany." What was new in this platform was the argumentation. "We demand, on the basis of the right of national self-determination, the union of all Germans to form one Greater Germany" (Point 1). There was also the popular demand for juridical equality for the German people and the abolition of the Peace Treaties of Versailles and St. Germain (Point 2). Hitler's later emphasis on the need for more "living space" was anticipated in the demand for "territory and soil [colonies] for the nourishment of our people and for settling our surplus population" (Point 3). Anti-Semitism was much emphasized. "No Jew may be considered a member of the nation" (Point 4). Jews were also to be barred from holding any official appointment on a federal, state, or local level. The parliamentary system was denounced as corrupt (Point 6).

The program reflected a new worship of power on a racialist basis. The individual lived for the nation-state and owed it his full allegiance, but the state in its turn had obligations to further the health and education of full citizens and to provide the means of livelihood for them. There should be state control of the press with the right to determine who may edit and contribute to newspapers (Point 23)—demands that were promptly implemented when Hitler came to power by the institution of the Reich Press Chamber and by a special law for the editors of the press. It was a program for national integration in which the German worker would also eventually find an honored though by no means a leading place. However, Hitler's party was then appealing much more to "the healthy middle class (*Mittelstand*)," the creation and maintenance of which was expressly demanded in Point 16. It is true that under the influence of an idealistic economist, Dr. Gottfried Feder, the program demanded "the abolition of incomes unearned by work, and emancipation from the slavery of interest charges" (Point 11), as well as "the nationalization of all business combines [trusts]" (Point 13). However, Hitler soon made a telling distinction between "destructive capital" and "productive capital," confining Jewish businesses and financial interests largely to the first category. As far as the Nazis had any clear-cut policy, their aim was said to protect the interests of the small shop keeper and businessman and the farmer and artisan from the onslaught of communism and the encroachment by the destructive (Jewish) capital.

Hitler was constantly haunted by fear of an international conspiracy of destructive forces that were threatening to destroy the physical and economic health of the German nation.[11] At the same time he took advantage of the economic crises that shook the German middle classes and other strata during the inflation of 1922–23 and again during the worldwide economic slump after 1929. Although mass unemployment on the second occasion played into his hands, it was largely the badly shaken middle classes who, under the spell of the "fear of freedom" [12] and in a desperate longing for security, listened to the crude but effective gospel of the one-party state and the simplification of all problems and worries according to "one Leader, one nation, one Reich [empire]."

What was new in the Hitler movement was its calculated dynamics—the use of fresh political techniques and tricks in which Hitler and his propaganda chief Goebbels proved past masters. The Nazis were, for instance, the first political party to make use of the airplane as a handy means of transportation that enabled the Führer to speak on the same day to several large audiences in towns hundreds of miles apart. It was then that Goebbels coined the propaganda slogan "Hitler über Deutschland" ("Hitler over Germany"). The fall of the Weimar Republic must be seen as the result of complex causes, and amongst them, the dynamics of the Nazi activists was of considerable importance in a period of widespread insecurity.

WHO VOTED FOR THE NATIONAL SOCIALISTS?

Two questions have to be asked here: First, who supported Hitler's party while it was still small and politically insignificant? It had only 27,000 members in 1925. Two years later the figure rose to 72,000 and by 1928 to 108,000. These members were a motley crowd, comprising many young people who were attracted by the aggressive dynamics and bold techniques of Hitler and of his henchmen. Others were disgruntled ex-officers and soldiers with a nostalgia for the glories of a better past. The bulk, however, belonged to the petite bourgeoisie and included many small shopowners, artisans, and

[11] See Ernst Nolte, *Three Faces of Fascism* (London, 1965), pp. 102–9.
[12] See Erich Fromm, *The Fear of Freedom* (London, 1960).

clerks who were often filled with both anticapitalist resentment and fear of proletarization. Manual workers, on the other hand, were as rare in the party as public servants and academics.[13] The unemployed joined in larger numbers only after 1928, when the new economic slump began to throw a sinister shadow onto the short-lived economic recovery. After 1930, we find a high percentage of unemployed in the ranks of Hitler's paramilitary force, the Stormtroopers (S.A.)—2,600 out of a total of 4,500 men in Hamburg, for instance. The electoral successes of his party between 1930 and 1932 differed a good deal in their regional and social composition. The Nazis polled highest in Protestant areas with strong agrarian and petite bourgeois elements. In Schleswig–Holstein, for instance, which had already experienced serious social unrest among the hard-pressed peasants before 1930, the Nazis gained 51 percent of the total vote in July, 1932. Of the remaining eight constituencies with the highest National Socialist vote in the same election, all except two—Chemnitz in industrial Saxony and the Palatinate in the west —had a predominantly agrarian and Protestant majority of voters. By contrast, in ten of the eleven constituencies with the lowest percentage of Nazi votes, the majority were Catholics; in one of them, Cologne–Aachen, Hitler's party scored just over 17 percent. Further in such major cities as Berlin, Hamburg, Leipzig, Düsseldorf, and Cologne, the Hitler vote constantly remained considerably under the average percentage for the whole of Germany. The same was true of Württemberg, an old citadel of South German liberalism.

On the other hand, there were many small towns in which the pro-National Socialist vote far exceeded the average. For instance, in Northeim in Lower Saxony (the position of which has been analyzed in a fascinating study), nearly two-thirds of the population voted for Hitler in March, 1933, as compared with an overall national figure of 41.1 percent.[14] The high correlation between the self-employed businessman in the small and medium-sized towns and the Nazi vote is perhaps not surprising. There was also a high percentage of Nazi votes among student organizations and teachers, which were just as much affected by nationalist ideology as by the fear of unemployment. In May, 1935, teachers provided just under

[13] See the informative memoirs of Alfred Krebs, the regional head of the National Socialists in Hamburg from 1926 to 1928, *Tendenzen und Gestalten der NSDAP* (Stuttgart, 1959).

[14] W. S. Allen, *The Nazi Seizure of Power: The Experience of a Single German Town, 1930–1935* (Chicago, 1965). The fictitious town "Thalburg" featured in the book has been identified as Northeim.

a third of all party functionaries; and by 1939, 97 percent of all German teachers were members of the party.[15]

Finally, what was the role of big business in the rise of Hitler? In the view of some Marxist writers, the Third Reich was entirely its creation. This dogmatic opinion is not borne out by the facts. Hitler undeniably had a great many contacts with some important sections of industry between 1927 and 1932. His main support came from leading coal and steel producers in the Rhineland such as Emil Kirdorf, Fritz Thyssen, and Albert Vögler. According to Otto Dietrich, who was a young pro-Nazi journalist in the Ruhr at the time, Hitler "suddenly decided to concentrate systematically on cultivating the influential economic magnates" in the summer of 1931.[16] A number of private meetings took place between Hitler and individual bankers and industrialists; but perhaps Hitler's most important move in this direction was his address before the Industry Club in Düsseldorf in January, 1932, in which he dealt at length with the threat of Communism and insisted that politics, not economics, was the decisive factor in national life. Fritz Thyssen has maintained that as a result of that meeting the Nazi Party obtained considerable sums from heavy industry.[17] Yet before 1933 most big businessmen did not support the National Socialists, but rather its conservative opponents and rivals. Big business was not kindly disposed to the republic, and was particularly hostile to the Social Democrats and the trade unions; Franz von Papen was much more its idol than Adolf Hitler. Even when the Hitler–Papen cabinet emerged on January 30, 1933, the big businessmen backed it more because they expected Papen to be the leading influence in it. They were, of course, as much mistaken in this as was Papen himself. It was undoubtedly a significant achievement for Hitler that big business, like the army, did not obstruct his rise to power; but, different from many small and medium-sized entrepreneurs, "the great majority of big businessmen had neither wanted a Nazi triumph nor materially contributed to it." However, once Hitler was in the saddle, he was fully backed by big business and received substantial sums from it. Altogether big business aided Hitler "significantly . . . in

[15] Hans Gerth, "The Nazi Party: Its Leadership and Composition," *American Journal of Sociology*, XLV (January, 1940), 25.

[16] Otto Dietrich, *With Hitler on the Road to Power* (London, 1934), p. 12.

[17] See Thyssen's book *I Paid Hitler* (London, 1941). However, the book is of questionable reliability as it is now known that large parts of it were written by a ghostwriter.

the early consolidation of his power, but not in its acquisition." [18]

The class that remained immune the longest from the Nazi virus were the workers. Only in 1933 did it affect the workers' vote, and even then only in areas with a high proportion of unemployment.[19] If the burghers of the small towns and elsewhere did not foresee that a National Socialist regime would allow them as little scope as it did the workers, it was due to the weakness of the latter that the socialist left was split and that Communists and Social Democrats criticized each other with much acrimony. However, even in November, 1932, the total percentage of votes cast for Social Democrats and Communists still amounted to 60.9 percent of the total in Berlin, 50.5 percent in Hamburg, and 52.9 percent in Leipzig.[20] It was largely this political attitude of the workers which, even after Hitler had come to power, prevented him from securing an absolute majority in the elections of March, 1933. Only with the support of Hugenberg's "German Nationalists" was he able to claim that more than half the population had voted in favor of a national revolution.

THE END OF THE REPUBLIC

The reasons for the downfall of the republic and Hitler's rise to power are complex indeed. They were the outcome of a plurality of factors. The serious economic crisis with 6 million unemployed both at the beginning of 1932 and of 1933 was a major contributing cause, especially since it came at a time when the trauma of the inflation in the early 1920s was not yet forgotten. While economic retrenchment would have made the task of any government extremely difficult and chancy, this is not sufficient in itself to account for the structural weaknesses of the republic. Nor is the circumstance that its president was an octogenarian, too old to cope with an emergency situation and much influenced by a camarilla in the wings. What seems more important in retrospect is the illusionary blindness displayed by all the parties, often divided amongst them-

[18] See the balanced article by Henry Ashby Turner, Jr., "Big Business and the Rise of Hitler," *American Historical Review*, LXXV (October, 1969), 56–70. For the subsequent period of 1933–1939, the work of the economic historian Albert Schweitzer, *Big Business in the Third Reich* (Bloomington, Ind., 1964), is relevant.

[19] Alfred Milatz, *Wähler und Wahlen in der Weimar Republik*, 2d ed. (Bonn, 1968), p. 113.

[20] R. I. McKibbin, "The Myth of the Unemployed: Who Did Vote for the Nazis?" *The Australian Journal of Politics and History*, XV (August 1969), 29.

selves, over the character of Hitler's movement and the lack of imagination and insight that prevented them from assessing Hitler's dynamic and untrustworthy personality, and from anticipating his likely behavior.

Before Hitler's coming to power and for some time after, all parties from the Communists to the German Nationalists refused to realize that they were facing the same fate of obliteration, and some of them persecution as well. Hitler could not have obtained control of the state and have consolidated it so quickly and easily if the parties had not been willing to eliminate themselves. This applies least, perhaps, to the Communists, most of whose deputies were in prison before the Reichstag meeting on March 23, which voted on the Enabling Law. But all the other parties facilitated the game of the National Socialists with astonishing blunders. This is equally true of both the members of the former Weimar coalition and the other parties, particularly of the German Nationalists under Hugenberg, who were officially allied with Hitler. With the exception of the Communists, they all believed in the truth of the German saying: "Things are not eaten as hot as they are dished up"—in other words, that the National Socialists would be more moderate than they had been in opposition.

The Communists expected that the Hitler movement would rule briefly and would then be followed more or less automatically by the dictatorship of the proletariat. Following Stalin's directives, the German Communists had proclaimed the existence of a fascist front that extended from the Nazis to the Social Democrats, which was labeled "Social Fascist" in Communist propaganda. Only a Communist proletarian mass party could break its power. The press agency of the German Communist Party, which had been transferred to Basel, Switzerland, after the suppression of the party in the Third Reich, wrote on April 1, 1933: "The momentary calm after the victory of fascism is only a passing phenomenon. The rise of the proletarian tide in Germany will inevitably continue. The resistance of the masses against fascism will inevitably increase." It was "a fantastic error as far as the German masses were concerned." [21]

The weaknesses of the Social Democrats were of a different kind. Well-organized and well-disciplined, the party was too heavily influenced by the traditions of the respectable but rather stodgy trade unions. The party had not basically changed its methods and much

[21] See F. Borkenau, *World Communism: A History of the Communist International* (Ann Arbor, Mich., 1962), Chapter 22.

of its outlook since 1890, when Bismarck's antisocialist law had been abolished. The party also suffered from too little contact between the leaders and the led. Many party leaders lost their working-class roots, having exchanged their proletarian jobs for white-collar positions in the party or the trade unions. They developed, in the words of Max Weber, "the physiognomy of prosperous innkeepers."

The bureaucratization of the party sapped its vitality. "The strict paternal regime provided by the elders was bound to sit poorly with the boisterous and radical new generation." [22] Moreover, as new middle-class supporters came in by the front door, old proletarian supporters left by the back door—mostly to the Communists. The party was, at best, what Eduard Bernstein had hoped it would be thirty years earlier, "a democratic socialist party of reform," but it was too often concerned with the maintenance of the status quo rather than with dynamic change and fresh goals.

Undoubtedly the SPD was in a difficult position after it had left the government in March, 1930. It soon accepted subsequent cabinets from Brüning to Schleicher as a minor evil compared with a Nazi dictatorship. This was probably an unavoidable policy, but it did paralyze the socialists. The acid test of the leaders' acquiescent courage came on July 20, 1932, when the socialist ministers Braun and Severing were ousted from the government of Prussia by Papen's emissary, Bracht. Though they protested, they made no effort to mobilize the millions of trade unionists and other supporters the SPD still had. Any resistance might have been only a heroic gesture, but it would have been a symbol of collective determination and the will to resist. Relieved, Goebbels wrote after July 20, in his diary: "The Reds have missed their great occasion. It will never return." Although nine months later the SPD politicians led by Otto Wells showed considerable courage as the only party present in the Reichstag to vote against Hitler's Enabling Law, it came too late.

With the exception of Brüning, the leading men of the Center Party erred in a different way. They seriously underrated Hitler's cunning and ruthlessness in the belief that they could come to terms with him. In the end, the parliamentary Center Party unanimously approved (with some misgivings) the Enabling Law, a consent which Chancellor Hitler was eager to obtain, for as he told his cabinet on March 20, he realized that it would mean "an increase in prestige

[22] Richard N. Hunt, *German Social Democracy: 1918–1933* (New Haven and London, 1964), p. 246.

vis à vis the outside world." Therefore, he was willing to give guarantees for a later return to the constitutional basis demanded by the Center Party.

The party leader, Prelate Kaas, declared in his speech before the vote that the consent was based on the understanding that Hitler's acceptance of the guarantees requested by the Center would direct future legislation—a pious wish, as Hitler had no intention whatsoever of keeping his promise. While the concordate between the Reich and the Vatican, brought about by Papen on July 5, was welcomed by many German Catholics, the self-dissolution of the Center Party on the following day stamped the seal on their policy of illusionary accommodation, which ended in political harakiri.[23]

The two liberal middle-of-the-road parties, the German People's Party and the Democrats, renamed *Staatspartei* in 1930, had lost nearly all their strength; in March, 1933, they only secured nine and five deputies to the Reichstag respectively. Their self-liquidation in June was therefore a matter of course and hardly caused a political ripple.

More unexpected and significant was the self-destruction of Hitler's ally in the cabinet, the German National People's Party. It is ironic that this party, which had campaigned for the destruction of the democratic parties, helped its own executioner to power. Its leader since 1928, Alfred Hugenberg, owner of a considerable mass media empire of newspapers and film studios, had systematically sabotaged the republic and, since his much-publicized joint conference with Hitler and his paladins in October, 1931, at Harzburg, had looked on his party as part of the "national opposition." Hitler, who wanted to come to power by legal means, needed the assistance of the German Nationalists—at least for the time being.

Hugenberg, the organizational bureaucrat, and his friends finally became aware of the ruthless methods of the National Socialists. There is reason to believe that Hugenberg expressed his doubts about Hitler's reliability as a coalition partner to President Hindenburg in January, 1933. It was only with some reluctance that he accepted Papen's plea to enter Hitler's cabinet as minister of economics at the end of the month. Goerdeler claims that Hugenberg told him on the day after the announcement of the new cabinet (Jan-

[23] See the final message from the leaders of the Center Party to their members, quoted in *Das Ende der Parteien 1933*, ed. Erich Matthias and Rudolf Morsey (Düsseldorf, 1960), p. 441.

uary 31), "Yesterday I committed the greatest folly in my life; I have allied myself with the greatest demagogue in world history." [24]

During February Hitler tried to allay Hugenberg's misgivings. He assured him repeatedly that the result of the forthcoming elections would not affect the composition of the cabinet. In fact, the Nazis did not secure an absolute majority with their 288 seats in the March elections, polling just under 44 percent of the total vote. They needed the 52 seats (8 percent of the total vote) that had gone to Hugenberg's party for a formal majority. Yet after the passing of the Enabling Law, Hitler quickly changed his tone to his junior partner. The arguments of the non-Nazis in the cabinet were ignored more and more by the new chancellor. Soon the houses of German Nationalists were also searched by the political police, and some of them were denounced by Nazi fanatics; even civil servants who were members of Hugenberg's party found themselves dismissed. The National Revolution first devoured the children of its ally and some of its own children a year later. On June 20, Hugenberg submitted his resignation as cabinet minister to Hindenburg, and the German National People's Party was obliged to dissolve itself, like its more democratic rivals. Hugenberg and his friends were bitterly disappointed, as they had hardly expected such unfair treatment. They had lived under the illusion of being respected fellow soldiers with equal rights in the national resurrection. However, the one-party system of the Nazis would not allow for any exceptions. Hugenberg and his friends realized too late that they had dug their own political graves.

[24] Quoted by Friedrich Hiller von Gaertringen in his essay on Hugenberg's party in *Das Ende der Parteien* (1933) p. 576.

9

Hitler's Third Reich

A Streamlined Society

It made an undeniable impression on millions of Germans, most of them not Nazis, that Hitler had come to power by legal means, having been duly appointed by the president. Officials and teachers in particular were more likely to acquiesce to the new regime because respect for lawfully appointed authority was deeply embedded in the traditional German attitudes. The skillful window-dressing that followed the March elections—the ceremony of opening the new Reichstag performed in the Garrison Church in Potsdam over the tomb of Frederick the Great—was intended to symbolize the synthesis between the old and the new National Germany, between the aged president in a field-grey uniform and the young chancellor, not very much at ease in a formal morning coat. Hitler paid a calculated tribute to Hindenburg, who seemed to have been deeply touched. The new chancellor also proclaimed that "a protective providence" had placed him over the new forces of the nation. The solemn cooperation of the leading officer of World War I and the former lance corporal, now head of a national mass movement, was propounded by Goebbels as a symbol for the new national synthesis that would transcend the gulf between generations as well as between classes.

Two days later on March 23, 1933, the Reichstag, with cohorts of S.A. men in its corridors, accepted by 441 to 84 votes the so-called Enabling Law, which had the promising title of "Law for Removing the Distress of the People and the Reich." In five paragraphs it transferred the power of legislation from parliament to the Reich cabinet for a period of four years. It was expressly stated that the laws enacted by the government were to be formulated by the chancellor and "might deviate from the constitution." Hitler promised in his soothing speech that neither the existence of the Reichstag nor of the Federal Council (Reichsrat) were menaced, and that the position and the rights of the president remained unchanged. The way was now open for the surprisingly rapid breakthrough of a totalitarian system based on the slogan: "one Führer, one Reich, one Nation." This breakthrough took place between March, 1933, and June, 1934. No coup d'etat occurred before June 30, 1934. By then Hitler had become angered by and suspicious of the demands of the Storm Troopers (S.A.)—under their leader, Ernst Röhm, now a member of Hitler's cabinet—for more power and perhaps another "social" revolution. Prodded by Himmler and Göring, the Führer had massacred a number of S.A. leaders in many towns to get rid of other and very different one-time opponents. They ranged from General von Schleicher and his wife to the former Bavarian Premier Gustav von Kahr and to Gregor Strasser, who had long fallen into disfavor with the Führer because of his contacts with Schleicher at the end of 1932. Once Hitler had established his dictatorship on the basis of the borrowed authority of the Enabling Law and the threats from the S.A. and S.S., it became obvious that he was not willing to give up his acquired power.

It is perhaps in the nature of a totalitarian dictatorship that its leading men have a passion for conformity. In the spring of 1933 it was generally expected that there would be a good deal of streamlining and many take-overs in Germany. However, few people outside the party anticipated the intensity and the speed with which this process of "coordination" (*Gleichschaltung*) was carried out. Less than six months after the formation of the Hitler cabinet, on July 14, 1933, the Nazi Party was declared by law to be the only political party in Germany and any attempt to maintain organized membership in other parties was considered a criminal offense, to be punishable with hard labor.

The centralization of the government meant the end of the federal structure of Germany, which was removed step by step. The diets of states in which the Nazis had no parliamentary majority were reshaped through special legislation, without any new elections, to make them conform with the distribution of the parties in the

Reichstag; and Hitler's special representatives (Reichsstatthalter) became permanent controllers of the entire administration of a Land. Exactly one year after January 30, 1933, the parliaments of the Länder were dissolved and their sovereign rights finally transferred to the Reich. Soon afterwards the Federal Council, the upper house of the Reich, was abolished in spite of Hitler's earlier solemn pledge to the contrary. A purge of the public service had already been enacted in April, 1933, by which officials with republican sympathies and others of Jewish descent were dismissed and replaced by "fighters" for the Nazi cause.

Yet the masses acquiesced. Although there was fear of terror and the State Secret Police, whose power constantly grew, and the knowledge of victimization and the concentration camps, this little affected the regime's wide popularity. Many Germans genuinely believed a true People's Community—that traditional idol of German romanticism—was about to be established. The ease with which the Nazi revolution was carried out and accepted during the first two years of the Third Reich cannot be explained solely in terms of the use of terror and violence. There is also little reason to believe that the results of the two early plebiscites were mainly the outcome of official pressure and intimidation. Hitler's decision to withdraw Germany from the League of Nations was approved in November, 1933, by 95 percent of those who went to the polls (or, by 88 percent of those entitled to vote). Nine months later in August, 1934, following the death of Hindenburg, 84 percent of all registered voters expressed themselves in favor of Hitler's amalgamation of the posts of president and chancellor. The progressive reduction of unemployment, together with a new feeling of belonging and integration, contributed much to the acceptance of the system. The idea of "National Community" especially attracted young people, and the introduction of a compulsory labor service was by no means unpopular. The fact that by the end of 1933 every cyclists' club or choir was remodeled on the lines of the regime, with old or new Nazis in leading positions, was accepted as an inevitable step on the road to a dynamic integration of the true people's community. Yet to untold numbers the millennium of a true people's community seemed to be round the corner. The claim that the old antagonism between workers and burghers was now forgotten, that both would gain a new status and dignity in the changed society was taken seriously by most people; it was, of course, constantly stressed by propaganda.

Hitler told Hanns Johst, President of the Reich Chamber of

Literature, in January, 1934, that "the burgher must no longer feel himself a king or pensioner of either tradition or capitalism, separated from the worker by the Marxist idea of property, but must aim to accommodate himself to work for the welfare of the community." [1] How far did this myth reflect German society? As has been convincingly shown, there remained in the Third Reich the discrepancy between objective social reality and its ideological interpretation that had bedevilled so much of Germany's previous history. By 1939, "objective social reality, the measurable statistical consequences of National Socialism, was the very opposite of what Hitler had presumably promised and what the majority of his followers had expected him to fulfill. In 1939 the cities were larger, not smaller; the concentration of capital greater than before; the rural population reduced, not increased. The East Elbian estates continued to be run by the gentry, the civil service by doctors, and the army by generals, all of whose names began with 'von.' " [2] From this perspective the history of the Third Reich can indeed be seen as "the history of an apparently betrayed revolution." [3]

On the other hand, the current interpretation of the social reality was different. "Like no world since 1914, it was a world of career civil servants and authoritarian paternalism, a world of national purpose and achievement where the Army was once again 'the school of the nation.' " It was no less a world where officers and men ate the same meals and conversed "as man to man." In sociological terms the Third Reich had a Janus face in that it was "a society that was New Deal and good old days at the same time"; [4] but above all it was a society geared to aggression and war, to conquest and the cult of racial superiority.

There has been a good deal of controversy on the attitude of the Reichswehr during the months prior to Hitler's coming to power with the consent of President Hindenburg—whose name meant so much in the traditions of the army. Some historians have agreed with Sir John Wheeler-Bennett's verdict that "nothing could have been more inglorious and inept than the record of the Army in the whole period." Even that part of the army leadership, represented by Generals von Schleicher and Kurt von Hammerstein, "which [was] allegedly anti-

[1] Max Domarus, *Hitler: Reden und Proklamationen 1932–1945* (Munich, 1965), I, 349–51.
[2] David Schoenbaum, *Hitler's Social Revolution: Class and Status in Nazi Germany, 1933–1939* (London, 1967), p. 298.
[3] *Ibid.*
[4] *Ibid.*

Nazi, was not 100 percent so." These men wished "to secure for the benefit of the Reichswehr, all that could be gained to advantage from the Nazi movement, while controlling and dominating it in policy." Undoubtedly they hoped to tame the Nazi lion while, as Wheeler–Bennett put it, "dreaming in their blindness of a martial State in which the masses, galvanized and inspired by modified National Socialism, would be directed and disciplined by the Army." [5] How could the Reichswehr have prevented Hitler's accession to power by the use of force? Another interpretation is more convincing. "In principle there seemed, at the most, only dubious justification for a putsch. In practice, the effects of the putsch could well have been negative." [6] Schleicher was intriguing, egocentric, and deceitful, but it can hardly be said of Kurt von Hammerstein that he exploited the circumstances for military ends. Moreover, since 1919 the army had regarded itself as a nonpolitical instrument, and it simply waited for the outcome of events.

Two different types of general tried to influence the shaping of the army in the prewar period of the Third Reich. For most of the time, Hitler interfered little with the running of the army; but at the same time he regarded the generals as a caste with both antipathy and apprehension. On the one side there were the pro-Nazis, the "political soldiers" in the ministry of defence, Reich Minister General von Blomberg, and his subordinate, Chief-of-Staff Walter von Reichenau. Energetic, with a touch of romantic idealism and with a good deal of naïveté, a kind of Wagnerian Siegfried, Blomberg's blind support for Hitler facilitated the steady infiltration of Nazism into the army. Hitler did not find it difficult to exploit Blomberg's odd idealism and make him comply with his own wishes. Reichenau was cooler and more calculating, an abler soldier, and, rather exceptionally, he greatly admired everything British.

On the other side there were the conservative traditionalists; professional soldiers with a conventional Christian background, men like Werner von Fritsch, Commander-in-Chief of the army, and Ludwig Beck, Hammerstein's successor as Chief of General Staff of the army from 1934 to 1938. The character of Fritsch has been called "perhaps the greatest enigma of the whole period." [7] Enjoying

[5] John Wheeler–Bennett, *The Nemesis of Power*, 2d ed. (London, 1964), p. 285.

[6] Robert John O'Neill, *The German Army and the Nazi Party, 1933–1939* (London, 1966), p. 12.

[7] *Ibid.*, p. 24.

both popularity and authority in the army, Fritsch was able to get along with people and yet maintain a good deal of reserve. A perfectionist in the military field, he was willing and able to perform the task that Hitler set him in 1934 when he took over the army command—i.e. to "create an army of the greatest possible strength, inner resolution, and unity, on the best imaginable foundations of training." Fritsch became the top army expert; but like so many experts in Germany, he remained utterly nonpolitical. During the famous secret meeting in the Chancellery on November 5, 1937, when the Führer revealed his expansionist plans and policies to the half-dozen top functionaries of state and party, Fritsch clashed with the Führer by daring to question the feasibility of his plans of aggression in the East. Subsequently, it seems, Fritsch stressed to Hitler the military impossibilities of the Führer's blueprint for war. The opposition of Fritsch, and to a lesser extent of Blomberg, annoyed Hitler and made him more amenable to the sordid intrigues of Himmler and Göring, who used the trumped-up charge of homosexuality to bring about Fritsch's downfall. Blomberg was also forced to resign after the discovery that his second wife, whom he had recently married in the presence of Hitler and Göring, was known to the police as a former prostitute. Though the officer caste was genuinely shocked by this "discovery," in the last analysis the removal of Fritsch and Blomberg was a political act. The remaining army leaders have often been criticized since for meekly accepting the removal of their chiefs. But it should be remembered that when Stalin carried out his much more drastic and sweeping purges of the Soviet Army at about the same time (May, 1937), "the masses of the army watched and waited for him to finish." [8]

In any case with few exceptions officers and men in the German Army felt bound by their oath of allegiance to the Führer. Its wording was drastic enough: "I swear by God this holy oath that I will render Adolf Hitler, Leader of the German Nation and people, Supreme Commander of the Armed Forces, unconditional obedience, and I am ready as a brave soldier to risk my life at any time for this oath." Had not Hitler modernized the army, astonishingly increased its strength in material, men and finance, and emphasized a new proficiency? Although there was local friction with minor officials and resentment of the growing inroads of the S.S. into the preserve of the army by the creation of three S.S. regiments, "there was much about

[8] Robert John O'Neill, op. cit., p. 150.

the Third Reich in its prewar years which seemed to the German Army at large to be wholly right and proper." [9]

HITLER OVER EUROPE

When Anthony Eden traveled to Moscow in April, 1935, and called on Stalin, he was surprised to discover that Stalin, unlike the British cabinet, was familiar with the content of Hitler's *Mein Kampf*. This hodgepodge of autobiographical resentment, hysterical contempt for the masses, shrewd political insight, recipes for propaganda, and racialist demands for a resurgent "Greater Germany" had by then become a compulsory bestseller in Germany. (Six million copies were sold by 1940.) Written by the imprisoned agitator in 1924–25, its main program in foreign affairs was the overthrow of the odious Treaty of Versailles, revenge for the German defeat of 1918, and the dynamic implementation of a German Empire in the East based on the need for more *Lebensraum*. In this blueprint Hitler contemplated the *Anschluss* (annexation) of Austria, the Sudetenland, and other territories with large German-speaking communities.

After the National Socialists had come to power, the brutal frankness of the agitator was replaced by the obsessive scheming of the leader of the one-party state, who camouflaged his ambitious plans in foreign politics with pacifist and cooperative protestations. Hitler was adroit in exploiting the widespread pacifist trauma in the West—an aftereffect of the First World War. Every surprise move by which he tore up a clause of the provisions in the Treaty of Versailles was accompanied by bland assurances of peace and cooperation and by repeated offers of bilateral or multilateral treaties.

Early in February, 1933, a few days after he had assumed power, Hitler told German army and navy commanders that building up a strong military force was "the most important prerequisite for attaining the goal of regaining political power." Yet he was still undecided how this political power was then to be used: "Perhaps fight for new export possibilities—perhaps—and this is undoubtedly better for the conquest of fresh *Lebensraum* in the East and its ruthless Germanization." Hitler operated as a gradualist during the first four years of his regime, which saw the building up of strong armed forces. Aware of the Englishman's guilt feeling towards Germany and his distrust of France, Hitler could also play on the widespread fear of

---

[9] *Ibid.*, p. 174.

Bolshevism in the West. Concentrating on Germany's right to
equality, he claimed that Germany had been unfairly treated, and
meanwhile gained time for his military preparations.

On October 14, 1933, Hitler shocked the world by his declaration that since France had refused to disarm, Germany was forced
by the denial of equal rights to withdraw from the Disarmament
Conference and the League of Nations. Four days afterwards, he told
the English journalist Ward Price that nobody in Germany desired
another war. In a well-calculated move, Hitler submitted his decision
on Germany's withdrawal from the League to a referendum in which
the voters approved of his decision by an overwhelming majority.
"All the long pent-up resentment of the German people against the
loss of the war and the Treaty of Versailles was expressed in the
vote." [10]

Hitler's role as champion of peace was further enhanced by the
unexpected conclusion of the German Nonaggression Pact with Poland in January, 1934. In common with many Germans, Hitler resented the loss of Danzig, Silesia, and Posen to Poland in 1919, but
he was prepared for the time being to acquiesce in it. The German
chancellor also developed the technique of taking advantage of actions by other governments as a pretext for his own military or
diplomatic coups. In March, 1935, the French government had
doubled the term of military service and lowered the age of enlistment
in the French Army to make up for the fall in conscripts, which had
resulted from the reduced birthrate during the First World War.
Hitler promptly argued that Germany had been deceived, and had no
alternative but to do the same. Therefore, he announced on March
16, the German government would reintroduce conscription and aim
at a peacetime army of 36 divisions with 550,000 soldiers. The German government had notified other governments a week earlier that
a German air force had been already established. In November, 1935,
the French ambassador in Berlin, François-Poncet, predicted that the
proposed pact between France and Soviet Russia would be used by
Hitler to denounce the Locarno Pact so that he could send German
troops into the demilitarized zone of the Rhineland. This was exactly what happened on March 7, 1936, after the French Chamber of
Deputies had ratified the Franco–Soviet Treaty. Hitler revoked Germany's signature under the Locarno Pact "on account of its incompatibility with the Franco–Soviet agreement." Trying to sweeten this

[10] Alan Bullock, *Hitler: A Study in Tyranny*, rev. ed. (London, 1962), p.
324.

drastic step by putting forward far-reaching peace proposals Hitler, as the French ambassador later observed in his memoirs, "struck his adversary in the face, and as he did so declared: 'I bring you proposals for peace.' " [11] England and France reacted with feeble protests. As a prominent "appeaser" in England put it, after all the Germans were only entering their own backyard. As for France, the French government then in power was fortunate in finding in the English resistance to any action a cover behind which to hide its own failure.[12] Hitler's gigantic bluff had come off.[13]

By 1937 Hitler felt he was in a strong position. The alienation of Italy from the Western Powers over their sanctions in the Ethiopian War, the close cooperation between Mussolini and Hitler in the Spanish civil war, the strong impression of German rearmament Mussolini received when visiting Germany in the autumn of 1937—all these events strengthened Hitler's resolve to develop and carry out much more ambitious plans for a policy of aggression. At a secret meeting with his military and political advisers in Berlin on November 5, 1937, the Führer declared it his "unalterable determination to solve Germany's problem of *Lebensraum* at the latest by 1943 to 1945." The first objective was to take over Czechoslovakia and Austria and secure Germany's eastern and northern flanks. Hitler predicted that England and France would acquiesce in this. In fact, only mild protests from Paris and London were uttered when in mid-March of 1938 German troops marched into Austria, removed the government of Chancellor Schuschnigg, and effected the incorporation of Austria into the German Reich. Although Hitler's later bid for the Sudetenland of Western Czechoslovakia met with some opposition in England and France, he achieved his goal without bloodshed at the Munich Four-Power Conference at the end of September, 1938. When France, England, Italy, and Germany agreed on the transfer of the Sudetenland to the Reich, without having consulted Czechoslovakia or the Soviet Union, it was a diplomatic triumph of the first order for Hitler, who was well aware that the German masses were not enthusiastic about a possible war. Yet the Führer felt thwarted, and told his commanders-in-chief two months after the Munich Conference that "this was only a partial solution." By mid-March, 1939, the solution was made "complete" when German troops

[11] André François-Poncet, *The Fateful Years* (London, 1949), p. 193.
[12] See Paul Reynaud, *In the Thick of the Fight, 1930–1945* (London, 1955), pp. 124–37.
[13] Paul Schmidt, *Statist auf diplomatischer Bühne* (Bonn, 1949), p. 320.

occupied Prague; Czechoslovakia ceased to exist as a state and became instead a German protectorate. Yet it was this cynical piece of power politics, without the fig-leaf of racial affinity with the annexed, that put an end to most of the illusions of appeasement in the West. The British government was at last galvanized into action and, a fortnight after the events in Prague, issued a declaration of guarantee for the frontiers of Poland, Rumania, and Greece. It was then rightly assumed that Poland would be the next victim on Hitler's list. On May 23, 1939, the Führer told his generals at a secret meeting that "leniency towards Poland was out of the question" and expressed his resolve "to attack Poland on the first suitable occasion."

Hitler was determined to avoid simultaneous operations against Poland and the Western powers who might come to her assistance. It was therefore vital for him to prevent Soviet Russia from joining the Western camp. Before the assault on Poland began on September 1, 1939, Hitler brought off what was easily his greatest diplomatic success—the German Nonaggression Pact with Soviet Russia, which was signed by Molotov and von Ribbentrop in Moscow on August 23, 1939. There were solid reasons for the two totalitarian states, which had long attacked each other so fiercely in propaganda, to conclude such an arrangement. Stalin, who had a high opinion of Germany's war potential, may well have regarded it as imperative to keep out of any forthcoming conflict between Nazi Germany and the Western capitalist powers. Hitler, for his part, knew of the aversion of his generals to entering a war on two large fronts. As he told his army chiefs on August 22, Poland was now in the position in which he wanted to see her. Germany need no longer fear a blockade. "The East will supply us with corn, cattle, coal, lead, and zinc." Undoubtedly Germany did profit considerably from the Russo–German Pact, and "great advantages fell to Stalin from an arrangement compounded of mutual perfidies." [14] When the German armies invaded Poland on September 1, 1939, Britain and—more reluctantly—France stood by her when she declared war on Germany on September 3. Yet they were unable to give any effective assistance to the Polish Republic. Poland was defeated by the German army and air force in eighteen days and was subsequently partitioned by Germany and the Soviet Union.

[14] John Erickson, *The Soviet High Command: A Military Political History, 1918–1941* (London, 1962), p. 565.

The year 1940 saw the triumph of German war preparations and of Hitler's concept of the *Blitzkrieg*, the intense war by lightning blows. Denmark, Norway, Holland, Belgium, and France were overrun within three months, with only minimal German losses. By the end of June, the war on the Continent appeared to have come to an end. There were both military and economic aspects of this *Blitzkrieg* warfare. "From Hitler's point of view there was everything to be said for the *Blitzkrieg* and not much against it." "Compared with her neighbours, in September, 1939, Germany's strength was very great. Her armaments were ready." [15] The control of the steel and oil of Austria, the steel and armament of Czechoslovakia, and the coalfields of the Saar (which was returned to Germany after a plebiscite in January, 1935) had made a considerable difference. "No nation had ever previously spent so vast a sum in peace time on preparations for war." [16]

Yet the impressive military successes of the German armed forces in early summer, 1940, did not extend beyond the English Channel. In the autumn of that year the attempt to break Britain's resistance through intense air attacks in preparation for a full-scale invasion failed. The Luftwaffe suffered crippling losses in the Battle of Britain, and the invasion never took place. "The attack of the Luftwaffe against England on her own island does not force England to capitulate in one day," Hitler had cautiously told the heads of his armed forces on May 23, "However if her fleet is destroyed capitulation will follow immediately." Hitler's love-hate relationship with the British Empire becomes evident from his words reported in General Halder's diary on July 13: "If we finish England militarily the British Empire will disintegrate. However Germany would not profit from this. What we would achieve by shedding German blood would only benefit Japan, America, and others."

It is quite obvious that, in accordance with his earlier views, Hitler had always regarded Soviet Russia and not Britain as his primary enemy. He argued in a roundabout way that England and America were putting their last hope in Russia and that "only if Russia is destroyed does England's last hope vanish." In July, 1940, Hitler decided to crush Russia "within five months," by the spring of 1941. The subjugation of Russia and the ruthless control of its population remained Hitler's constant objective throughout his

[15] Alan S. Milward, *The German Economy at War* (London, 1965), pp. 76–77

[16] *Ibid.*

career. This becomes evident from *Mein Kampf*, from Hitler's later important conversations with Hermann Rauschning (1932–34), from his *Table Talk* of 1942–43, and from the epilogue to his talks with Martin Bormann during the last few months of his life in the spring of 1945.[17] In November, 1940, six months before the German armies marched at dawn into Russia, Soviet Foreign Minister Molotov visited Berlin. In order to impress his foreign guest, Hitler conjured up an image of the disintegrating British Empire and promised the Russians that they could participate in the partition of the British Empire." Yet Molotov, cold and factual, was not impressed by such "world historical perspectives of the future"; he came back with irritating persistence to the existing points of conflict between Germany and the Soviet Union concerning Finland, Rumania, and Bulgaria. Although Hitler and Ribbentrop evaded these issues, Molotov refused to budge from his line of concrete complaints and demanded their rectification. After Molotov's return to Moscow, the Russians were willing to fall in with Hitler's plans—at a price—but they never received a reply to their written proposals. By his secret directive, "Operation Barbarossa," issued on December 18, Hitler fixed the military attack on the Soviet Union for May 15, 1941.

Owing to Italian involvement in Greece, the attack had to be postponed by five weeks to June 22, 1941.[18] In spite of the spectacular initial successes of the German armies, which by the middle of July had advanced 450 miles into Russia and stood outside Leningrad and Moscow in the autumn, these major cities were not taken; the war was not ended "within five months," before the onset of the severe Russian winter. In spite of very heavy losses, the Russians were able to start a large-scale counteroffensive in December and force the German troops to withdraw from the environs of Moscow. After serious disagreements with his leading generals, who favored a strategy of concentration rather than of dispersal, Hitler took over the direction of the armies in the East himself. A breakdown of their

[17] See the Bibliography on p. 263. A second work, written by Hitler in 1928 and mainly concerned with his ideas on foreign affairs, was not published during his life time. The manuscript, discovered in May, 1945, by an American officer in Munich, is now available in English as *Hitler's Secret Book*, introduction by Telford Taylor (New York, 1961).
[18] When the collapse of his regime was imminent, in his table talk in February, 1945, Hitler blamed the failure of the Russian campaign on the loss of these five weeks due to his Axis partner. See the "Testament of Adolf Hitler," in the *Hitler-Bormann Documents, February–April, 1945*, ed. François Genoud (London, 1961), p. 84.

morale was prevented, and after some retreating the German line was held. In the summer of 1942, a new German advance began pushing forward in the south along the corridor formed by the Don and Donetz rivers. German military power had reached its peak and controlled most of Europe to the Volga and the Caucasus, and to the Nile in the Middle East, under General Rommel's astute leadership. It was in Russia that Hitler overreached himself. "Overestimating the German strength, he did not limit himself to his original objective, to reach the Volga and capture Stalingrad, but tried to break into the Caucasus with its valuable oilfields as well, thus dividing his forces and ending by gaining neither Stalingrad nor the oil." [19]

When the battle of Stalingrad began in September, the Russians held the city because they had been able to obtain further troops. The Russian net surrounding the German Sixth Army at Stalingrad under General von Paulus was drawn tighter and tighter. Hitler did not allow von Paulus to break the ring from within nor later to capitulate. On January 31, 1943, the Russian command was able to announce that they had completed the capture or annihilation of the remainder of the Sixth Army and the Fourth Panzer Army. Von Paulus, recently promoted to Field Marshall, was among the prisoners.

Following upon the important successes of the British-American troops in North Africa at the end of 1942, Stalingrad must be seen as the turning point of the war. A few men at the top such as Goebbels and Albert Speer were shocked by the tragedy of the Sixth Army and soberly asked themselves how it could have happened under the Führer's command. In the past, setbacks had been followed by new successes, but this was a defeat without an equivalent win.[20] Goebbels galvanized a mass meeting of selected party members in Berlin into action in February, 1943, with his defiant slogan of "total war," requiring drastic measures among the civilians. He even spoke to Speer and Ley of a "Leader crisis." " His criticism showed what Stalingrad really meant." [21] Immense and successful as the German war effort had been from 1939 to 1941, the attack on the Soviet Union and the entry of the United States into the war after Pearl Harbor made Hitler's concept of the *Blitzkrieg* outdated. "Russian ability to

[19] Alan Bullock, op. cit., p. 685.
[20] Albert Speer, *Memoirs* (New York, 1970), Chapter 18.
[21] *Ibid.*, p. 258.

survive the 'first five months' committed Hitler to struggle on two fronts. One front was primarily military, the other naval and aerial. Thus the *Blitzkrieg* became impossible." [22] And Germany's plight reached unexpected dimensions.

PROPAGANDA AND THE MOOD OF THE PEOPLE

Like all totalitarian movements, the National Socialists regarded propaganda as a major activity. Hitler's psychology was crude. He was convinced that in order to influence the masses, one had to paint in black and white and avoid all the finer shades. In *Mein Kampf* he declared it a basic tenet of all propaganda that it "confine itself to little and to repeat this eternally." The masses were slow and their intelligence limited, and they were only accessible to thousandfold repetitions of the simplest ideas. As with commercial life, the criterion of propaganda was its effectiveness and success. Joseph Goebbels, Hitler's ablest performer in this field, told the regional subleaders of Berlin in January, 1928: "If a brand of propaganda has won over a circle of people then I imagine it has been good; if not, then I imagine it has been bad." The National Socialists favorite technique was to build up images and counterimages by the use of both the spoken and the written word. Their propaganda thrived on the contrast between villains and heroes. During the last years of the republic, Goebbels deliberately nicknamed Jewish vice-president of the Berlin police, Dr. Bernhard Weiss, "Isidor" and portrayed him as a wicked specimen of Jewish destructiveness. It was an exercise in cynical aggressiveness. Looking back on it later, Goebbels told Werner Stephan privately that it had been great fun: "How grand it was to transform Isidor into the most brutal bailiff of the Weimar Republic, into the grinning mask of the eternal Jew—although this Deputy Commissioner of the Berlin Police and former Captain of the Royal Bavarian Army Reserve was actually only a harmless fool." [23]

Goebbels carefully groomed Hitler's image among the masses in his annual addresses and articles on the Führer's birthday.[24] If the masses were to identify themselves with the Führer and his regime, it

[22] Alan S. Milward, op. cit., p. 53.
[23] W. Stephan, *Joseph Goebbels* (Stuttgart, 1949), p. 68.
[24] See Ernest K. Bramsted, *Goebbels and National Socialist Propaganda, 1925–1945* (East Lansing, Mich., 1965), Chapter 9, "The Projection of the Hitler Image."

was imperative to describe Hitler as both human and superhuman, as a genius in politics yet full of kindness and understanding for the man in the street. Hitler's superhuman quality was stressed more after the Third Reich had begun, but it had been by no means neglected in the earlier propaganda. On the eve of the first ballot for president in 1932, Goebbels presented his candidate under the head-line: "Hitler—the Greater German—the Führer—the Prophet—the Fighter." Before the second ballot on which Hindenburg and Hitler competed again, Goebbels struck a different note: "Adolf Hitler as a human being" was now the caption of a highly slanted portrait. The readers were told that Hitler was "fundamentally an artist—an architect and painter—whom only the misery of the German people had called into politics."

Appeal to sentiment was always present, particularly when Hitler had brought off one of his coups. Referring to a radio address by Hitler after the occupation of the Rhineland in March, 1936, Goeb-bels pontificated: "We saw in Cologne hard and strong men who had overcome many a danger burst into tears during the last words of the Führer. This was religion in the deepest and most mysterious sense of the word." In a 1939 speech on Hitler's birthday Goebbels added a further feature to the portrait. The Führer was now presented as a good European loved also by many non-Germans. The great initial successes of the German armies during the first two years of the war made Goebbels' job of eulogizing the incomparable Führer easy. If it was comforting for the masses to identify themselves with Hitler, the victorious dictator of most of Europe for the first half of the war, Goebbels had to change the approach when the tide turned against Germany. By 1944 when Hitler was almost isolated from the people, the Führer was presented as a worthy successor to Frederick the Great. Like the Prussian king, he had suffered reverses and hardships; but as Frederick had finally triumphed in the difficult days of the Seven Years War, so, it was suggested, would Hitler lead the German nation to final victory over a coalition of pernicious enemies.[25]

The propaganda was ubiquitous, and the same theme was played simultaneously in different variations by the hard working departments of the Ministry of Propaganda and People's Enlightenment. Goebbels claimed that the press was an orchestra that had to play the same melody on different instruments as directed by the conductor's baton. In fact, he regarded the various mass media in just

---

[25] See Chapter 3, pp. 89–90.

this way. In each propaganda campaign that was planned by and carried out under the supervision of his ministry, the various mass media were allotted different voices and tasks. Goebbels was well aware of the considerable variations in levels of education and interest among the public, and he knew that the daily press, periodicals, broadcasts, films, books, and plays appealed in different ways to their respective publics. Dubious statements over the radio were less risky than when they appeared in the daily or weekly press.

Each mass medium had its specific function in the frequent anti-Semitic campaigns of the regime. Polemics that exploited current news items had to be voiced by the daily press and supported by anti-Jewish editorials. Weekly or monthly periodicals, on the other hand, had to justify anti-Semitic ideology and official contempt for the Jewish race with racialist and pseudoscientific theories. Film producers were asked to assist in tendentious productions such as "Jew Süss," the story of a Jewish court financier in Württemberg in the eighteenth century, or the history of the house of Rothschild; these films were used to implant negative Jewish and positive Germanic images on the masses.[26] The raido served to spread dubious or false news of Jewish or anti-Semitic events for most of which it would have been difficult, if not impossible, to provide documentary evidence.

The party press, headed by the *Völkischer Beobachter,* was regarded as the journalistic backbone of the system. It was much strengthened by the buying up or the confiscation of former socialist or nonpolitical newspapers. Yet it speaks for Goebbels's skeptical ingenuity that he realized the party papers were ill-equipped to satisfy a more educated and sophisticated public. While most of the former high-class liberal newspapers were closed down, the most famous liberal organ, the *Frankfurter Zeitung,* was allowed to continue for ten years, though, of course, it had to toe the official line. The continuation of this newspaper with a high prestige abroad allowed the regime to influence the foreign public with its policy of earnest endeavor and sweet reasonableness, particularly during the heydays of "appeasement." [27]

All newspapers had to pursue the official line and follow the confidential daily press directives issued by the propaganda ministry

[26] The anti-Semitic propaganda films produced under Goebbels's close personal supervision are discussed in David Stewart Hull, *Film in the Third Reich* (Berkeley and Los Angeles, 1969), pp. 157–77.

[27] See E. K. Bramsted, op. cit., Chapter 5, "The Strange Case of the Frankfurter Zeitung."

during the twelve years of the regime.[28] These directives were first issued at the daily press conference in the ministry, but were also made available to editors of provincial newspapers. A salient feature of the directives was their insistence on frequent repetition of the same line, particularly if it was one of abuse and attack. To give only one example, the press directive of February 2, 1940, said: "The term 'plutocracy' has to be discussed by all newspapers once by next Monday, including that day. Every newspaper has to send a copy of the issue in question as proof to the ministry. There is much to be said for the uniform work of indoctrination and instruction, as they use it in the army. It should serve as a model for the press." Another feature of the directives was the technique of suppressing inconvenient news or keeping silent. More than 25 percent of about 50,000 confidential directives were orders to enforce silence on specific issues and themes. The reasons for enforcing such taboos varied. On January 19, 1938, all references to war preparations inside Germany were forbidden. During the serious British crisis in December, 1936, over the abdication of King Edward VIII, Goebbels advised the German press to ignore the issue altogether. He allowed a mere mention of the change on the British throne only after the abdication. He then ordered that the Duke of Windsor, as the former king was now called, must not be mentioned for the next ten years.

Although the fight against Jewry occupied Nazi propaganda with increasing intensity, there was a strict embargo on reports of arrests and transportation of Jews. A directive of December 11, 1936, declared the mentioning of events in concentration camps as undesirable, as this would draw the attention of the public and the foreign press. Other taboos (*Verbote*) during the years 1934 to 1937 prohibited news on strike movements, the frequency of suicides, the Nazification of the "People's League for Germans Abroad," and above all the position of the Protestant Church. Apart from publishing an official statement, the editors were told in February, 1936, not to refer to the trial of Pastor Niemoeller, the courageous anti-Nazi leader of the Protestant "Confessional Church." As far as trials were concerned, in principle they should be confined to the local press of the areas in which they had taken place. The publication of sentences should act as a deterrent but not create unrest. However, certain events that were disquieting or deplorable from the party's point of view could not be entirely ignored in the local press since many

[28] E. K. Bramsted, op. cit., Chapter 4.

readers had heard of them through eyewitnesses, rumors, and so on. When, for instance, the Reich Representative (*Reichstatthalter*) of Oldenburg had the crucifixes removed from the schoolrooms in 1937, a measure that caused much unrest and indignation among the Catholics of the area, cautious reports were allowed to appear in the local newspapers because thousands of people were aware of what had happened. However, the press in other parts of Germany never mentioned the incident, and thus few Germans outside the region of Oldenburg knew of it.

Sultan Harun al-Rashid is reported to have mingled in disguise with his subjects to discover how they felt and what they thought. A modern dictator and his lieutenants cannot do the same, yet they depend even more upon reliable information on public opinion when there are no open channels for self-expression. The reactions of the masses to events and orders from above and the degree and nature of possible resistance and opposition have to be studied by the rulers in a system that does not allow for public opinion polls. As Heinrich Himmler told his masseur, Felix Kersten, in September, 1942, it was the task of the Security Service (S.D.) as a branch of the S.S. "to present an impartial picture to leaders of the party and the government, to show the effect of their measures on every department of life—the economic, the cultural, the administrative, the legal, and others." [29] With a goodly number of confidential agents in all walks of life reporting on what they saw and heard, a fairly accurate picture of changing public moods in times of peace and war was put together for the benefit of the leading men in the state and party, although Hitler himself does not seem to have seen or been interested in these intelligence reports.[30]

THE SPIRIT OF AUSCHWITZ

One of the most striking features of Hitler's Third Reich was the dualism of power between the state and the party. Hitler, who after the death of President von Hindenburg in August, 1934, appointed himself "Führer and Reich Chancellor," thus becoming the total fountain of power, never allowed the state and the party movement, and the state bureaucracy and the party machinery to merge into one; he deliberately kept them apart.

[29] Felix Kersten, *The Kersten Memoirs, 1940–1945* (London, 1956), p. 210.
[30] For a selection of these confidential reports see *Meldungen aus dem Reich*, ed. Heinz Boberach (Neuwied and Berlin, 1965).

Corresponding to the dualism of party and state, and of the Reichswehr and the "protective squads" of the S.S., there soon developed a dualism of orders and *mores*, one based on the more rational and traditional type of rule, the other a by-product of a fanatical Nazi *Weltanschauung*. In the words of Hans Buchheim: "Hitler had harnessed state and party like two horses to the chariot of his policy. Both could be used at will." The state still carried out many of its traditional "normal" functions, and the old courts continued in the field of justice. Yet their power was often curtailed by the extranormative powers of the Secret State Police (*Gestapo*) and the People's Courts, against whose decisions there was no appeal.

Whereas the Reichswehr was trained to counter any external threat to the Reich, Hitler felt the need for a relatively small body to combat the enemies within Germany, and this was founded in January, 1929, with only 280 men. Hitler had directed Heinrich Himmler to shape this organization, the *Schutzstaffel*, or S.S., which was first part of the Storm Troopers (S.A.), into an elite troop of the party that would always be dependable. Unlike the S.A., the S.S. was based on a strictly selective system, a strong ideological indoctrination, and a rigorously enforced marriage code. The S.S. men wore smart black uniforms and shining jackboots.

The S.S. had the political task of tracing and persecuting all real or alleged enemies of the Third Reich. Hitler seems to have envisioned the S.S. half in terms of Nietzsche's superman and half as a ruthless political police force. The two most important divisions of the S.S. were the *S.S. Verfügungstruppe* and the S.S. Death Head Unit—both soon legitimized as "organizations in the service of the state." The former, conceived as Hitler's praetorian guard, developed more and more along military lines, while the latter provided most of the ruthless and often brutal guards in the concentration camps. The *Verfügungstruppe* became a forerunner of the *Waffen S.S.* ("armed S.S.") of the Second World War.[31]

In an address to the senior officers of the S.S. in October, 1943, Himmler described the expansion of the armed S.S. since the beginning of the Second World War as "fantastic." Before the war it had comprised at most 25,000 to 28,000 men, yet within the first year of the war it had risen to nearly 150,000. Soon afterwards, Himmler established the *Waffen S.S.* as "the fourth branch of the Wehrmacht." He wanted to make the armed S.S. the military van-

[31] George H. Stein, *The Waffen S.S.: Hitler's Elite Guard at War, 1939–1945* (New York, 1966), p. 15.

guard of National Socialism, which would be a model for the army; but despite its valorous deeds in the battles of the Second World War it did not become a serious rival of the latter. Nevertheless, the armed S.S. was transformed in the course of the Third Reich from the Führer's militarized police force to "the elite combat arm of Hitler's Wehrmacht." But though it was never officially a branch of the Wehrmacht, its divisions "were among the most effective in the German war machine." [32] Its immense losses led to a large-scale recruitment of pro-Nazi foreigners during the second half of the war. By 1945, of the thirty-eight S.S. divisions, none of which was confined exclusively to Germans, at least nineteen consisted mostly of foreigners from nearly all the prewar states of Europe. Eugen Kogon, a former inmate of Buchenwald, as well as a sociologist, detected "much naïve and boyish idealism in the ranks of the *Waffen S.S.*, coupled with a savage soldier-of-fortune spirit." [33] They did not bother much about Himmler's pedantic fantasies of the S.S. superstate. They were the *Condottieri* of the Third Reich, and most of them perished with it.

The "Secret State Police," or *Gestapo*, was also a new institution in the history of Germany. First established in Prussia in 1933 under Göring, it soon spread its tentacles all over the Third Reich. The *Gestapo* could arrest people at any time and for any reason without allowing redress to the arrested through ordinary courts. There was no appeal from its decisions, and the law courts were forbidden to question or reexamine them. A 1936 report by the *Gestapo* in Bavaria lists such vague reason for arrest as "antistate attitudes" or "attitudes hostile to the state," "preparations for high treason or being suspected of such preparations," "activities in or propaganda for the Communist or Socialist Parties," and "forbidden activities as Jehovah's Witnesses." Other reasons for arrest were "disturbing or endangering public security" and "behavior damaging to the nation." Finally, there was the charge of homosexuality or of being suspected of it, which must have reminded many of Hitler's denunciation of Röhm and other S.A. leaders when he publicly justified their execution on that account after the purge in the summer of 1934.

Although justice, or the lack of it, was utterly irrational in this system, there was an oddly high degree of rational bureaucratization. To distinguish the various types of prisoners in the concentration

[32] *Ibid.*, p. 286.
[33] Eugen Kogon, *The Theory and Practice of Hell* (London, 1950), pp. 260–61.

camps inmates were made recognizable by different-colored triangles fixed on their clothing.[34] For political prisoners there was red, for Jehovah's Witnesses lilac, for "antisocial elements" black, and for criminals green. Jews had to wear the yellow star of David, and emigrés who had imprudently returned to Germany from abroad a triangle in blue. Homosexuals were branded with pink. Of all the groups, anti-Nazis and Jews usually fared the worst, and there was practically no limit to the extent to which the S.S. guards could maltreat them. There was a deliberate policy behind these sadistic indulgences in the concentration camps, the number of which grew with the expansion of Nazi rule until by April, 1944, there were 20 of them, with 167 affiliated labor camps. The aim was to break all possible opposition, to isolate and humiliate adversaries and to destroy their spirit by physical violence and despair intensified through the prospect of indefinite detention.

During the twelve years of the Third Reich, the function of the concentration camps changed to some extent.[35] There had always been places in the Third Reich in which a multitude of prisoners vegetated at the mercy of the system and its often fanatical and sadistic henchmen. But mass extermination on a large scale came with the war and took place mainly in camps erected outside the Reich in occupied territories, particularly in the east. Ten thousand Jews were taken to Buchenwald in 1938, but the great majority were soon released from the camp, provided they were willing and able to emigrate and left most of their property to the Nazis. The war years led to a large increase in the number of victims detained in concentration camps and also to systematic killing *en masse* by means of modern chemical methods used on an unprecedented scale. Only a small percentage in the camps were then Germans, and by 1945 they accounted for only about 5 to 10 percent of all inmates. The great majority of detainees were non-Germans—Russians, Poles, Belgians, Greeks, Serbs, Croats, French, and Dutch—men and women, and, above all, an immense number of Jews deported from most European countries.

What Hitler and Himmler did was to establish a primitive tribal ethics in a highly industrialized society that had developed novel technological instruments for mass killing. The slogan on large signboards at the entrance to the concentration camp of Buchenwald

[34] See Eugen Kogon, *The Theory and Practice of Hell* and *Anatomy of the S.S. State*, by Hans Buchheim and others (London, 1968), p. 458.
[35] See Chapter 1, "The Concentration Camps, 1933-45," by Martin Broszat in *Anatomy of the S.S. State*.

near Weimar was characteristic: "My Country, Right or Wrong." The whole system encouraged cruelty, especially the unfeeling and barbarian behavior of criminal types, among both the S.S. guards and some of the "Capos," prisoners with a criminal record who were often put in charge of others. There was a premium on inhuman hardness and systematic hatred. Yet it has been rightly pointed out by Martin Broszat that while these primitive outbursts of barbarism were encouraged by the system, they were not the reason for its existence.[36] Arbitrary tormenting of prisoners by individual S.S. functionaries, satisfying of personal lust, and robbing captives were all regarded by Himmler as "weaknesses"—as were all feelings of pity.

Himmler's tribal ethics—proclaiming one type of behavior for those *inside* the group and another for those *outside*—is clearly illustrated when he was *Reichsführer S.S.* in an address to the assembled S.S. group leaders in Posnan on October 4, 1943.

"One principle must be absolutely valid for the S.S. man," Himmler asserted, "we have to be honest, decent, loyal, and comradely to those who share our own blood and to no one else. How the Russians fare, how the Czechs are, is a matter of total indifference to me. We shall take over the good blood of our kind that exists in these people by robbing them of their children, if necessary, and by bringing them up with us. Whether other nations live in prosperity or whether they perish from hunger only interests me as far as we need them as slaves for our culture. I have no other interest in them." [37]

These cruel ethics were imbibed by thousands of S.S. men, among them Rudolf Hoess, commandant of the Auschwitz concentration and extermination camp from 1940 to 1943. We have his revealing autobiographical notes, written after 1945 when he was in detention before the trial by the Polish government that ended in his execution.[38] In the camp at Auschwitz, a little town between Kattowitz, then in German Silesia, and Cracow in Poland, at least two and a half million people were gassed, shot dead, killed through injections, or starved to death standing in little bunkers during the Second World War. About 60,000 people managed to survive. During the second

[36] *Ibid.*

[37] Translated from *Der Nationalsozialismus: Dokumente 1933–1945*, ed. Walther Hofer (Frankfurt, 1957), pp. 113–14.

[38] *Commandant of Auschwitz: The Autobiography of Rudolf Hoess* (London, 1959). There is an introduction by Martin Broszat to the German edition of this book, *Kommandant in Auschwitz* (Stuttgart, 1958), from which a few sentences have been translated and quoted here.

half of the war, the camp contained an average of 100,000 at one time. The cold terror of eliminating hundreds of thousands of "national" and "racial" "subhuman" prisoners was carried out on a routine, organized basis. The dedication of men like Hoess, who never reflected on the moral basis of their actions but obeyed orders from above without question, was an important factor in the system. For it was only through their devotion and unceasing activity that it functioned. Owing to their conscientiousness, "an instrument of terror could give the appearance of an institution of order and education" [Martin Broszat].

Rudolf Hoess was pleased when it turned out that Cyclon B gas could be used to effect mass killings in a very simple, noiseless, and bloodless manner. He claims that he had always had a horror of execution by shooting, thinking of the countless women and children. The regime put a premium on "orderly" elimination of "racially and biologically alien bodies and enemies of the nation" (*Volksschädlinge*). It becomes clear from Hoess's autobiography that those who developed and carried out the technique for mass murder were not just perverted criminals but, in the words of Martin Broszat, "ambitious, duty-obsessed, authoritarian-minded, and prudish philistines who, having been brought up in blind obedience, without a critical sense and without any imagination, told themselves, and allowed others to talk themselves into believing, that the 'liquidation' of hundreds of thousands of people was a service to the nation and the fatherland." A man like Rudolf Hoess, who supervised the murder of thousands of Jews, saw himself as a self-disciplined manipulator acting in accordance with the Hitler–Himmler ideology. After 1945 he maintained that he felt no personal hatred for the Jews; he had simply regarded them as "the enemies of our people."

"In the spring of 1942 hundreds of healthy human beings passed under the blossoming fruit trees of the farm to the gas chamber, into death, mostly without a presentiment of things to come," the oddly sentimental executioner explained, "This picture of growing and perishing is still squarely before my inner eye." It was a grim travesty of Goethe's *Stirb und Werde*, of the great poet's belief in the cycle of life and death. If one can accept the notes of a mass murderer with the mind of a bookkeeper and an obsession with duty, it seems that he was sometimes plagued by doubts as to whether the killing of hundreds of thousands of women and children was really necessary. But he quickly overcame such scruples, and those of some of his subordinates, by referring to the Führer's order and by reiterating that "the destruction of the Jews is necessary in order to liberate Germany and future German generations for all time from our toughest opponents."

Hoess watched while bodies were burnt, gold teeth were broken out of the victims' mouths, and the hair was cut from female heads. He also witnessed through a peephole the grim spectacle of his charges dying in the gas chambers. Hoess was obliged to fulfill this and other unpleasant duties because he was "the person to whom all looked up," because he had to show to everybody that he "not only issued orders and gave the instructions, but was also ready to be present everywhere." His superiors, who do not seem to have envied Hoess his job, impressed on him that any consideration for the victims of the "Final Solution" would be dangerous. After some talks with Eichmann, he predictably felt that the traces of human feeling left in him came close to "a betrayal of the Führer." Hoess felt sorrier for himself than for his innumerable victims. As he observed in retrospect, "all the people in Auschwitz thought: the Commandant has it good." Yet this was only true of his wife and children.

The so-called Auschwitz trial before a German court at Frankfurt-on-Main, which from December, 1963, to August, 1965, threw a grim posthumous light on the practices of mass death in this concentration camp.[39] Twenty years after the events it proved difficult to disentangle the complexities of organized destruction and to establish detailed facts of what had happened. But there could be no doubt about the calculated ruthlessness with which the armed few could torture and dispose of the helpless many in a totalitarian dictatorship.

GERMAN RESISTANCE

It is one of the ironies of twentieth-century German history that the resistance to the Hitler regime emerged largely from the conservative circle that had put the Nazis into power. In 1938, a section of the old guard of aristocrats, generals, and diplomats first tried somewhat half-heartedly to bring Hitler's regime to an end. These men paved the way for a more determined and revolutionary effort to assassinate Hitler and overthrow the Nazis during the second half of the war. Most of the earlier members of the resistance were "de-

---

[39] See Hermann Langbein, *Der Auschwitz Prozess: Eine Dokumentation,* 2 vols. (Vienna, 1965).

liberate or unintentional defenders of the *ancien regime*" [40] (before 1914).

Once the National Socialists were established in power, the majority of the workers acquiesced or supported the regime like the rest of the population. It has been estimated that after 1933 only 10 percent of the former members of the two workers' parties, the Social Democrats and the Communists, were prepared to fight the Hitler regime so far as it was possible within the obvious limits.[41] Moreover, the old disunity and antagonism between the Social Democrats and the Communists did not even stop in the underground struggle. Although the headquarters of the Social Democrats continued to operate from Prague and sent anti-Nazi material surreptitiously into Germany, it received a very small response from the former rank-and-file of the party. The urge and the pressure to conform proved far too great. After a few years, the Social Democrats, shaken by the arrests and murders of their friends in concentration camps, gave up any hope of being able to influence the masses decisively in a state where the army was admired and the secret police had the upper hand.

The Communists, on the other hand, were much more familiar with small-scale methods of conspiracy than were the order-loving Social Democrats. Although the first Communist groups were wiped out by the *Gestapo* rather quickly, the party produced new groups again and again to spread anti-Nazi literature. This clandestine work stopped during the period of cooperation between Hitler and Stalin, but it became active again after the German attack on the Soviet Union in June, 1941. In spite of the overwhelming odds, some Communist propaganda was distributed and some groups were trained in sabotage. During the last years of the war, the presence of a great number of foreign workers in Germany could be utilized. There was an extreme-left socialist resistance group in Berlin around Dr. Arvid Harnack, an official in the ministry of economics, Harold Schulze–Boysen, a lieutenant in the air ministry, and Rolf von Schelia, an official in the foreign ministry. Part of that group was in regular intelligence and radio contact with the Red Army. This circle and its spy ring, to which the National Socialist judges gave the name of "Red Chapel" (*Rote Kapelle*), was detected and destroyed in

---

[40] See Ralf Dahrendorf, *Society and Democracy in Germany* (London, 1968), pp. 414–15.

[41] *Der deutsche Widerstand gegen Hitler*, ed. Walter Schmitthenner and Hans Buchheim (Cologne, 1966), p. 209.

August, 1942. Many executions followed. After that debacle, the remaining underground Communists were more prepared to cooperate with socialist idealists like Adolf Reichwein, an educator, and Julius Leber. But again, many of these socialists and Communists were also arrested later by the *Gestapo* (Reichwein and Leber early in July, 1944). Other high-minded young socialists had joined the Kreisau circle (named after the estate of one of the members, Count Helmuth James Moltke) with which the former socialist trade-union leader and state minister Leuschner also had contacts. The Kreisau circle differed from the older set of opponents, who were as hostile to parliamentary democracy as they were to the National Socialist dictatorship. Men like Carl Goerdeler, the former Lord Mayor of Königsberg and Leipzig, Ulrich von Hassel, German Ambassador to Rome until 1937, and General Ludwig Beck, Chief of the General Staff from 1935 to 1937, had their roots in Prussia before World War I. Earlier, they had all longed for a revision of the Treaty Versailles, a strong German power in the heart of Europe, and an authoritarian regime free from the taint of democracy and permissiveness. The Prussian sense of discipline and law and order and a sense of responsibility now prompted these men to question the destructive willfulness and inhumanity of the National Socialists, the vulgar impact of their mass formations, and their disregard of the rights of the individual. "Moral values, and frequently their reality in the past, were held up against the arbitrariness of the Nazis." [42]

General Beck was more guarded and sceptical, compared with the overoptimistic and sometimes indiscreet Goerdeler. Neither was a born rebel—if such a type exists—but each gradually and reluctantly felt a strong aversion to a regime they had at first welcomed for reasons of national prestige. It has been rightly said of Beck that "he was the epitome of the virtues of the German General Staff, but he also suffered . . . from their inability to see beyond the interest of their own calling." [43] Although Beck was without any political experience, he was not irresolute and half-hearted in his opposition, as were so many of his colleagues.

Goerdeler, who traveled abroad a good deal in the years before the Second World War, believed that a revision of the Treaty of Versailles in Germany's favor by the Western powers was by no means impossible. He hoped that this breakthrough would be granted not to Hitler but to members of the more trustworthy and more easily

[42] R. Dahrendorf, op. cit., p. 414.
[43] John Wheeler–Bennett, op. cit., p. 299.

satisfied conservative circles. The view was shared to some extent by the ambitious and ambiguous Dr. Schacht and by certain officials in the German Foreign Ministry. These men were deeply worried in the summer of 1938, when Hitler deliberately brought the international crisis over the Sudetenland to the boiling point. Beck, who resigned from his post as Chief of the General Staff of the Army in August, 1938, and his successor, General Franz Halder, were convinced that a European war, fostered by Hitler, was imminent and that it would be a catastrophe for Germany. General von Witzleben worked out a plan in which troops would quickly take over the Reich Chancellory in Berlin, remove the Führer, and hold him at an unknown place as soon as he had given the order for the attack on Czechoslovakia. He was to be put before a people's court, and on the strength of a certificate from a panel of psychiatrists, be declared insane. Through an emissary, Ewald von Kleist, the group managed to contact Sir Robert Vansittart and Winston Churchill. At the same time, the German Chargé d'Affaires in London, Theodor Kordt, approached Sir Horace Wilson, who had the ear of Neville Chamberlain, and the British Foreign Secretary Lord Halifax, with the message that the Berlin conspirators were prepared to strike on the day of German mobilization. They asked Britain and France to stand firm against Hitler and his war policy because it was the only way to avert European conflict. Mr. Chamberlain was not prepared to listen to the uncertain voices of a handful of Germans with a grievance. Instead he pertinaciously pursued the road to Berchtesgaden, Godesberg, and Munich, and by doing so, nipped the plans for the revolt in the bud. However it is doubtful whether these plans would have succeeded, as the conspirators lacked a clear and resolute leader.

After 1945, General Franz Halder, Beck's successor as Chief of the General Staff, and others alleged that the only prewar attempt to remove Hitler with any chance of success was frustrated by Neville Chamberlain's readiness to go to the Munich conference. Is this true? One historian maintains that "this apology for failure, circulated by interested parties, does not hold water for a moment." [44] Another, however, argues that Chamberlain's announcement of the forthcoming Four-Power conference made all the difference. By this action "the basis for the popular support necessary for such a putsch had been pulled away." [45] The conspirators were suddenly faced with Hitler's tremendous triumph. Our judgment in this case depends on

[44] John Wheeler-Bennett, op. cit., p. 421.
[45] R. J. O'Neill, op. cit., p. 165.

whether or not one believes in the genuiness of the anti-Hitler plot. There is the strong argument that "even if Chamberlain and Daladier had decided not to come to Munich, such a putsch would have been an extremely risky undertaking." [46]

The Blitzlike advances of the German armies in the West in the spring of 1940 took the wind out of the plotters' sails, but it was only the turn of the tide. The catastrophies of Stalingrad and North Africa at the end of 1942 and the intense bombing of German cities activated a younger set of German resisters and prompted some of them to action. Doubts of the Führer's halo of infallibility grew among the military experts, while others felt that the war could only end in disaster for Germany. Moreover, some officers on the Eastern front became aware of the mass murders of Jews, Russians, and others by the S.S. inside and outside the concentration camps. They felt ashamed as well as alarmed by the wave of hatred of everything German brought on by such enormities. In their plans for a better post-Nazi Germany, the members of the Kreisau circle were oriented more toward Europe than were the older, more conservative set of plotters.

Some aristocrats like Count Moltke and Adam von Trott zu Solz, a former Rhodes scholar at Oxford, had British–American affiliations, while others like the Jesuit fathers Delp and Röscher and the remarkable Protestant theologian Dietrich Bonhoeffer were moved to turn against the tyrant by the dictates of their Christian conscience. Idealistic socialists like Leber, Reichwein, and Haubach added a further element and contributed to a synthesis of Christian, conservative, and socialist values.

This group also tried to make contact with the Western Allies and convince them that there was an internal opposition to Hitler in Germany. When Dr. Bell, the Bishop of Chichester, visited Stockholm on church business in May, 1942, he met Dietrich Bonhoeffer and another German Protestant pastor. Their message, which was conveyed by Dr. Bell afterwards to the British Foreign Secretary, revealed the aims of the German opposition, which was working for a nation governed by law and social justice and was willing to join the Federation of Free European Nations, including a free Poland and Czechoslovakia. However the Stockholm meeting bore no fruit. When Dr. Bell reported his discussions to the foreign secretary after his return to England, Mr. Eden felt that "he must be scrupu-

[46] *Ibid.*

lously careful not to enter into even the appearance of negotiations with the enemy and to be able to say truthfully that this was so both to Russia and America." [47] He was obviously afraid that at a time when the Western powers were still on the defensive and hard-pressed on all fronts, secret contacts with a handful of resisters would create suspicion among Britian's allies.

The attempt to forcefully put an end to Hitler's intolerable tyranny was finally carried out by a few young and desperately deter-mined officers. Several of their attempts on Hitler's life in 1943 mis-carried. In July, 1944, after the Allies had established themselves in France, some of the conspirators doubted whether it was the right moment to do away with Hitler. Major General Henning von Tresckow, who had organized the earlier attempts on Hitler's life, sent them this message from the Eastern front: The assassination of Hitler "must take place whatever the cost. Even if it does not succeed, the Berlin action must go forward. The point now is not whether the coup has any practical purpose but to prove to the world before history that German resistance is ready to stake its all." On July 20, 1944, operation "Valkyrie" was put into effect in Berlin and in other centers; the initial move was made by thirty-seven-year-old Colonel Claus Count Schenk von Stauffenberg, Chief of Staff of General Fromm's Replacement Army. During a routine report to Hit-ler at his headquarters in East Prussia, he placed a bomb in a briefcase under the conference table close to the Führer's seat. Stauffenberg managed to leave and catch a plane to Berlin after watching the explosion from a distance. Although several people were killed or seriously injured, Hitler himself was hardly hurt and soon recovered. As it turned out, some serious mistakes of omission were made by the conspirators. Unfortunately, operation "Valkyrie" in Berlin was started three hours after the explosion at the Wolfsschanze (after Stauffenberg had reached the capital). Although the conspirators secured control of the war ministry and other important points in the city, the telephone lines between the Führer's headquarters and the propaganda ministry were only briefly blocked, and the news that Hitler had survived created consternation among the plotters and a feeling of relief among his supporters.

As soon as General Fromm, an ambiguous and opportunistic figure who had neither hindered nor helped the resisters, realized that the plot of his subordinates had failed, he turned against them. A

[47] Quoted in R. C. D. Jasper, George Bell Bishop of Chichester (London, 1968), p. 271.

court-martial was set up; and as a result of Fromm's findings, four of the conspirators were executed the same evening in the courtyard. They included Colonel Stauffenberg who, when facing the firing squad, exclaimed, "Long live our sacred Germany." [48] Predictably, Hitler and Himmler took a fearful revenge on the conspirators. All the resistance cells were wiped out, and many of the plotters suffered a shocking death at the hands of the *Gestapo*. The valiant attempt had failed; and the masses—half-frightened and half-reassured— continued to back the regime. If some of the conspirators had suffered from lack of resolution and illusions, this cannot be said of the determined Colonel Stauffenberg. He had been close to the socialist members of the circle and had been opposed to the selection of the conservative Goerdeler as Reich Chancellor. Though he wanted social justice for the masses, he was not oriented towards Soviet Russia, as later Communist propaganda in East Germany made out. With all his dash and daring, Stauffenberg had few illusions. Only a few days before July 20, he told a sympathiser: "It is now time that something be done. But he who has the courage to do it must do so in the knowledge that he will go down in German history as a traitor. If he does not do it, however, he will then be a traitor to his own conscience." [49] Stauffenberg and his friend, Adam von Trott zu Solz, shared a similar outlook. Both favored an egalitarian society without class warfare but with a common purpose. They were "conservative revolutionaries," as Adam von Trott's English biographer has said.[50]

German opponents of Hitler were often torn by "troubled loyalties"—between the duty to support the war effort of their own nation and the moral imperative to resist a barbarous system which, they felt, was based on inhumanity and racial arrogance and would in the long run prove as disastrous in their own nation as they had proved in others. There was a difficult dividing line between the duty to resist and the danger of high treason. Major General Oster of the German counterintelligence department, *Abwehr*, warned Dutch and Belgian authorities of the impending German attack on their countries in 1940. The pro-Communists of the "Red Chapel" later transmitted important intelligence to the Soviet Union and the

---

[48] General Beck was allowed to end his own life, though a sergeant had to give him the *coup de grace*. Goerdeler was a fugitive for some weeks, but was detained in the end and executed after lengthy interrogation.

[49] Joachim Kramarz, *Stauffenberg* (London, 1967), p. 185.

[50] Christopher Sykes, *Troubled Loyalty: A Biography of Adam von Trott zu Solz* (London, 1969), p. 408.

Red Army. These were perhaps exceptional cases, but they reveal a realm of inner conflict unknown to the resistance movements in countries under German occupation.

Stauffenberg and other progressives like Carl Mierendorff, Theo Haubach, and Julius Leber would have been a great asset to their nation and to Europe in the post-Hitler era. In spite of their failure, the men of July 20 should be assured of an honorable place in the annals of European history.

10

Literature and Politics: 1914-1949
Thomas Mann and Bertolt Brecht

THOMAS MANN

Thomas Mann is undoubtedly the most representative German novelist and writer of the first half of the twentieth century. His international fame is reflected in the fact that by 1956 translations of his works had appeared in thirty-one countries. There exist alone forty-eight different translations of his first long novel, *Buddenbrooks*, and twenty-eight of *The Magic Mountain*. In addition, over 200 books and theses have been written by now on his personality and work.

Thomas Mann (1875–1955) was only twenty-five when *Buddenbrooks: Decline of a Family* appeared. This German counterpart to John Galsworthy's *Forsyte Saga* is the story of four generations of merchants in Mann's birthplace, Lübeck. Largely based on the story of his own family, it combines rich documentation with graphic descriptions of people and conditions, comedy and melancholy, bold characterization and pessimistic philosophy. The progressive refinement of the later Buddenbrooks—their artistic abilities and philosophical understanding—had to be paid for by a decline in wealth and the early death of the last of them, the young and sensitive Hanno. He is the artist in a family of burghers, and the discrepancy between these types also forms the theme of some of Mann's subtle short stories such as *Tonio Kröger* and *Death in Venice*.

His second major novel, *The Magic Mountain*, was written twenty years later; and its locale, a Swiss tuberculosis sanatorium,

226

is very different. Yet decline and death are even more emphatically the central issues. The main figure, Hans Castorp, also comes from a Hanseatic patrician family; he is well-mannered, thoughtful, and passive, and often an astute observer of that specific world far away from the ordinary routine "down under." Though he intended to stay at the sanatorium for only three weeks in order to visit a sick relative, he remains seven years on the *Magic Mountain*. There are superb sketches of the doctors and their patients, and medicine and psychoanalysis play their part in this mammoth work of eleven hundred pages. Above all, there is also a long and extensive confrontation between two opposite attitudes to society and life, represented by the Italian freemason, Settembrini, the humanist, the firm believer in progress, democracy, and world peace, and his opponent, Naphta, born as an East European Jew, trained in the Talmud, but later brought up by the Jesuits, and now an ardent convert to the Catholic Church. Each of them, Settembrini, the eloquent educator, and Naphta, the shrewd dialectician, who, by the way, also favors terror and the dictatorship of the proletariat, wants to win over the politely listening Hans Castorp, but in vain, for he favors a compromise between the two extremes. The last we hear of Castorp after he has left the curious atmosphere of the sanatorium is that he has volunteered for military service in the First World War and is involved with other soldiers in bravely storming a hill; we never learn whether or not he survived the ordeal. With this end to a long but fascinating story, Mann perhaps wanted to indicate the watershed that the war of 1914 formed for German and European society.

It was towards the end of that war that Thomas Mann caused a stir by a book on politics, the *Reflections of a Nonpolitical Person*. Deeply steeped in the German romantic and conservative tradition, Mann came to the defense of the German cause. His guiding light was then Frederick the Great, to whom he had devoted a lengthy essay. Mann drew a sharp dividing line between the profoundness of German culture and the shallowness of Western civilization. In doing so, he clashed with his brother, Heinrich, a distinguished novelist in his own right, who, in an essay on Zola, had defended the Western approach to democracy and socialism. Heinrich Mann symbolized for Thomas the hideous type of *Zivilisationsliterat*, the shallow man of letters without roots in the culture of his country. In the foreword to his *Reflections*, Thomas Mann confessed that he was deeply convinced the German people would "never be able to love political democracy" and that the much maligned "authoritarian state"

(*Obrigkeitsstaat*) was and would remain the kind of government suited to the German people "and fundamentally desired by them." Yet Mann was no cheap jingo patriot or annexationist. In a letter to a friend in 1915, he had already stated that for his part he "would find little pleasure in belonging to a nation which puts its foot on the neck of Europe." He admitted that the German character was "vexatiously problematical." Yet Mann still declared anyone "who desires that the Germany way should disappear from the earth in favor of *humanité* or *raison* is guilty of an outrage." [1]

However, Thomas Mann realized by 1917 that democracy was inevitable in Germany too, and he came gradually round to supporting it. As with the historian Friederich Meinecke, Mann's attitude was changed by the German defeat and the feeble attitude of the Kaiser and of the old ruling class in 1918. This individualistic moralist, so steeped in the tradition of Richard Wagner, Schopenhauer, and Nietzsche, accepted the Weimar Republic. In an address in 1922 Mann declared that "democracy can be something more German than an Imperial gala opera. Does the possibility of harmony dawn today, despite all the misery? Is not the Republic only another name for the popular happiness of the unity of state and culture?" Cool and practical, Mann now pursued a middle course between the anti-republican doctrinaires of the nationalist right and the critics on the republican left, who in weeklies such as *Weltbühne* and *Das Tagebuch* bitterly lamented the discrepancy between their ideal of a truly democratic and social-minded state and its blurred and fragmentary reality. Thomas Mann now favored a synthesis of tradition and progress, of the legacy of Goethe and Wagner with the modern trend towards the welfare state. While respected by the critics on the left, Mann was mercilessly attacked by the nationalists on the right. They accused him of having betrayed his former attachment to the eternal German values and to romanticism for the pottage of a transitory concern with the hapless republic and "Father Ebert."

Mann had no illusions from the beginning about the nature and aims of the Hitler regime. Nor was he surprised when in March, 1933, his own works, together with those of other independent minds, were publicly burned in Berlin on Goebbels' orders. A few days after Hitler came to power, Mann went on a previously arranged lecture tour in Switzerland. Thomas Mann and his family never returned to Nazi Germany. During the first few years of the Third Reich, he

---

[1] For his changing attitudes to Germany and the Germans, see K. Sontheimer, *Thomas Mann und die Deutschen* (Munich, 1961).

remained silent on politics. But in January, 1936, he published a sharp attack on the regime in a Swiss newspaper. The Nazi government replied in the autumn by depriving him of his German citizenship, a distinction he shared with his brother, Heinrich Mann, and with two of his children. Moreover, the dean of the faculty of arts at the University of Bonn informed him soon afterwards that he had forfeited his honorary doctorate. Thomas Mann answered in a famous letter to the dean that was translated into many languages and was later clandestinely circulated as a pamphlet in Germany. "I could not have lived," he declared in it, "nor have worked, I would have been stifled . . . without frankly expressing from time to time my fathomless disgust for the wretched words and the more wretched deeds that have happened at home. . . . You have the incredible effrontery to confuse yourselves with Germany! Yet perhaps the moment is not very far away when the German people will give their utmost not to be confused with you." [2]

The writer and his family went for a short while to Czechoslovakia and then to the United States, where they lived from 1938 until 1952. On an earlier visit to Washington in 1935, he was received by President Franklin D. Roosevelt. Mann was impressed. "When I left the White House at that time," he wrote later, "I knew Hitler had lost." In 1944, he became an American citizen. Thomas Mann was soon invited to give lectures at Princeton; later he settled in California. Unlike most of his fellow emigrés, he took an active interest in the life of the United States. Erika Mann, his daughter, has reported that by doing so "he made many friends, and some enemies." Yet the great writer remained basically German, and once proudly wrote to his brother, "Where I am there is German culture." In the turmoil of the Second World War, he became a hard-working political propagandist, regularly recording broadcasts for the German Service of the British Broadcasting Corporation. Mann never proved more outspoken and pugnacious than in his "Addresses to the German Radio Listeners." There was no sitting on the fence, so characteristic of his earlier writings. The radio talks were filled with a cold hatred of Hitler, the destructive tyrant, and were inspired by the belief that, though German people had gone astray, Germany and National Socialism were not identical. The Third Reich was portrayed as the dynamic incarnation of Satan, as "the malice of Hell," and the fight against it as "a sacred defense." The addresses were in-

* Walter A. Beréndson, *Thomas Mann* (Lübeck, 1965), p. 141.

tended to reveal to the German audience the stark reality in which they had allowed themselves to become involved. The detached artist of former days had turned into a semireligious crusader against an evil that endangered both his own nation and the entire world. "In this war," he said in one of the last broadcasts, Germany's opponents "were from the first faced with the entire German inventive power, valour, intelligence, love of obedience, military prowess—in short with the whole German national strength that as such backed the regime and fought its battles—Hitler and Himmler would be nothing at all were it not for the strength and blind loyalty of German men presently fighting and dying with a fatal lion's courage for these rascals." In a lecture, "Germany and the Germans," delivered in Washington in 1945 on the occasion of his seventieth birthday, Thomas Mann pointed to the paradoxes of German introversion (*Innerlichkeit*). Whereas it had given a great and profound impetus to European thought through the Reformation and the romantic movement, it had prevented a more balanced approach by its refusal to accept the spirit of European humanism and democracy. In his last major work, the novel *Dr. Faustus*, there is a constant parallel between the tragic fate of its hero, the musician of genius, Adrian Leverkühn, who makes a pact with the devil and ends in madness, and the German people, who entrusted themselves to the seducer, Adolf Hitler, and by doing so find themselves finally in a catastrophic abyss.

When the demonic dream of Hitler's hegemony over Germany and Europe had vanished, leaving behind a trail of ruin and misery, Thomas Mann considered whether it was possible to turn the more positive aspects of the German national character to productive account. He felt that postwar Germany could and should participate in the awakening of mankind to an awareness of its practical unity, in the new trend towards a world government and a broader kind of social humanism. The Cold War and the growing division of the world into Western and Communist spheres distressed him. While appreciating the contribution the United States had made against the Axis Powers, he later deplored the growth of McCarthyism in the States and had serious misgivings about the attitude of some German-American groups. On the other hand, he sympathized with the new approach of the first Labor government in postwar Britain and with its ideal of the modern welfare state and justice for all.

It was only natural that Thomas Mann should want to spend the last few years of his life where it had begun—in Europe. (He died in Zurich in August, 1955). He had gone to Germany in 1949 without settling there. As Germany was to him a spiritual unity in spite of the sharp political divisions now running through it, he insisted on visiting both German states, the Federal Republic and the German Democratic Republic. Some West German writers who had lived through the Third Reich, such as Frank Thiess, now blamed him for not having shared their "inner emigration" in Nazi Germany instead of spending the years in the safety and comfort of California. Other critics in West Germany as well as in the United States disapproved of Mann's visit to East Germany and suspiciously viewed him as a fellow traveler. Mann followed his own path, and in 1949 decided to deliver the same address on the 200th anniversary of Goethe's birth in West *and* East Germany—in Frankfurt-on-Main where the great poet had been born and had spent his carefree youth, and in Weimar, the city of his greatest achievements and maturity. In Weimar the Communist Party leaders made much of their illustrious guest. Mann's visit was thoroughly organized; he was awarded the Goethe Prize and declared an honorary citizen of the town. Flags, garlands, and flowers appeared everywhere, and school children and bands lined the streets for his welcome.

In contrast, Mann's reception in Frankfurt was not politically manipulated, but it was sincere. In a speech of welcome delivered by the Lord Mayor of the town, Walter Kolb, but actually written by a local author, Gottfried Stein, an independent mind with a fine understanding of Mann's works, Thomas Mann was presented as a bridge-builder between Germany and the United States, and as a complex but great writer who allied German cultural traditions with a worldwide outlook. In his reply, he explained that it was the memory of the sage of Weimar that had caused him to return to Germany. "I know no occupation zones," he said, "my visit is directed towards Germany, to Germany as a whole. Who should guarantee and represent the unity of Germany if not an independent author whose true language is German, unaffected by occupation forces?"

Thomas Mann had traversed a long and difficult road. At first he had known only Germany, then Europe, then the New World across the Atlantic. He had been able to learn from hard and bitter experiences. The onetime champion of Frederick the Great and admirer of the German romantic tradition had gradually developed into a cosmopolitan humanist. If, despite her political divisions, he regarded Germany essentially as one, he now equally stressed the oneness of Europe and the world. The former Hanseatic burgher and the sensitive artist had long merged in him and so had the German patriot, the citizen of the United States, the visionary of one civilized world.

BERTOLT BRECHT

Like Thomas Mann, Bertolt Brecht (1898–1956) is one of the very few writers in German of the first half of the present century to reach worldwide fame (Rainer Maria Rilke and Franz Kafka are other examples). If the patrician Thomas Mann developed gradually from a conservative to a progressive humanist, Brecht shocked and entertained the world as a forceful playwright and a sardonic critic of the establishment. Brecht began as a somewhat cynical anarchist, evolved into a rather unorthodox Marxist, and ended with a humanistic pessimism of his own.

As a schoolboy, Brecht, the son of a middle-ranking business manager in Augsburg, Bavaria, was asked during the first year of World War I to write an essay on the classic tag that "it is sweet and fitting to die for one's country." He dismissed it promptly as a mere piece of propaganda: "To depart from life," he declared, "is always hard, in one's bed as well as on the battlefield and certainly most so for the young in the flowering of their days." Only the plea of an understanding teacher that this was the case of a confused youngster saved him from dismissal from the school. But when, on another occasion, his class was asked to prove that Goethe was a greater writer than Schiller, he promptly maintained the opposite and was severely disciplined. In the troubled years from 1917 to 1920, this young pupil of Frank Wedekind wavered between the worship of a chaotic but grand life and sardonic rejection of the social order. His first play, *Baal*, written in 1918 and performed in Munich in 1923, has been described as "a passionate acceptance of the world in all its sordid grandeur." The theater audience of his second play, *Drums in the Night*, was confronted with streamers ordering them, "Don't stare so romantically" and proclaiming, "Every man feels best inside his own skin." It is the the story of Kragler, the soldier returned from the war who does not join the Spartacus rising and puts up with the fact that his bride has become pregnant while he was away; he is unheroic, but also genuine. "I am a swine and the swine goes home," is his final comment. A leading German critic, Herbert Ihering, wrote at the time, "Brecht feels the chaotic and putrid decay of the age. Hence the unparalleled force of his images."

It was not by chance that Brecht's *The Threepenny Opera*

(1928) became a popular success. This brilliant and trenchant adaption of John Gay's *Beggar's Opera* reflected the cynical mood of many Germans during the closing years of the Weimar Republic. "For man is not clever enough for life," runs one of his biting comments. What in Gay is a contrast between high society and the underworld become in Brecht a confrontation between the bourgeoisie and the very human underworld of criminals. The story focuses on the marriage between a highwayman, Macheath, and the attractive Polly Peachum, daughter of London's king of the beggars. In a later version Brecht gave the play a more definite anticapitalist twist by letting Macheath end up as the director of a national bank. When earlier, Macheath intends to change from street robbery to bank robbery, he tells his gang wistfully: "What is a jemmy compared with a share on the stock exchange? What is the murder of a man compared with employing a man?" Brecht knew his types, and he was at home at race tracks and boxing matches. The provocative music by Kurt Weill, with its mixture of cockney songs, jazz, and parodies of classic carols, was a great public success. Willy Haas has described the author of *The Threepenny Opera* as "uncanny. He had the profile of a Jesuit, the steel-rimmed spectacles of a schoolteacher, the short haircut of a prisoner, and the shabby leather jacket of an old-party Bolshevik. . . . He spoke in a very superior, harsh, and abstract manner." [3]

Later the cynical outlook of Brecht the anarchist gave way to the Puritanism of a disciplined Marxist who wrote "didactic plays" with a purpose. The first of them, *The Measure Taken* (*Die Massnahme*), anticipates the dilemma of totalitarian Communism with astonishing insight. There is a controlling chorus that symbolizes the collective conscience of the Communist Party and that listens to four soloists from a group of party workers that had been sent on an illegal mission to China in the 1920s. One by one they justify the liquidation of the fifth member of the group who did not return. There was no alternative; for when all had descended into anonymity by wearing masks, he had disclosed his identity as an agent and had symbolically torn off his mask. In the end, the chorus acquits the four of any guilt and approves of the measure they had taken in the interest of the party. Purposeful collectivism triumphs over the erring individual. Indeed this play "transcends the author's intention" by expressing "years before the great Soviet purge trials the essential nature of Sta-

---

[3] Willy Haas, *Die literarische Welt* (Munich, 1960), p. 144.

linist Communism." [4] The totalitarian belief that man can be manipulated and his character changed into a different mold had been
anticipated in Brecht's play, *Man's A Man*. Though funny, the
story has serious implications. Man is malleable for better or worse,
runs the lesson, his brain can be washed, his whole outlook on life
can be redirected.

Brecht left Germany with Hitler's coming to power. From 1933,
he lived abroad in exile for the next fourteen years. Settling first in
Denmark, he went to Finland in 1940 and in the following year
traveled from there through the Soviet Union to the United States.
Although he was joint editor of an antifascist monthly published in
Moscow in German, he preferred not to reside in Stalin's Russia,
where so many foreign communists, including some Germans,
perished during the 1930s. Brecht seems to have realized that the
attitudes of the Russian party bureaucracy was a far cry from true
socialism. Unlike Thomas Mann, Brecht did not take a very active
part in the fight against the Third Reich. However, some of the
pessimistic "Svendborg" poems he wrote in Denmark during the
period of appeasement are telling:

> The Governments are drafting nonaggression pacts—
> Little man,
> You should make your testament.
>
> .   .   .   .
>
> It is night. The couples lie down in their beds;
> The young wives will give birth to orphans.

In his later sequence of twenty-eight scenes, *Fears and Miseries
of the Third Reich*, of which seventeen appeared in English under
the title *The Private Life of the Master Race* (1948), the hopeless
plight of the people as mere cogs in the totalitarian wheel is well
depicted. The brutality of the Storm Troopers, the fear of parents
who dread being reported to the party by their son, who is in the
Hitler Jugend, the tragedy of a Jewish wife who plans to kill herself
to make things easier for her "Aryan" husband—these events, based
on newspaper clippings and eyewitness reports, run true to life. *The
Resistible Rise of Arturo Ui* (1941) is a scathing satire on the career
of Hitler and his lieutenants who are disguised in the plays as a

---

[4] Martin Esslin, *Brecht, A Choice of Evils* (London, 1959), p. 259.

Chicago underworld gang; by the "protective" bullying of business people, the gang eventually takes over their combine. Though not exactly a piece of history, the play shows remarkable insight into the weird mentality of Hitler. In the character of Arturo Ui, Hitler learns from a faded Shakespearean actor how to conduct himself and how to strut, sit, and speak in order to impress the masses. In exposing Hitler as an hysterical but cunning adventurer from the gutter, Brecht combats what he calls "the romantic concept of history" of the petite bourgeoisie. This story of organized crime perhaps throws more light on the blood bath of June 30, 1934, than many history textbooks.

Convinced that all history is the history of class struggle, Brecht's sympathy lies with the exploited masses, the little man, the servants, albeit he did not make heroes out of them. In his play *The Caucasian Chalk Circle*, the servants steal and plunder after their masters have fled—a feature severely criticized in the East German press. Yet the proletarians in his works are always natural, and Brecht clearly approves of their will to live and fight for existence. On the other hand, his capitalists and governors are more often caricatures than real people, or too complex like the eccentric rich Finnish landowner, Puntila. Brecht's secular, near-Confucian wisdom is neatly expressed in *Stories of Herr Keuner*, which comment on many aspects of everyday life as well as on friendship, religion, and human behavior. "What do you do," Herr Keuner was asked, "when you love a person?" "I make a pattern [*Entwurf*] of him and see to it that he becomes similar." "Which? The pattern to the man?" "No," said Keuner, "the man to the pattern."

Brecht had a good deal of the chameleon in him. He knew how to adjust to changing circumstances and how to make the best of most worlds. He liked to keep an escape route open. When he settled in East Berlin after World War II, he acquired Austrian nationality and had a bank account in Switzerland. Politically, he sided with Communism, though he was not uncritical of the Ulbricht regime. Artistically, he found much more understanding for his work in the West, and his publisher resided in West, not East Germany. There were no Utopian trends or expectations in Brecht's work, and in later years his outlook was basically that of a pessimistic humanist. His attitude to life had been largely conditioned by the turmoil in Germany after the First World War, when the bourgeoisie began to totter, and violence and terror became commonplace. "The world is poor, and man is bad," runs a statement in *The Threepenny*

Opera; and in another of his early plays man is called "the meanest thing al've, and the weakest." The main character Shen Te in *The Good Woman of Setzuan* asks trenchantly:

> Something must be wrong with your world,
> Is there a reward for wickedness?
> Why do the good receive,
> Such hard punishment?

Joan Dark of the Chicago stockyard is doomed because she is innocent and good. In many ways, Brecht is in the great European tradition of pessimism. Evil prevails in his plays, and there is no God to defuse the time bombs placed by irrational forces. The role of fate in classical tragedy is replaced "by the unscrutable workings of the social order which molds the life of the characters and tosses them into misfortune or happiness." [5] Men and women can be manipulated and brainwashed by them. Brecht's pessimistic humanism, helped by this simple, drastic diction, is forcefully revealed in one of his best plays *Mother Courage*. A cockney profiteer in the Thirty Years War, Mother Courage sells food, drink, and comfort to the soldiers behind the lines. She lived by the war and must therefore lose by it. In fact, her three children tragically perish one by one. But *Mother Courage* is open to different interpretations. Anyone who saw the impressive acting by Therese Giese in the main role will view her as a brave woman of the people who fights against heavy odds and yet refuses to give in. To Brecht himself, her behavior is a warning against the stupidity of supporting any war. "What I am at," she says, "is the survival of myself and my children with my wagon." War is all round her and yet she is oblivious to its destructive force. Virtue is questioned and remains without reward. At the end of one scene, amidst the ruins of a destroyed village, Kattrin holds a living baby in her arms, a symbol of "triumphant compassion which could not abolish, and yet stood out against the greed, malice, and uncharitableness on every hand." [6]

If Mother Courage, the embodiment of the lower orders, is by no means always good, the main character of *Herr Puntila and His Man Matti*, the personification of the capitalist ruling class, is not altogether bad. Rather, he is amusingly complex; for Puntila, the Finnish landowner, displays good humor, kindness, and generosity

---

[5] Martin Esslin, *Brecht*, op. cit., p. 231.
[6] Ronald Gray, *Brecht* (Edinburgh and London, 1961), p. 97.

when he is drunk, but lives only for making money and calculation when he is sober. Only rarely does a positive moral emerge from Brecht's sophisticated plays. The exception is *The Caucasian Chalk Circle*, where two women bid for the possession of a child. Grusha, a kitchen maid who saved the infant earlier, competes with his mother, the wife of a tyrannical governor who had left it behind during an insurrection and now claims the boy back. In the end, Judge Azdak, a grotesque and far from admirable figure, gives the boy to Grusha, because whereas the mother uses violence to secure her child, Grusha does not. The moral is that "things should belong to those who are good for them: the children to those who are motherly . . . and the valley to those who will irrigate it and make it fruitful." If this is utilitarian ethics, it is at least ethics without reference to a party dogma.

11

Major Issues of Foreign Policy Since 1949

The emergence of the two German states after World War II and their internal development and structure have been discussed in the first chapter of this book. In this final chapter we return from the long and complex path of German history to the contemporary scene. The major issues in foreign policy as they have developed in the two German republics since their creation in 1949 will be considered briefly. The two Germanies have been deeply affected by the tensions of the Cold War and the formation of rival power blocs arising from it. The problems of individual freedom and the question of national reunification or coexistence of the two Germanies have been vital issues during the last twenty years, issues of truly international significance.

Dr. Adenauer's Western Orientation (1949–1963)

The fact that the first chancellor of the Federal Republic, Dr. Adenauer, sided from the beginning with the Western Allies is as important as the skill with which he managed to exact more and more concessions from them. The paradoxical international situation that dissolved the Four-Power alliance of the war in less than two years became midwife to the birth of the two German republics. In 1945, all military installations and organizations in Germany were destroyed, and even toy soldiers for children were looked upon with official disfavor by the occupation authorities. By 1950, leading circles in the United States, Britain, and France insisted that German soldiers were required as part of an overall front to defend Western Europe against a possible Russian invasion. The Western Powers also felt that they could not justify the continued presence of their troops on German soil to their taxpayers without the West Germans themselves contributing their share to the joint defense effort. The 1948 coup d'état in Czechoslovakia in Prague, the Berlin crisis of the same year, and the impact of the Korean War in 1950 accelerated the change of West Germany's status from an object of interallied occupation policy to an associated power in the Western camp.

Dr. Adenauer knew what he was doing when, in November, 1949, he agreed that the Federal Republic should join the Council of Europe and become a member of the proposed International Ruhr Authority. A further step toward recognition and cooperation was his joint demarche in May, 1950, with the French Foreign Minister, Robert Schumann, for a European Coal and Steel Community. This step allayed the French fear of a German military comeback in the Ruhr and, at the same time, put an end to the planned International Ruhr Authority. On the other hand, it placed the new Federal Republic on a wider canvas and helped towards German rehabilitation. Dr. Adenauer believed that reunification could only be brought about by a policy of strength and by the integration of the young republic into Western Europe. This view was sharply contested by Kurt Schumacher and other Social Democrats who were opposed to German rearmament and still believed that the way to reunification lay in a rapprochement with the Soviet Union, though Schumacher was a decided anti-Communist. Christian pacifists like Martin Niemoeller and Dr. Gustav Heinemann, Adenauer's minister of internal affairs, were against any new military games.[1] From 1949 to the middle of the 1950s, the Socialists remained opposed to West Germany's integration with Western Europe, partly from fear that this would lead to the formation of a Catholic, clerical bloc, and partly because they thought it would make unification more difficult. To the satisfaction of the German Social Democrats and of both Communists and Nationalists in France, the proposed European Defense Community (EDC) was not ratified by the French

[1] Dr. Heinemann even left the federal cabinet and the CDU over the issue and later joined the Social Democrats. (In 1966, he became minister of justice in the coalition cabinet, and in 1969 he was elected the third federal president of the republic.)

Parliament in August, 1954. However, other channels were found to integrate the new West German armed forces in an overall Western military structure; and by October, 1954, the Federal Republic became a member of NATO.

A corresponding development took place in the East German Democratic Republic when its new National People's Army was integrated with the Warsaw Security Pact organization, which was formed by the Soviet Union and East European Communist states. With the participation of West German forces in NATO and of East German military units in the Warsaw Pact, the partition between the two German states became more and more marked and the Iron Curtain an almost physical reality. The rulers of the Democratic Republic (GDR) erected a "protective belt" along the frontier with the Federal Republic (FRG). High heaps of rubble and barbed-wire fences put an end to the local border traffic, which until then had still been flowing at many points of the frontier.

Between 1952 and 1955, the Soviet Union made repeated efforts to arrive at a solution of the German problem other than by the coexistence of two rival German states. Its motives were the desire for security from a possible further German nationalist threat and the wish to gain a Communist foothold in West Germany. In March, 1952, the Soviet government sent notes to its former Western allies in which it expressed its willingness to conclude a peace treaty with Germany, to be prepared "with the participation of Germany, represented by an all-German government." Stalin proposed that Germany should be restored as a uniform state. All foreign troops then stationed in Germany would have to leave within one year after the ratification of the peace treaty. Germany was "not to enter into any coalition or military alliance." Although Stalin suggested free elections for the whole of Germany, he would allow only "democratic parties and organizations" to take part in them and ban all parties "hostile to democracy and the preservation of peace"—a concept obviously molded after the pattern of the GDR and other Communist states. While Stalin might then have agreed to the formation of a neutralized united German state like the one formed by the Austrian Peace Treaty of 1955, he definitely wanted to prevent the reappearance of a strong, independent, and potentially aggressive Germany of the kind the world had known between 1870 and 1945. Haunted by memories of the German invasion of Russia of 1941–44, the Soviet Union was prepared to promote a politically "neutral" united Germany that would be deprived if the chance to join any coalitions or military alliances directed against any state that had fought Germany." Adenauer was often criticized later by his opponents for failing to test the substance of the Soviet Union's offer of reunification in 1952 at the negotiating table. In any case Konrad Adenauer preferred West Germany's "safe" integration with the West—politically, economically, militarily—to the hazards of a doubtful accommodation with Moscow. He and his cabinet feared that after agreeing to a neutralized Germany, American, British, and French troops would depart from German soil and the new, reunited state would be gradually drawn into the orbit of the Soviet power bloc.

From 1952 to 1955, the frequent exchange of notes between Soviet Russia and her former allies revealed a marked discrepancy of approach. The West insisted on the need for free elections in both German states before the conclusion of a peace treaty, whereas the Soviet Union was only interested in such elections if they culminated in the establishment of an all-German government with the participation of the "democratic mass organization," as in East Germany. The integration of the two German republics with opposite blocs led the Soviet Union (and the GDR as its satellite) to increasingly stress the need for accepting the status quo in Germany and the coexistence of two separate German states. In retrospect, the question has been asked whether Stalin ever did "consider a reunited, neutral Germany between the two big power blocs more important than Communist rule between the Oder and Elbe Rivers." [2] Adenauer's signature to the EDC Treaty had relieved the Communists of the need to prove that their offer was more than window-dressing, and soon after, Ulbricht proclaimed the "construction of socialism in the GDR" at the Second Communist Party Conference in East Germany in July, 1952. He even claimed that this was a direct preparation for all-German elections. Ulbricht's attitude gradually changed. Whereas in 1946 he had still declared: "Every true German wants reunification. Our people cannot live without unity. Saxony cannot exist without the Ruhr, Bavaria not without Saxony," this inter-German dependence no longer mattered to him, at least from 1955 onwards. As was mentioned earlier, the economic position of the GDR had by then fundamentally altered from that of a mere object of Russian exploitation to the second most important industrial state within the Communist bloc in

[2] Carola Stern, *Ulbricht: A Political Biography* (New York, 1965), p. 183.

Europe. The German Democratic Republic had become fully integrated in COMECON.[3]

However, in the summer of 1955, the Soviet government again made an important demarche; this time it invited Bonn to open negotiations on establishing diplomatic relations between their two countries. Although the Four-Power summit meeting at Geneva that summer (the first of its kind since 1945) brought few concrete results, it led to some détente in the relations between the Soviet Union and the Western Powers; and the chance for negotiations between Moscow and Bonn seemed more propitious. The German chancellor visited Washington for consultations with President Eisenhower and John Foster Dulles before he went to Moscow. Though aware of the obstacles confronting them, Dr. Adenauer was more optimistic than the leading members of the delegation who accompanied him to Moscow in September, 1955. Kurt Georg Kiesinger, then chairman of the diet's committee on foreign affairs; Professor Carlo Schmidt, a prominent Social Democrat parliamentarian; and Heinrich von Brentano, Adenauer's minister of foreign affairs, were all sceptical about the wisdom of entering into diplomatic relations with Soviet Russia.[4] Adenauer thought differently and achieved his aim in spite of the uncertain and moody attitude displayed by Khrushchev and some of his colleagues. Later, in Adenauer's own words, the protracted negotiations appeared more like "an open quarrel than a diplomatic conference." When the German chancellor pleaded for the release of thousands of German war and civilian internees still held by the Russians, Khrushchev argued with some justification that their plight was due to Hitler. If millions of Germans had lost their lives, so had millions of Russians. And he added an acid warning: "If someone dares in the future to talk to us from a position of strength and to repeat what Hitler did, he will end equally badly or even worse."[5] After much frank talking on both sides, an agreement was finally reached; the Soviet leaders promised to release the German detainees, and diplomatic relations between the two powers were established. The Russians kept their promise, and soon nearly 10,000 German prisoners of war, followed by nearly 20,000 German civilian detainees could return home. No progress had been made towards German reunification. On the other

[3] See Chapter 1, pp. 32–33.
[4] Konrad Adenauer, *Erinnerungen, 1953–1955* (Frankfurt, 1968), Chapter 13.
[5] *Ibid.*, p. 500.

hand, the Russians had been sufficiently realistic not to suggest that the Federal Republic leave the Western camp. And at least Adenauer acknowledged after his return from Moscow that the Soviet Union had "a strong desire to feel secure." [6]

Yet Adenauer's hazardous journey to Moscow (during the year that the Federal Republic achieved full national sovereignty) was to remain an isolated episode. His foreign policy continued to be oriented solely towards the West. It rested mainly on two fundamental tenets: first, on the close ties between the Federal Republic and the United States, and second, on her desire to bury the traditional hatchet of enmity with France and become her partner instead of her foe. Although the defeat of the European Defense Community in 1954 seemed a major setback to Adenauer's policy, it did not in the long run prove a stumbling block to a rapprochement with France. The important agreements signed by the foreign ministers of the six member-states of the Coal and Steel Community at Messina opened the way for setting up the European Economic Community, or Common Market, by the Treaty of Rome in 1957. Soon after it came into effect on January 1, 1958, General de Gaulle once more took control of France and quickly established a close understanding with Dr. Adenauer. In the days of the Weimar Republic, Konrad Adenauer, then Lord Mayor of Cologne and President of the Prussian State Council, had as a Rhinelander never been an enemy of France. Moreover, he shared a measured authoritarian conservatism and a Catholic legacy with General de Gaulle, soldier, diplomat, and patriot. The cooperation between the two men reached its peak in 1962, when as the first German statesman to visit France since 1945, Adenauer was well received by the French people. A few months afterwards, de Gaulle on his part carried out a triumphant tour in West Germany, addressing Munich burghers, Hanseatic patricians, and Ruhr workers in German, a language he had acquired while a prisoner of war in Germany during World War I. Meetings and consultations between the West German and French prime ministers, foreign secretaries, and ministers of defense have taken place periodically since the signing of the Franco-German Friendship Treaty of January, 1963. Although many ups and downs in Franco-German relations occurred under Adenauer's successors, the fundamental improvement in the relationship has remained.

Adenauer sincerely tried to make amends as far as possible for

[6] *Ibid.*, p. 543.

the mass destruction of German and foreign Jews by the Hitler regime and to establish firm and friendly relations with the state of Israel. Together with Theodor Heuss, the urbane first president of the republic from 1949 to 1959, Adenauer achieved far-reaching restitution measures for Jews who had suffered and for their relatives. During his visits to the United States and other Western countries, Dr. Adenauer realized the extent to which the Nazi extermination of the Jews and the diabolical spirit of Auschwitz had damaged Germany's image and prestige abroad. Both the Federal Restitution Act of July, 1957, and the agreement with Israel, concluded in September, 1952, and accepted with a considerable majority by the federal diet in March, 1953, were important landmarks in the policy of reconciliation.

Tough, unsentimental, foxy, occasionally cynical, and noticeably contemptuous of human stupidity and weakness, Dr. Adenauer pursued his main lines of policy with rare skill and a specific mixture of idealistic and realistic motives, which still await a full analysis.

THE HALLSTEIN DOCTRINE AND ITS AFTERMATH

Chancellor Adenauer's visit to Moscow in 1955 did not lead to any change in the Soviet Union's attitude towards its satellite, the German Democratic Republic. In fact, two days after the departure of the West German delegation from Moscow, an East German delegation arrived and soon afterwards concluded a treaty with the Soviet Union under which the GDR obtained sovereignty and was expressly authorized to have diplomatic relations with other states. The post of High Commissioner of Soviet Russia in Germany was abolished at the same time and instead a Soviet Russian ambassador made his bow in East Berlin.

With the arrival of the new "third world" of nonaligned states in Asia and Africa, the two German states soon vied with each other for their recognition. The Federal Republic left no doubt that the newly emerged postcolonial states would have to choose between it and its East German rival. Bonn refused to maintain diplomatic relations with any state that recognized the GDR, excepting the Soviet Union. This is the essence of the Hallstein Doctrine, named after Professor Walter Hallstein, who was an undersecretary of state in the German foreign ministry in the early 1950s. Recognition of the GDR was viewed in Bonn as "an unfriendly act" because it implied acquiescence in the system of two Germanies, which was then unacceptable to the West German government. The test came in 1957 when Tito's Yugoslavia, which entertained diplomatic relations with Bonn, decided to exchange ambassadors with the GDR as well. Bonn broke off diplomatic relations with Yugoslavia at once. Due mostly to the growing economic strength of West Germany and its readiness to grant credits and subsidies to many underdeveloped countries, nearly one hundred states preferred for political and economic reasons to recognize the Federal Republic rather than East Germany during the next ten years.

Seen in retrospect, the Hallstein Doctrine proved to be a double-edged sword. Although it contributed greatly to the diplomatic isolation of the East German state, the doctrine prevented the formation of economic ties between West Germany and Communist-controlled countries like Rumania and Bulgaria. A kind of diplomatic no-man's-land also developed in which many Arab states who disapproved of the friendly relations between West Germany and Israel severed their ties with Bonn in the early 1960s without immediately taking the further step of recognizing the GDR. However the situation had changed in two ways by the late 1960s. After the formation of the Great Coalition, the Hallstein Doctrine was no longer applied by Bonn one hundred percent. In February, 1967, West Germany agreed to establish diplomatic relations with Rumania, a country that had shown a growing spirit of independence within the East European Communist camp. In the same year, Bonn and Belgrade once more exchanged ambassadors.

In 1967 the new foreign minister, Willy Brandt, also began his policy of "little steps" toward the German Democratic Republic, trying to make contacts short of diplomatic recognition. The response was not encouraging. Ulbricht answered with "a kind of Hallstein Doctrine in reverse" (Th. Sommer) by insisting that full recognition of the East German state should be made a condition in order for West Germany to have diplomatic relations with Communist countries. In fact, each of the two German governments since 1949 has claimed to be the sole representative of Germany (*Alleinvertretungsanspruch*). This claim was one of the basic principles of Adenauer's foreign policy and the decisive factor in the Hallstein Doctrine. Bonn was backed by her Western allies in this intransigent attitude. In an interview wtih the American newspaper owner William Hearst on April 26, 1968, Ulbricht declared that "the government of the German Democratic Republic as the only German government represents consistently the national interests of the German people." Similarly at the Fifth Party Congress of the Socialist Unity Party (SED), a declaration of principle was issued that contained the sentence: "The GDR is the legitimate sovereign German state." In 1969, East Germany scored successes on the diplomatic chessboard through the decision of some Arab states to recognize the GDR. They included Nasser's United Arab Republic (which had broken off relations with West Germany in 1967) Syria, Iraq, Sudan, and South Yemen. In the same year, Cambodia changed sides by breaking ties with West Germany and recognizing East Germany instead. Libya, Morocco, and Tunisia have retained their diplomatic ties with Bonn, while the Republic of Yemen, which had broken off her relations with the Federal Republic, restored them in the summer of 1969. It is possible, though not easy to prove, that some of the non-committed states in Africa and Asia used the threat of a possible recognition of East Germany to make West Germany more inclined to give them economic support.

During the fourteen years of his chancellorship, Dr. Adenauer was successful in many ways, for his country became both prosperous and integrated with Western Europe. Yet he made little progress in improving inter-German relations or the chances of reunification. Adenauer's policy of acting from strength achieved little in this respect. Although President de Gaulle backed the German chancellor by refusing to recognize the GDR, he expressly recognized the Oder–Neisse Line during a visit to Poland in 1965. By doing this, he endorsed the policy of East Germany, which had already accepted the Oder–Neisse Line as the frontier in an agreement with Poland in July, 1950. During a visit to the city of Wrocklav (formerly Breslau), President de Gaulle left the Poles in no doubt that he approved of the Oder–Neisse frontier. Dr. Adenauer's stiff attitude toward the recognition of the German Democratic Republic (which he continued to call "the Soviet Zone") can partly be explained by the necessity of not alienating millions of refugees who had organized themselves into a number of very vocal associations, and partly because the chancellor hoped that such recognition might prove a valuable bartering item for a future international settlement.

In the early 1960s two contrasting attitudes towards East Germany could be detected among the West Germans. There were those who simply closed their eyes to the existence of a second Germany and viewed visits to the GDR by West Germans as pernicious, even as treasonable. There were others who regarded this diehard attitude as unrealistic—the byproduct of the Cold War, which in their eyes no longer existed. However, even these critics of West German official policy realized that twenty years after the collapse of the Reich the two German states that had taken its place had little in common apart from the language and some traditions and folk customs. The alienation between the two Germanies had become so obvious that in 1964 some prominent liberal writers on the staff of the Hamburg weekly *Die Zeit* could call their report on a tour of East Germany *Journey to a Distant Country*.[7]

While at the western boundary and along the Berlin wall the threatening machine guns of the frontier police spoke a language of their own, posters of Marx and Lenin at the Eastern frontier with Poland proclaimed solidarity with the other East European Communist states. The visitors found that, apart from some substantial houses and streets in East Berlin, there had been little rebuilding in the towns and villages. Yet the general standard of living had unmistakably improved. Not only was there enough food for everybody, but even the problem of obesity, characteristic of Western society, had begun to appear. The regime appeared to the Hamburg visitors as "a kind of second-class welfare state." Judged by Western standards, life in East Germany was dull; but in 1964 Professor Norden, a leading spokesman of the GDR, claimed that the former *tristesse* was gradually being eliminated and that socialism would become "a very enjoyable affair." Some criticism of institutions and measures has been permitted as long as it does not include the basic principles of the system. Continuously supported by the Soviet Union, the GDR regime can now afford to ignore some things and be more lenient towards the masses, although not to dissenting party members.

Many of the elderly Communist leaders who were either in concentration camps or in exile in Moscow during the Third Reich have died or retired. They are being replaced by a younger generation of effective technicians who take their Marxism and their society for granted without becoming hysterically insistent over it. Although the antagonism of capitalism and Communism is accepted without reflection and Communism remains a dogma, it is no longer a gospel.

[7] Marion Doenhoff and others, *Reise in ein fernes Land* (Hamburg, 1964).

The Problem of Reunification

For some years the idea of reunification continued to be sponsored by the Bonn government as well as by a West German all-party foundation "Indivisible Germany"—parodied by some critics as "Invisible Germany." Moreover, toward the end of his tenure in office, Konrad Adenauer seems to have realized that reunification had become a somewhat unreal and academic issue. In October, 1962, the chancellor told parliament that the Federal government would be prepared to make concessions if more humane conditions could prevail in the other German state.

It was not a statesman but a philosopher who realized that for the second time in a hundred years the Germans were faced with a choice between national unity and individual liberty. In several provocative and controversial books Karl Jaspers, the eminent Basel philosopher, clearly recognized this basic issue.[8] When German refugee organizations clamored loudly for the return of Pomerania, East Prussia, and Silesia to a united fatherland and some of the former Sudeten Germans living in West Germany even demanded the incorporation of the Sudetenland, Jaspers had no illusions about the chances of such pleas. He was convinced that a realistic policy had to be based on two "inescapable premises," however hard it might be to accept them. The first was the finality of the Oder–Neisse Line. The second was that the special status of the German Democratic Republic as the "Soviet zone of occupation," had to be considered final so long as Soviet Russia wanted it to be.[9] While sympathizing with the suffering of the expellees from the former German territories east of the Oder–Neisse Line, Jaspers emphasized that reunification by violence was out of the question. He shared the conviction of many experts that if there were truly free elections in the German Democratic Republic, the majority of voters would reject Communism and would probably favor a democratic socialist party. For this reason alone the Communist rulers could not be expected to concede a free and unhampered expression of the will of the people. The issue therefore demanded a choice in the priority of values. As far as Jaspers was concerned, political freedom was an absolute, and reunification was only a relative value. It was possible

---

[8] See in English Karl Jaspers, *The Future of Germany* (Chicago and London, 1967). Jaspers died in Basel in 1969.

[9] K. Jaspers, op. cit., p. 132.

to obtain one without the other. Reunification without political freedom of the people would be undesirable because it would lead to a Communist-controlled Germany. On the other hand, in order to achieve political freedom for the people in East Germany, the idea of reunification would have to be given up. Jaspers maintained that greater freedom in East Germany could be obtained—at a price. The price was a definite renunciation of reunification by the West German government and the acceptance of a guaranteed neutrality in world affairs by the Federal Republic on the lines of the Austrian State Treaty of 1955, underwritten by the four victorious powers of 1945. Jaspers admitted that this would be a big price to pay. Yet a realistic view led him to the conclusion that this condition could not be avoided if there was to be greater popular freedom in East Germany.

It has long been obvious that both West Germany and East Germany would have to make concessions for a fundamental improvement of the German situation. These would have to include the removal of the Berlin wall, as both a physical and a symbolic barrier, by the East German regime, and a recognition of the de facto frontier between the two Germanies and the Oder–Neisse Line by the government of the Federal Republic. Moreover, unless this rapprochement is accompanied by a general détente between the NATO powers and those of the Warsaw Treaty, perhaps by way of a European Security Pact, the situation is likely to remain insecure.

Meanwhile, Willy Brandt's "small steps" toward an improvement of the situation that he began as foreign minister in 1966 gathered momentum after he became chancellor in October, 1969. In retrospect, it is now clear that the basic change in the attitude of the Federal Government toward Eastern Europe goes back to the beginnings of the Great Coalition in December, 1966. It has been rightly said that Bonn's policy entered a new path in three important respects.[10] First, the rulers in Bonn now showed "a real and sustained interest in reconciliation with the countries of East Europe." This was particularly so toward Poland. In his first statement as chancellor, Dr. Kiesinger declared that "large sectors of the German people" very much wanted "reconciliation with Poland, whose sorrowful history we have not forgotten and whose desire ultimately to live in a territory with secure boundaries we now . . . understand better than in former times." However, as Bonn was not willing to

---

[10] See James Richardson, "Germany's Eastern Policy: Problems and Prospects," *The World Today*, IXIV (September, 1968).

recognize the Oder–Neisse Line, this gesture of good will was not reciprocated by Warsaw.

Second, the West German government under Kiesinger realized that "an East–West *rapprochement* in Europe" was "a prerequisite for German reunification." Bonn no longer linked the German question formally with any measure of European arms control or relaxation. Third, the government favored increased contact between the two Germanies. The chancellor then suggested greater freedom of travel, trade and credit facilities, joint economic projects, visits and cultural exchanges, and the exchange of newspapers. In a letter to Willi Stoph, Prime Minister of East Germany, sent in June, 1967, Kiesinger proposed that each of them should appoint commissioners to "recommend practical steps towards easing the daily life of people in both parts of Germany." The East German response to these proposals was not positive, and little came of them. In any case, Bonn's merely legalistic approach during the era of Adenauer and the Hallstein Doctrine had now definitely been abandoned.

OSTPOLITIK: BRANDT'S NEW LINE IN FOREIGN AFFAIRS

When in October, 1969, the Great Coalition between the CDU and the SPD was replaced by the "minicoalition" of Social Democrats and Free Democrats, the ministry for foreign affairs was one of the three ministries to go to the Free Democrats; and Walter Scheel succeeded Brandt as its head. Yet one can speak of a new "Brandt–Scheel" course in foreign affairs, for Brandt's prestige had increased so much at home and abroad that he continued to determine the foreign policy of his government to a large extent. The policy statement of the new government by Chancellor Brandt to the Federal Diet on October 28, 1969, contained this key paragraph.

> We are determined to preserve the security of the Federal Republic of Germany and the cohesion of the German nation, to maintain peace and to cooperate in a European Peace Order, to enlarge the rights of freedom and the welfare of our people, and to develop our country so that its rank will be acknowledged and assured in the world of tomorrow. The policy of this government will be run on the lines of continuity and renovation.[11]

[11] For the general text of this policy statement, so far as it refers to foreign affairs, see "Ziele und Absichten der neuen deutschen Bundesregierung im Bereich der auswärtigen Politik," *Europa Archiv*, XXIV (November 10, 1969), 499–506.

The striking feature is the omission of both the traditional demand for "the reunification of Germany" and the usual reference to the disastrous events before 1945. It should be remembered that Chancellor Brandt, "who from 1933 until the end of the National Socialist regime lived as an emigré abroad, does not regard himself as representative of the defeated but rather as one of the liberated Germany." His conduct is therefore "less determined by traditions and visions and more by the given realities of the situation in Europe." [12]

Brandt's emphasis has not been on confrontation or on bloc policy. He hopefully visualizes a growing détente between East and West and a greater degree of cooperation with both. The Federal Republic's Western and Eastern policies are not separated in different pigeon holes as was the case under Chancellor Adenauer and his first two successors, but are combined in an overall approach to European problems. Willy Brandt thinks in terms of a "European order of peace" and tries accordingly to integrate the various sectors of policy—the European policy in the traditional sense, the Eastern policy, and the problems of the Common Market and of its enlargement. To do so requires both firmness of purpose and tactical skill. A decrease of existing tension rather than the expectation of quick agreement has been the short-term aim of this approach, but its long-term goals are more comprehensive. While sincerely determined to continue close ties with the West through both the European Economic Community and the Western European Union, the Brandt government has simultaneously pursued a policy of peace and reconciliation with the Soviet Union and the Communist states of Eastern Europe.

In his first major speech before the Federal Diet on October 28, 1969, Chancellor Brandt made a point of declaring that his government would "continue the policy introduced in December 1966," of offering negotiations to the government of the GDR "which should lead to cooperation." Herr Brandt argued that "even if two states exist in Germany, they are nevertheless not foreign territory to each other. Their relations can only be of a special nature." For the time being, in Brandt's words, it has to be "the task of practical politics to preserve the unity of the nation by dissolving the existing cramp in the relationship between the portions of Germany."

[12] Wolfgang Wagner, "Aussenpolitik nach dem Regierungswechsel in Bonn," *Europa Archiv*, XXIV (November 11, 1969), 776.

Brandt's new formula of "two States of the German Nation" is certainly noteworthy.[13] While Bonn has continued to refuse the recognition of the other German state in international law, it has emphasized what all Germans have in common. As Brandt formulated it: "The Germans are not only connected by their language and their history, with its splendor and its misery; we have still common tasks and a common responsibility: for peace between us and Europe." Twenty years after the founding of the two German republics, the Chancellor stressed the need for "preventing a further drifting apart of the German nation." This meant an effort "to try to arrive, via a regulated relationship side by side, at a position of togetherness." One of the first moves Brandt made was to change the rather pompous title of the "Ministry of All-German Affairs" in Bonn to the more modest description of "Ministry for Inter-German Relations," a clear indicator that his government no longer claimed to speak in the name of all Germans. From its inception, Bonn's *Ostpolitik* has aimed at a simultaneous improvement of West Germany's relations with Eastern Europe on a threefold level: in its attitudes towards the German Democratic Republic, in its negotiations with Poland, and in those with the Soviet Union. The two meetings of Brandt with East German Prime Minister Willi Stoph at Erfurt (East Germany) on March 19, and at Kassel (West Germany) on May 21, 1970, were of historic significance even if they yielded few concrete results.

By the end of 1970, the prickly relationship between the two German states had not basically changed, although the fact that meetings between some of their top representatives and public officials had taken place was a measure of détente. More progress had been made in improving relations between the Bonn government and Soviet Russia and Poland. In November, 1969, the Federal German government had already given proof of its good will by signing the Nonproliferation Treaty on Nuclear Weapons, sponsored by the Soviet Union and the United States. After some lengthy negotiations, a treaty on the mutual renunciation of the use of force was signed in Moscow on August 12, 1970, by Brandt and Scheel and Premier Kosygin and Andrey A. Gromyko. Both powers tried to solve the controversial questions between them solely by peace-

---

[13] In the Constitution of the German Democratic Republic of 1968 the country is described as a "Socialist State of the German Nation."

ful means. At the same time they agreed to respect the territorial integrity of all European states within their present frontiers. There was a significant reference to the mutual recognition of the Oder–Neisse Line as the western frontier of Poland.[14] This pointed to the protective role of the Soviet Union towards Poland and anticipated an identical clause in the agreement between Poland and the Federal German Republic that was concluded in Warsaw four months later. Both treaties specifically stipulated that they did not affect any bilateral or multilateral international agreements concluded by or involving one of the parties. Thus each party is able to continue its alliances or contractual obligations.

The Polish–West German Treaty "on the normalization of mutual relations" was signed by Chancellor Brandt and Polish Premier Jozef Cyrankiewicz on December 7, 1970. There are some emotional undertones in its preamble, which states that the treaty was concluded: "considering that over twenty-five years have passed since the end of the Second World War, the first victim of which was Poland, and which has brought heavy suffering to the peoples of Europe" and in the knowledge that "a new generation has grown up in both countries for which a peaceful future shall be safeguarded." [15] Youth was further emphasized by the fact that representatives of three German youth organizations, Catholic, Protestant, and socialist, accompanied the German delegation to Warsaw.

As could be expected, the recognition of the Oder–Neisse Line, so vital to Poland, met with indignation and criticism from the refugee organizations; and Herr Brandt was eager to show his sympathy with the former German inhabitants of the provinces lost to Poland in 1945.[16] "Our Polish conversation partners know what I should also like to say to you at home in full clarity," the German chancellor said in a TV talk from Warsaw to Germany on December 7, "This agreement does not mean that we subsequently legitimize expulsions." Stressing that it had not been easy for the German government to come to the decisions laid down in the agreement,

---

[14] A similar recognition was expressly given to the existing frontier between the Federal Republic of Germany and the German Democratic Republic.

[15] Text of the treaty in *Bulletin*, No. 171 (Bonn, December 8, 1970).

[16] For the arguments in favor of recognition of the Oder–Neisse Line by the Federal Government, see Ulrich Scheuner, "Die Oder–Neisse Grenze und die Normalisierung der Beziehungen zum Osten," *Europa Archiv*, XXV (June 10, 1970), 377–86.

Brandt declared that they "must not forget that what had been done to the Polish people after 1939 was the worst they had experienced in their history. This wrong has not remained without its consequences. Our people, particularly our East German fellow countrymen, have also suffered great grief. We must be just; the greatest sacrifices were brought by those whose fathers, sons, or brothers lost their lives. But after them, those who had to leave their homeland paid most bitterly for the war." [17]

In spite of some criticism from the CDU, the party in opposition, and violent attacks by the extreme rightists, the great majority of Germans have acquiesced in this treaty. The long-term success of *Ostpolitik* depends on whether Soviet Russia is prepared to make concessions and pressure the German Democratic Republic into being more accommodating on questions concerning West Berlin. In this context the Four Power Agreement on Berlin, initialled by the Ambassadors of France, Great Britain, the United States of America, and the U.S.S.R. in Berlin on September 3, 1971, is of considerable significance. It was welcomed in a Declaration by the Government of the Federal Republic of Germany.[18]

Fears in the West that the "opening" of the German window to the East would impair the previous commitments of the Federal Republic have not been substantiated. This position was emphasized as early as December, 1969, by West German Minister of Defense, Hellmuth Schmidt. In a speech to the Western European Union in Paris he said, "It would be sheer folly if one attempted to conduct one's policy towards the East from any other basis than that of firm Western solidarity. NATO remains the indispensable prerequisite for both the safeguarding of our policy and for any efforts towards an East–West rapprochement." [19] The Brandt–Scheel government has been opposed to any "bloc" policy as was favored by Adenauer and Dulles. A sense of balance and open-mindedness is regarded as indispensable. "We are certainly agreed that our community should not be a new bloc but rather an exemplary unit and a worthy element of an all-European structure," Chancellor Brandt declared at the summit meeting of the European Common Market countries in the Hague early in December, 1969. "It is in this spirit that the

---

[17] *Bulletin*, No. 171 (Bonn, December 8, 1970), 1814.
[18] *Bulletin*, No. 127 (Bonn: September 3, 1971), p. 1359.
[19] *The Times* (London), December 11, 1969.

Federal Republic of Germany seeks an understanding with the East and cooperation with the West." [20] An extension of the European Common Market to include Great Britain and the Scandinavian countries would be welcomed by the Brandt–Scheel government because it might further the East–West detente and make Bonn less dependent on Paris.

It remains to be seen how far the recent rapprochement between Bonn and the Soviet Union and the more far-reaching one with Warsaw will induce the East German government to a less intransigent attitude. The aim of Ulbricht and his successor Erich Honecker is undoubtedly the diplomatic recognition of the East German state by the Federal Republic. For the time being Bonn is inclined to maintain its policy of "acceptance without recognition" and emphasize both caution and flexibility. There is a good deal of support for this policy from the younger people in West Germany, who are often critical of both superpowers—the Soviet Union and the United States—and have no memory of the Cold War.[21]

In 1962 the national program of Ulbricht's Socialist Unity Party (SED) still emphasized that "two hostile Germanies confront each other on German soil today." The East German formulations a decade later are somewhat less drastic but the antagonism continues to be reinforced by their mass media and by their stubbornness over West Berlin.

One thing is certain: "The exclusiveness of [Bonn's] Western integration in the style of the 1950s can no longer be the principle of orientation today because the East–West antagonism has not been the only issue in world affairs for a considerable time." [22] Yet only the future can show whether the Brandt–Scheel policy of strong ties with the West and friendly relations with the East will prove as wise and fruitful in the 1970s as did Adenauer's orientation towards the West alone in the 1950s. The new *Ostpolitik*, although a commendable attempt toward a greater détente between East and West, cannot square the circle. It has to reckon with the obvious limits to reconciliation between the more diehard Communist regimes and the non-Communist "liberal" states. There is room today

[20] *The Times* (London), December 2, 1969.
[21] See Wolfgang Wagner, "Voraussetzungen und Folgen der deutschen Ostpolitik," *Europa Archiv*, XXV (September 10, 1970).
[22] Waldemar Besson, *Die Aussenpolitik der Bundesrepublik: Erfahrungen und Maasstäbe* (Munich, 1970), p. 445.

for a sober and practical rapprochement in a changing situation; at the same time, the weight of contrasting geographical, political, and ideological facts and factors cannot be dismissed simply by gestures of good will.

Suggested Readings

GENERAL WORKS

There is no up-to-date standard work in English dealing with the whole of German history. Two reliable handbooks by German specialists covering the whole field are: Peter Rassow, ed., *Deutsche Geschichte im Überblick*, 2d ed. (Stuttgart, 1962); and Bruno Gebhardt, *Handbuch der Deutschen Geschichte*, ed. Herbert Grundmann, 8th rev. ed., 4 vols. (Stuttgart, 1954–1960). A lively textbook in English, with the main emphasis on the cultural development, is Kurt F. Reinhardt's *Germany: 2000 Years*, 2 vols. 2d ed. (New York, 1961).

MEDIEVAL GERMANY

The Pelican History of Medieval Europe, by Maurice Keen (London, 1968), puts the development of Germany and the clash between the Holy Roman Empire and the Papacy in its overall European setting. Friedrich Heer, *The Holy Roman Empire*, trans. Janet Sondheimer (London, 1968), is a stimulating, though sometimes rather subjective account with many illustrations. Geoffrey Barraclough's *The Origin of Modern Germany* (Oxford, 1957) is the outstanding book in English on the rise of the German Empire. The same author has also edited *Medieval Germany*, 2 vols. (Oxford, 1961). The early medieval setting is brilliantly dealt with by R. W. Southern, *The Making of the Middle Ages* (London, 1953).

The rule of Charlemagne is examined in the works by M. Fichtenau, *The Carolingian Empire*, trans. P. Munz (Oxford, 1963); and by

257

D. Bullough, *The Age of Charlemagne* (London, 1965), with many illustrations. There is no relevant biography of Frederick Barbarossa, but an illuminating primary source from the period is now available in an English translation: Otto of Freising, *The Deeds of Frederick Barbarossa* (New York, 1953). Another important original source is the *Chronicles of the Crusades*, trans. M. R. B. Shaw London: Penguin Books, Ltd., (1963).

We have two important works in English on Frederick II and his age: the subtle and colorful study by Ernst Kantorowicz, *Frederick II*, trans. E. O. Lorimer (New York, 1957); and the shorter, but very readable account by Georgina Masson, *Frederick of Hohenstaufen* (London, 1957).

The standard works on the socioeconomic pattern by Marc Bloch, *Feudal Society* (London, 1962), and by J. W. Thompson, *Economic and Social History of Europe in the Late Middle Ages* (New York, 1960), should be consulted. The growth of the towns and commerce has been dealt with brilliantly in *Medieval Cities* by the eminent Belgian historian, Henri Pirenne, trans. F. D. Halsey (Princeton, 1925).

GENERAL WORKS ON MODERN HISTORY

K. Pinson, *Modern Germany: Its History and Civilization* (2d ed., New York, 1966), is of special value for the insight it offers on political ideologies and traditions. M. Dill, *Germany* (Ann Arbor. University of Michigan Press, 1961), is informative and reliable but somewhat pedestrian. Golo Mann's *The History of Germany since 1789* (London, 1968), is a stimulating and well-written critical account by a German liberal. Agatha Ramm, *Germany, 1789–1919: A Political History* (London: Methuen & Co., Ltd., 1967), is competent and judicious if not inspiring.

The most detailed survey in English are the three important volumes by the late Hajo Holborn of Yale, *History of Modern Germany* (New York: Alfred A. Knopf, Inc., 1959–69, which cover the period from the Reformation to 1648, from 1648 to 1840, and from 1840 to 1945 respectively. Holborn's strength was his conspectus of political history, social history, and the history of ideas, which is particularly impressive in the second volume. E. J. Passant, *A Short History of Germany, 1815–1945* (London: Oxford University Press, 1959), is useful for the general reader.

REFORMATION AND COUNTER-REFORMATION

Of the several general surveys that put German developments in an overall European setting, G. R. Elton, *Reformation Europe* (London, 1963), and H. J. Grimm, *The Reformation Era, 1500–1650* (New York,

1965), are the most recent. Vol. II, *The Reformation 1520–1559*, ed. G. R. Elton (1958), and Vol. III, *The Counter-Reformation and Price Revolution, 1554–1610*, ed. R. B. Wernham (1968), of the *New Cambridge Modern History* contains many relevant chapters by specialists. There are two original surveys in German, *Das Werden des neuzeitlichen Europa 1300–1600* (Braunschweig, 1959), by E. Hassinger, and the lucid account of German politics of the period, *Reich und Reformation*, by S. Skalweit (Berlin, 1968).

There is a wealth of biographies of Luther. Only the following can be mentioned here: R. H. Bainton, *Here I Stand* (London, 1950); James Atkinson, *Martin Luther and the Birth of Protestantism* (London: Penguin Books, 1968); Gerhard Ritter, *Luther: His Life and Work* (New York, 1959); and Heinrich Boehmer, *Martin Luther: Road to Reformation* (London, 1946), which only goes to 1521. An interesting, if controversial interpretation is *Young Man Luther* by the psychoanalyst Eric Erickson (New York, 1959).

There is a short work in English translation on the Swiss reformer H. Zwingli by his biographer O. Farner, *Zwingli, the Reformer: His Life and Work* (London, 1962). C. L. Manschreck, *Melanchton: The Quiet Reformer* (Nashville, Tenn., 1958), is instructive. On the radical left we have the comprehensive study by G. H. Williams, *The Radical Reformation* (London, 1962), and the relevant chapters in Norman Cohn's *The Pursuit of the Millenium* (London, 1957). For a Marxist approach see Roy Pascal, *The Social Basis of the German Reformation* (London, 1933). The work by the Catholic historian J. Lortz, *Die Reformation in Deutschland*, 3d ed. (Freiburg, 1949), is fair to the Protestant side and very informative on the Catholic counterrevival. Contrasting examples of the Catholic, Protestant, and secular interpretations of the Reformation have been assembled in *The Reformation: Revival or Revolution?* ed. W. Stanford Reid (New York, 1968). *Ideas and Institutions in Western Civilization: Renaissance and Reformation 1300–1648*, ed. G. R. Elton (New York: The Macmillan Company, 1963), is a collection of documents from the period. R. Ehrenberg's standard work on the economic aspects of the period, *Capital and Finance in the Age of the Renaissance*, English trans. (London, 1928), can now be supplemented by the illustrated study in German by G. von Pölnitz, *Die Fugger* (Frankfurt, 1960).

The Seventeenth and Eighteenth Centuries

The standard work on the period of the Thirty Years War is by C. V. Wedgwood, *The Thirty Years War*, 2d ed. (London: Jonathan Cape, Ltd., 1964). The negotiations for peace and the peace treaties of 1648 are carefully considered in Fritz Dickmann, *Der Westfälische*

Frieden (Münster, 1959), and the impact of the war in Günther Franz, *Der Dreissigjährige Krieg und das Deutsche Volk,* 3d ed. (Stuttgart, 1961).

THE RISE AND ROLE OF PRUSSIA

Indispensable for the earlier centuries is F. L. Carsten's *The Origins of Prussia* (Oxford: Clarendon Press, 1954). Sidney B. Fay's *The Rise of Brandenburg–Prussia to 1786,* rev. Klaus Epstein (New York, 1964), is a useful textbook. Two works on Frederick the Great, the first by an Englishman, the second by a German historian, complement each other: G. P. Gooch, *Frederick the Great: The Ruler, the Writer, the Man* (London: Longmans, Green & Company, Ltd., 1948); and Gerhard Ritter, *Frederick the Great: An Historical Profile,* trans. Peter Paret (Berkeley: University of California Press, 1968). The role of the aristocracy and the civil service in Prussia is astutely discussed in Hans Rosenberg, *Bureaucracy, Aristocracy, Autocracy: The Prussian Experience, 1660–1815* (Cambridge: Harvard University Press, 1958). The lucid and judicious survey by W. H. Bruford, *Germany in the Eighteenth Century* (London: Cambridge University Press, 1935); and the penetrating work, *A History of Political Thought in Germany, 1789–1815,* by R. Aris (London: George Allen & Unwin, 1936), are helpful.

THE NINETEENTH CENTURY

Works on Economic and Social History

Valuable general surveys are by John Clapham, *The Economic Development of France and Germany, 1815–1914* (London: Cambridge University Press, 1936); and by F. Lütge, *Deutsche Sozial-und Wirtschaftsgeschichte,* 2d ed. (Berlin, 1960). W. O. Henderson, *The Zollverein,* 2d ed. (London: Frank Cass, 1959), is a thorough investigation of the German Customs Union. The last third of the century is covered by G. Stolper, *The German Economy, 1870–1914* (London, 1940); and by W. F. Bruck, *Social and Economic History of Germany from William II to Hitler,* 2d ed. (New York, 1962). Two important special studies in German are Hans Rosenberg, *Grosse Depression und Bismarckzeit, Wirtschaftsablauf, Gesellschaft und Politik in Mitteleuropa* (Berlin, 1967), an original work by an American historian; and Helmuth Boehme, *Deutschlands Weg zur Grossmacht, 1848–1881* (Cologne and Berlin, 1966), an analysis of the relations between economic interest groups and the political establishment of the period.

1815–1871

The connection between economic trends and political developments has been skillfully analyzed by Theodore S. Hamerow, *Restoration, Revo-*

lution, Reaction: Economics and Politics in Germany, 1815–1871 (Princeton, N.J.: Princeton University Press, 1958).

The Revolutions of 1848–49

Veit Valentin, *1848: Chapters from German History* (London: George Allen & Unwin, 1965) Priscilla Robertson, *Revolutions of 1848: A Social History* (Princeton, N.J.: Princeton University Press, (1952); and Frank Eyck, *The Frankfurt Parliament, 1848–1849* (London and New York, 1968), should be consulted. For a variety of interpretations of the 1848 revolutions, see Melvin Kranzberg, ed., *1848: A Turning Point? Problems in European Civilization* (Boston: D. C. Heath & Co., 1959). The influx of German immigrants into the United States after 1848 is examined by Carl Wittke, *Refugees of Revolution: The German Forty-Eighters in America* (Philadelphia: University of Pennsylvania Press, 1952).

Bismarck and German Unification

Otto Pflanze, *Bismarck and the Development of Germany: The Period of Unification, 1815–1879* (Princeton, N.J.: Princeton University Press, 1963), is the first of two volumes. See also the essay by the same author, "Bismarck and German Nationalism," *American Historical Review*, LX (1954–1955), pp. 548–66. E. N. Anderson, *The Social and Political Conflict in Prussia, 1858–64* (Lincoln, Neb., 1964), throws much light on the clash between King William and the Prussian liberals, which led to Bismarck's appointment as prime minister.

Considering the complex personality of Bismarck and the many facets of his role, it is advisable to read different accounts. The following works are relevant: Erich Eyck, *Bismarck and the Second Empire* (London: George Allen & Unwin, 1950), A. J. P. Taylor, *Bismarck: The Man and the Statesman* (New York, 1955); and Werner Richter, *Bismarck*, trans. B. Battershaw (London, 1962).

1871–1918

In spite of a somewhat misleading title Arthur Rosenberg's *The Birth of the German Republic, 1871–1918* (London: Oxford University Press, 1931), is still an important sociological survey of the period. Andreas Dorpalen, *Heinrich von Treitschke* (New Haven, Conn.: Yale University Press, 1957), offers a balanced account of the development of the influential nationalist German historian. Volume I of N. Rich's *Friedrich von Holstein: Politics and Diplomacy in the Era of Bismarck and William II* (London: Cambridge University Press, 1965), is a well-documented account of this rather enigmatic adviser behind the official curtain. *The Kaiser and His Times* (London: Cresset Press, 1964), by Michael Balfour, is perceptive and readable.

A lively controversy on German political aims before and during World War I has been sparked by Fritz Fischer's well-documented study *German War Aims in the First World War* (New York: W. W. Norton & Company, Inc., 1967). For differing opinions in this context, see the articles by Golo Mann, "1914: The Beast in the Jungle, Dr. Fritz Fischer's Thesis," *Encounter* (November, 1968); and by Fritz Stern, "Bethmann Hollweg and the War: The Limits of Responsibility," *The Responsibility of Power: Historical Essays in Honor of Hajo Holborn*, ed. L. Krieger and F. Stern (New York: Doubleday & Company, Inc., 1967). Ludwig Dehio's *Germany and World Politics in the Twentieth Century* (London: Chatto & Windus, Ltd., 1959), is still useful.

THE WEIMAR REPUBLIC, 1918–1933

The best general account of its political history so far is the work by Erich Eyck, *A History of the Weimar Republic*, 2 vols., trans. Harlan Hansons and Robert G. L. Waite (New York: John Wiley & Sons, Inc., 1967). The earlier volume by S. W. Halperin, *Germany Tried Democracy: A Political History of the Reich from 1918 to 1933* (Hampden, Conn., 1963), is useful.

There are a number of judicious monographs on Stresemann in English: Hans W. Gatzke, *Stresemann and the Rearmament of Germany* (Baltimore, 1964); Henry L. Bretton, *Stresemann and the Revision of Versailles* (Palo Alto, Calif.: Stanford University Press, 1962); H. A. Turner, *Stresemann and the Politics of the Weimar Republic* (Princeton, N.J.: Princeton University Press, 1963). The penetrating essays on leading issues and personalities of the republic by Theodor Eschenburg, *Die improvisierte Demokratie* (Munich, 1963), deserves an English translation. John W. Wheeler Bennett's *Wooden Titan: Hindenburg in Twenty Years of German History, 1914–1934*, new ed. (Hamden, Conn.: Anchor Books, 1963); and Andreas Dorpalen, *Hindenburg and the Weimar Republic* (Princeton, N.J.: Princeton University Press, 1964), give different interpretations. The biographies of Walter Rathenau by Harry Count Kessler (London: Gerald Hore, 1929) and of Erzberger by Klaus Epstein, *Matthias Erzberger and the Dilemma of German Democracy* (Princeton, N.J.: Princeton University Press, 1959), throw much light on the chaotic conditions after 1918. *Germany's New Conservatism*, by Klemens von Klemperer, 2d ed. (Princeton, N.J.: Princeton University Press, 1968); and *Anti-Demokratisches Denken in der Weimar Republik*, by Kurt Sontheimer (Munich, 1962), are helpful guides through a bewildering labyrinth of nationalist ideologies. There is an abridged edition in English of Oswald Spengler's *Letters 1913–1936* (London: George Allen & Unwin, 1966).

For the left-wing parties the perceptive book by Richard N. Hunt,

German Social Democracy: 1918–1933 (New Haven, Conn.: Yale University Press (1964); Ruth Fischer (a former Communist deputy in the Reichstag), *Stalin and German Communism* (London: Oxford University Press, 1948); and *World Communism: A History of the Communist International,* by Franz Borkenau (Ann Arbor: University of Michigan Press, 1962), are indispensable. The social and cultural history of the Weimar Republic remains to be written. The small, lively book by Peter Gay, *Weimar Culture: The Outsider as Insider* (New York, 1968), offers an introduction to a complex theme.

Penetrating studies of the decline of the republic and the rise of National Socialism before 1933 are A. J. Nicholls, *Weimar and the Rise of Hitler* (London and New York: St. Martin's Press, Inc., 1968), with a valuable bibliography; and the symposium by Theodor Eschenburg and other German authors, *The Road to Dictatorship: Germany, 1918–1933* (London: Oswald Wolff, 1964). A standard work on the decline of the republic is Karl Dietrich Bracher's *Die Auflösung der Weimarer Republik* (Stuttgart, 1965). A fascinating study of the political behavior of the inhabitants of a typical small German town in Lower Saxony during the period 1930–35 has been done by W. S. Allen, *The Nazi Seizure of Power: The Experience of a Single German Town, 1930–1935* (New York, 1966).

THE THIRD REICH

The Rise and Fall of the Third Reich by William L. Shirer (New York, 1959), is popular and fairly comprehensive. As a former newspaper correspondent on the spot, Shirer is familiar with the atmosphere of the Hitler regime in the 1930s. Yet his readable account is not always balanced and sometimes lacks historical perspective. The interesting work by Ernst Nolte, *The Three Faces of Fascism* (London, 1965), treats the National Socialist ideology and practice from a comparative point of view. The best general survey of the National Socialist era is *The German Dictatorship: The Origins, Structure, and Consequences of National Socialism* by Karl Dietrich Bracher (New York: Praeger Publishers, Inc., 1970).

There are several editions in English of Hitler's major book, *Mein Kampf,* written in 1924–25. A second work by him written in 1928 but only published in recent years, is *Hitler's Secret Book,* introduction by Telford Taylor (New York, 1961). *Hitler's Secret Conversations, 1941–44* (New York, 1961), is a record of his table talk in his headquarters, which throws much light on his outlook and ideology. See also *The Testament of Adolf Hitler: The Hitler–Bormann Documents, February–April, 1945,* ed. François Genoud (London, 1961). Primary sources of considerable interest are Herman Rauschning's *Hitler Speaks* (London, 1939), based on some intimate conversations between Hitler and the author in 1932–34; and for the war years, the recollections of Albert Speer, English edition, *Inside the Third Reich* (London: Weidenfeld and Nicolson, 1970). Speer, a member of Hitler's inner circle, was his minister of armaments after 1942.

The best biography of Hitler is Alan Bullock's *Hitler: A Study in Tyranny*, rev. ed. (London: Penguin Books, Ltd., 1962). For the impact of the Nationalist Socialist system on German society, we have the important book by David Schoenbaum, *Hitler's Social Revolution: Class and Status in Nazi Germany, 1933–1939* (London: Weidenfeld & Nicolson, 1967). E. Robertson's *Hitler's Pre-War Plans* (London: Longmans, Green & Company, Ltd., 1963); and Alan S. Milward, *The German Economy at War* (London: Macmillan & Co., Ltd., 1965), are valuable studies. A thorough examination of Hitler's foreign policy in the prewar period is *Nationalsozialistische Aussenpolitik: 1933–1938* (Frankfurt 1968), by the German historian H. A. Jacobsen. Hitler's war aims have been differently interpreted by A. J. P. Taylor in his *The Origins of the Second World War* (London: Penguin Books, 1969); and by H. R. Trevor–Roper, "Hitler's Kriegsziele," *Vierteljahrshefte für Zeitgeschichte* (Munich, April, 1950). The nature and techniques of propganda in the Third Reich have been analyzed by E. K. Bramsted, *Goebbels and National Socialist Propaganda, 1925–1945* (East Lansing: Michigan State University Press, 1965). The monograph by Prof. Oran James Hale, *The Captive Press in the Third Reich* (Princeton, N.J.: Princeton University Press, 1964), throws light on the Nazi take-over of former non-Nazi newspapers. The machinery of terror—the S.S. and the concentration camps—are authoritatively examined in a symposium by the German historians H. Krausnick, H. Buchheim, Martin Broszat, and H. A. Jacobsen, *Anatomy of the S.S. State* (London: Collins, 1968). See also the book by George H. Stein, *The Waffen S.S.: Hitler's Guard at War* (New York, 1966).

On the Auschwitz trial itself, the two volumes by Hermann Langbein *Der Auschwitz Prozess: Eine Dokumentation* (Vienna, 1965), are sadly revealing, and so is the autobiography of Rudolf Hoess, *Commandant of Auschwitz* (London: Weidenfeld & Nicolson, 1959).

There is a biography, *Heinrich Himmler*, by Roger Manvill and Heinrich Fraenkel (London: William Heinemann, Limited, 1965). The same authors have also written *The July Plot* (London: William Heinemann, Limited, 1964), an account of the anti-Hitler revolt in 1944. Of the numerous books on the German resistance, the following are available in English translation: Gerhardt Ritter, *The German Resistance: Carl Goerdeler's Struggle Against Germany* (London: George Allen & Unwin, 1950); E. Zeller, *The Flame of Freedom* (London: Oswald Wolff, 1968); *The German Resistance to Hitler* is a collection of essays on various aspects of the resistance movement by H. Graml, Hans Mommsen, H. Reichhardt, and Ernst Wolf (London: Betsford, 1970). A useful collection of relevant documents is *Deutscher Widerstand 1938–1944: Fortsehritt oder Reaktion?* ed. Bodo Schurig (Munich: Deutscher Taschenbuch Verlag, 1969). There are biographies in English of two leading personalities in the resistance—Joachim Kramarz, *Stauffenberg* (London, 1967); and Christopher Sykes, *Troubled Loyalty: A Biography of Adam Trott zu Solz* (London, 1969).

For German–Italian relations, the following are indispensable: Elizabeth Wiskemann, *The Rome–Berlin Axis*, rev. ed. (London: Collins, 1966); and F. W. D. Deakin, *The Brutal Friendship* (London: Weidenfeld & Nicolson, 1962) an account of relations between Mussolini and Hitler during the war.

For German–Russian relations, see G. Hilger and A. G. Meyer, *The Incompatible Allies: German–Soviet Relations, 1918–1941* (New York, 1953); and G. Weinberg, *Germany and the Soviet Union* (Leiden, 1954). On the relations between Nazi Germany and the United States, see S. Friedländer, *Prelude to Downfall: Hitler and the United States, 1939–1941* (London: Chatto & Windus, 1967); and James A. Compton, *The Swastika and the Eagle: Hitler, the United States, and the Origins of the Second World War* (New York: Houghton Mifflin Company, 1968).

Germany After 1945

A lucid and thoughtful survey by Michael Balfour and John Mair, *Four Power Occupation of Germany and Austria, 1945–1946* (London: Oxford University Press, 1956), discusses the problems of the occupation powers and their varying attitudes towards them. Particularly good on the rebirth of education and on the mass media.

For the American occupation in Germany, the memoirs by the U. S. Commander-in-Chief, General Lucius D. Clay, *Decision in Germany* (New York, 1950), are important. Harold Zink's, *The United States and Germany, 1944–1956* (Princeton, N.J.: Princeton University Press, 1957) is an historical account. The author was able to draw on his own recollections while in Germany in addition to much documentary evidence. Eugen Davidson, *The Death and Life of Germany: An Account of the American Occupation* (New York, 1959), is the work of a journalist. John Gimbel, *The American Occupation of Germany: Politics and the Military 1945–1949* (Stanford: Stanford University Press, 1968) is a valuable historical analysis.

On the British attitudes during the occupation period, see Raymond Ebsworth, *Restoring Democracy in Germany: The British Contribution* (London and New York: St. Martin's Press, Inc., 1960). Also relevant are Richard Hiscocks, *Democracy in Western Germany* (London: Oxford University Press, 1957), and Edgar McInnis, Richard Hiscocks, and Robert Spencer, *The Shaping of Post-War Germany* (London and Toronto: J. M. Dent & Sons, Ltd., 1960).

The developments leading up to the formation of the Federal Republic of Germany have been ably discussed by John Golay, *The Founding of the Federal Republic of Germany* (Chicago, 1958); and Peter Merkl, *The Origin of the West German Republic* (New York, 1963). A comprehensive work in German is Hans Peter Schwarz's *Vom Reich zur Bundesrepublik* (Neuwied: Luchterhand, 1966).

Helpful surveys of the political and economic development of the Federal Republic have been provided by Michael Balfour, *West Germany* (London: John Murray, Publishers, Ltd., 1968); and by the French political scientist Alfred Grosser, *The Federal Republic of Germany: A Concise History* (London, 1964), and *Die Bundesrepublik Deutschland: Bilanz einer Entwicklung* (Tübingen, 1967). A symposium on various political and sociological aspects of life in the Federal Republic, *The Politics of Post-War Germany*, ed. Walter Stahl (New York: Frederick A. Praeger, Inc., 1963), is uneven but rich in material.

For the period from 1949 to 1963, the *Memoirs* by Konrad Adenauer are indispensable. There are four volumes in German, but so far only the first, *Memoirs, 1945–1953*, has been translated by Beate Ruhm von Oppen (New York and London, 1966). Adenauer's great socialist opponent has found a judicious biographer in Lewis J. Edinger, *Kurt Schumacher: A Study in Personality and Political Behavior* (Palo Alto, Calif.: Stanford University Press, 1965); the book is based on many interviews with Schumacher's former friends and colleagues. A masterly survey of Bonn's foreign policy between 1944 and 1969 is Waldemar Besson's *Die Aussenpolitik der Bundesrepublik* (Munich: K. Piper, 1970). Special periods and issues are dealt with by Alistaire Horne, *Return to Power: A Study of West Germany's Emancipation, 1952–1955* (New York: Frederic A. Praeger, Inc., 1956); and by James Richardson, *Germany and the Atlantic Alliance: The Interaction of Strategy and Politics* (Cambridge: Harvard University Press, 1966). Arnulf Baring's *Aussenpolitik in Adenauers Kanzlerdemokratie* (Munich: R. Oldenburg, 1969), is the first major critical examination of Adenauer's foreign policy from 1949 to 1954 and its relationship to his domestic policy.

EAST GERMANY: THE GERMAN DEMOCRATIC REPUBLIC

Important for the early years is J. P. Nettl's *The Eastern Zone and Soviet Policy in Germany, 1945–50* (London: Oxford University Press, 1951). A. J. Heidenheimer, *The Government of Germany* (London: Methuen & Co., Ltd., 1965), contains chapters on the governmental set-up in both East and West Germany. Carola Stern's *Ulbricht: A*

Political Biography (New York, 1965), is critical and reliable. Among the speeches and writings by Karl Ulbricht, there is *Die Entwicklung des deutschen volksdemokratischen Staats, 1945–58,* 2d ed. (Berlin, 1958). The text of the Constitution of the German Democratic Republic of 1968 is to be found in *Ulbrichts Grundgesetz: Die sozialistische Verfassung der DDR* (Cologne: Verlag Wirtschaft und Politik, 1968). Two attempts by West German authors to give a fair account of conditions and of the people in East Germany are: Marion Doenhoff and others, *Reise in ein Fernes Land* (Hamburg, 1964); and Ernst Richert, *Das Zweite Deutschland* (Gütersloh, 1965).

Of the many books and articles on the history of Berlin since 1945, only the following can be mentioned here: Julius Mander, *Berlin: Hostage for the West* (London: Penguin, 1962); W. Phillips Davison, *The Berlin Wall Blockade* (Princeton, N.J.: Princeton University Press, 1957); Hans Speyer, *Divided Berlin* (The RAND Corporation, 1961); Elizabeth Barker, "The Berlin Crisis, 1958–1962," *International Affairs* (January, 1963). See also Willy Brandt's autobiographical account, *Mein Weg nach Berlin,* ed. Leo Lenia (Munich, 1960).

On the issue of reunification the following works are particularly relevant: Karl Jaspers, *The Future of Germany* (Chicago: University of Chicago Press, 1967); F. H. Hartmann, *Germany Between East and West: The Unification Problem* (Englewood Cliffs, N.J.: Prentice-Hall, Inc., 1965); and Philip Windsor, *German Reunification* (London: Elek Books, 1969). The origins of the reorientation of Bonn's attitude towards the East European states are lucidly discussed in Kurt Kaiser's paperback, *German Foreign Policy in Transition: Bonn Between East and West* (London: Oxford University Press, 1968).

SOME SPECIAL TOPICS

Hans Kohn, *The Mind of Germany: The Education of a Nation* (New York: St. Martin's Press, Inc., 1961), is a brilliant attempt to analyze how the alienation of Germany from the West came about. It relates German intellectual history to the political development of the nineteenth and twentieth centuries.

Four different works by American historians trying to disentangle the complex ideological factors in German thought since 1800 are: Leonard Krieger, *The German Idea of Freedom: The History of a Political Tradition* (Boston: Beacon Press, 1951); G. L. Mosse, *The Crisis of the German Ideology: Intellectual Origins of the Third Reich* (New York, 1964); Fritz Stern, *The Politics of Cultural Despair: A Study in the Rise of the German Ideology* (Berkeley: University of California Press, 1964), with penetrating essays on Lagarde, Langbehn, and Moeller van der Bruck; and Georg G. Iggers, *The German Concept of History:*

The National Tradition of Historical Thought from Herder to the Present (Middletown, Conn.: Wesleyan University Press, 1968). Fritz Ernst, *The Germans and Their Modern History* (New York, 1966), offers some sincere reflections by a German historian looking back on two disastrous world wars. The role of authoritarian traditions and patterns in German society in the nineteenth and twentieth centuries has been astutely analyzed by Ralf Dahrendorf in *Society and Democracy in Germany* (London: Weidenfeld & Nicolson, 1967), translated by the author from the German.

P. G. J. Pulzer, *The Rise of Political Anti-Semitism in Germany and Austria* (New York: John Wiley & Sons, Inc., 1964), pursues the theme with insight and clarity through the nineteenth century to 1914.

GERMAN MILITARISM AND THE HISTORY OF THE GERMAN ARMY

The role of the Prussian and German armies from the middle of the seventeenth century to the downfall of Hitler has been penetratingly examined by Gordon Craig, *The Politics of the Prussian Army, 1660 to 1945* (New York: Oxford University Press, 1964), and Karl Demeter, *The German Officer Corps in Society and State, 1650 to 1945* (London: Weidenfeld & Nicolson, 1965). The standard work in German is Gerhard Ritter's *Staatskunst und Kriegshandwerk*, 4 vols. (Munich, 1959–68), a masterly discussion of the problem of "militarism" in Germany during the last three hundred years.

The following works are important for the role of the German army during the Weimar Republic and the Hitler period: J. W. Wheeler–Bennett, *The Nemesis of Power: The German Generals and Politics 1918–1945*, rev. ed. (London: Macmillan & Co., Ltd., 1964); F. L. Carsten, *The Reichswehr and Politics, 1918–1933* (London: Oxford University Press, 1966); and Robert J. O'Neill, *The German Generals and the Nazi Party, 1933–1945* (London: Oxford University Press, 1966).

GERMAN LITERATURE AND SOCIETY

A perceptive general survey of German literature is to be found in *Periods in German Literature*, ed. J. M. Ritchie (London: Oswald Wolff, 1966). For a sociological approach, see Ernest K. Bramsted, *Aristocracy and the Middle Classes in Germany: Social Types in German Literature, 1830–1900*, rev. ed. (Chicago: University of Chicago Press, 1964).

Goethe

The following are valuable guides: W. H. Bruford, *Culture and Society in Classical Weimar, 1775–1806* (London: Cambridge University Press, 1963); Barker Fairley, *A Study of Goethe* (London: Oxford University Press, 1947); and Fritz Strich, *Goethe and World Literature* (London: Routledge & Kegan Paul, Ltd., 1949).

Wilhelm von Humboldt

For English translations of some of his writings see: *The Limits of State Action,* ed. J. W. Burrow (London: Cambridge University Press, 1969); and *Wilhelm von Humboldt: Humanist Without Portfolio,* an anthology translated and edited by Marianne Cowan (Detroit, Mich.: Wayne State University Press, 1963). See also the introductory essay by Joachim H. Knoll and Horst Siebert, *Wilhelm von Humboldt: Politician and Educationalist* (Bad Godesberg: Inter Nationes, 1967).

The German Romantics

R. Aris, *A History of Political Thought in Germany from 1789 to 1815* (London, 1936); and H. Reiss, ed., *The Political Thought of the German Romantics* (Oxford, 1954).

Heine

E. M. Butler, *Heinrich Heine: A Biography* (London: Cambridge University Press, 1956); and William Rose, *Heinrich Heine* (London, 1956).

Fontane

Joachim Remak, *The Gentle Critic: Theodor Fontane and German Politics, 1848–1898* (Syracuse, N.Y.: Syracuse University Press, 1964); and E. K. Bramsted, *Aristocracy and the Middle Classes in Germany* (Chicago: University of Chicago Press, 1964), Chapter 7.

Thomas Mann

Letters of Thomas Mann 1889–1945, 2 vols. (New York: Alfred A. Knopf, 1970). Walter A. Berendson, *Thomas Mann* (London, 1965); and Erich Heller, *The Ironic German: A Study of Thomas Mann* (London, 1958), are major studies; see also Georg Lukacs, *Essays on Thomas Mann,* trans. Stanley Mitchell (London, 1964); and Kurt Sontheimer, *Thomas Mann und die Deutschen* (Munich, 1967).

Bertolt Brecht

Martin Esslin's *Brecht—A Choice of Evils: A Critical Study of the Man, His Work and His Opinions* (London, 1959) is excellent; and Ronald Gray's *Brecht* (Edinburgh and London, 1961), with a bibliography, is a useful introduction.

Index